W9-BQM-036

BEYOND SURVIVAL

BEYOND SURVIVAL:

AFRICAN LITERATURE & THE SEARCH FOR NEW LIFE

EDITED BY

KOFI ANYIDOHO
ABENA P. A. BUSIA
ANNE V. ADAMS

Africa World Press, Inc.

P.O. Box 1892

Trenton, NJ 08607

P.O. Box 48

Asmara, ERITREA

Africa World Press, Inc.

P.O. Box 1892
Trenton, NJ 08607

P.O. Box 48
Asmara, ERITREA

Cover design: Jonathan Gullery

Library of Congress Cataloging -in-Publication Data

Beyond survival : African literature & the search for new life /
    edited by Kofi Anyidoho, Abena P. A. Busia, Anne V. Adams
        p. cm. -- (Annual selected papers of the ALA, ISSN 1093-2976
    ; no. 5)
    Includes bibliographical references and index.
    ISBN 0-86543-708-4. -- ISBN 0-86543-709-2 (pbk.)
    1. African literature--History and criticism Congresses.
    1. Anyidoho, Kofi. II. Busia, Abena P. A. III. Adams, Anne V.
    IV. Series.
    PL8010. B48 1999
    809'.896--dc21   99-15525
                                                                                    CIP

ANNUAL SELECTED PAPERS OF THE ALA

20th Annual Meeting of the African Literature Association
held in Accra, Ghana from March 24 to 31, 1994
and at Rutgers University from April 15 to 17, 1994

Series Editor: Hal Wylie

The ALA is an independent professional society founded in 1974.
Membership is open to scholars, teachers and writers from every
country. The ALA·exists primarily to facilitate the attempts of a
world-wide audience to appreciate the creative efforts of African
writers and authors. The organization welcomes the participation of
all who are interested and concerned with African literature. While
we hope for a constructive interaction between scholars and artists,
the ALA as an organization recognizes the primacy of African
peoples in shaping the future of African literature.

The ALA publishes the quarterly *ALA Bulletin* for its members.
Membership is for the calendar year and available on the following
terms (U.S. funds): African students studying in Africa, $5; Income
under $15,000, $15; Income from $15,000 to $35,000, $30; Income
over $35,000, $40. ALA Headquarters: Contact Prof. Anne Adams,
Director, Africana Studies and Research Center, Cornell University,
310 Triphammer Road, Ithaca, New York 14850-2599; Tel. 607-255-
0415; Fax: 607-255-0784; e-mail: ava2@cornell.edu.

TABLE OF CONTENTS

SECTION A: Introductory

SECTION B: Shifting Paradigms

SECTION C: New Life I:

Language & Artistic Tradition

SECTION D: New Life II:

Resistance Strategies/Performing Resistance

SECTION A:
INTRODUCTORY

Literature and the Burden of History:

An Introduction

Creative writers and masters of verbal art bring to us an unusually intimate
and perceptive understanding of society and the individual .... Literature,
whether written or oral, printed or performed, is an art that forces us to think
or reflect as it stimulates our imagination and excitement, awakens our
sensibility as well as our aesthetic appreciation of language and its surrogates.

With the above words, J.H. Kwabena Nketia, in his capacity as one of
Africa's most celebrated cultural spokespersons and as Chairman of the
Board of Directors of the newly opened National Theatre of Ghana, venue
for the 1994 ALA Annual Conference, welcomed the more than 300
participants to another major milestone in the history of the association.
That the conference was taking place in Ghana and at that particular time
in history, could very well be considered a miracle. Less than a decade
earlier, hardly anyone could have dreamt of bringing such a gathering to
Ghana. Once the leading light for the African independence movement,
Ghana had suffered such tragic turn of fortune that by 1984, the country
had become, in the prophetic words of Kofi Awoonor, a "revolting
malevolence," from which even the most devoted patriots had to seek
refuge in every corner of the globe. In 1983, in the midst of extreme
conditions of deprivation arising from a totally depleted economy caught in
an extended period of drought marked by devastating bushfires, well over a
million Ghanaians poured back into a battered motherland following their
summary expulsion from Nigeria.

That Ghana was able to survive those years of widespread hunger and
humiliation and was already beginning to be hailed as a new model for a
probable African renaissance, could not but be regarded as a significant
lesson for the continent as a whole. Yet, there were many who would not
give in so readily to another period of euphoria, believing most
passionately that African people need much more than survival. Indeed,
many of our artists, especially our creative writers, had reacted in similar
manner to the uncontrolled jubilation that greeted those heady years of

African independence—the late fifties into the early sixties. If only society had paid a little more attention to their visionary alarm! It was this line of thinking that guided the choice of a theme for the 1994 conference in Accra: *Beyond Survival: African Literature and the Search for New Life.* Even in the best of times, the artist is constantly reaching beyond the present; the severity of Africa's present situation of crisis must urge our artists even farther into their vision of a new life. In *Beyond Survival,* some of the best interpreters of African Literature focus on "the role of the creative artist as a critical assessor, confidence builder and inspirer to excellence." The central theme of this important collection of essays is inspired by the belief that given the severity of the current crisis of life for African peoples, and given the intuitive and cultivated ability of the creative artist to monitor and accurately capture the complexities of any human situation, a close attention to the work of African and African-heritage writers should provide not only important insights into various dimensions of the problem, but also and perhaps even more crucial, subtle but reliable pointers to probable solutions. More than any other group of people, it is perhaps to the artists we must turn for a creative but ultimately realizable vision of the future.

The gathering in Accra was blessed with the presence of several writers and a number of scholars, especially those based at home in Africa, many of whom would normally not have been able to participate in the association's annual meetings. It was a special pleasure for most members of the association to meet again or for the first time, such writers as Margaret Busby, Syl Cheney-Coker, Fatoumata Diakhite, O. Onuora Enekwe, Ezenwa-Ohaeto, Harry Garuba, Odia Ifeimum, Monique Ilboudo, Festus Iyayi, Mzamane Mbulelo, Atukwei Okai, Tanure Ojaide, Femi Osofisan, Niyi Osundare, keynote speaker Ngugi wa Thiong'o, Ken Saro-Wiwa, Mabel Segun, Zulu Sofola, Efua Sutherland, and Veronique Tadjo. This may have been the largest gathering of African writers at any ALA annual conference, a fact made possible by the choice of an African country as venue for the conference.

Regretably, this may also have been the last time many members of the association saw three of these writers—Ken Saro-Wiwa, Zulu Sofola, and Efua Sutherland—all of whom died within a year following the conference. Zulu Sofola, whose plays have been a source of delight and debate among various generations of students, teachers and theatre goers across English-speaking Africa, was in Ghana for the first time in several years for a formal appearance before countless admirers of her work. Efua Sutherland, a widely-acknowledged pioneer of the theatre movement in Africa, out of personal choice, hardly ever responded to invitations to conferences on African literature. But on this rare occasion, she was very much a part of our program. Indeed, she went on to Rutgers University as a keynote speaker in the "After Accra" Conference which immediately followed the annual meetings in Ghana. Our original guest list had included Flora Nwapa but she had died in 1993 while we were still finalizing preparations for the conference. With the death, soon after the Accra conference, of Sofola and Sutherland, the world lost three of the founding female voices in African literature.

Now, in retrospect, we must count ourselves blessed that the Accra conference also saw the formal launch of the *Women Writing Africa* project, under the auspices of the Feminist Press. The project has since then developed into a very comprehensive and innovative attempt to promote the study of African women's writing and to bring African women's literature to readers around the world. The ultimate objectives of the Women Writing Africa project include:

— publishing six anthologies of African women's written and oral compositions, organized by region (North, East, Southern, Central, West, and the Sahel);

— publishing a series of individual books by and about African women;

— creating repositories in Africa for the narratives that have been collected;

— establishing a computer network for experts in African women's history and culture;

— promoting egalitarian partnerships between African and non-African writers and scholars.

The *Women Writing Africa* project is co-directed by two ALA members—Abena Busia and Tuzyline Jita Allan, together with Florence Howe, Publisher/Director of The Feminist Press. Much progress has already been made, and it is expected that the first volumes in the series will be ready for publication in the near future.

Almost against all odds and in spite of severe "state security restrictions," Ken Saro-Wiwa managed to get out of Nigeria to travel to Accra for a brief one-day visit, during which he received the Fonlon-Nicols Prize at a very moving ceremony held at the W.E.B. DuBois Memorial Centre for Pan African Culture. In his acceptance speech, he spoke, among other issues, of his detention in 1993 for caring and daring enough to use his personal resources and his talents as spokesperson for the Ogoni people. Following that earlier arrest and imprisonment, Ken Saro-Wiwa later recorded for us in *A Month and a Day: A Detention Diary*, the

following resolve which was to lead him to his tragic but heroic death in
the name of democracy, human rights and justice for his people:

> They had been sleepwalking their way towards extinction, not knowing what
> internal colonialism had done and was doing to them. It had fallen to me to
> wake them up from the sleep of the century and I had accepted in full the
> responsibility for doing so. Would they be able to stand up to the rigours of the
> struggle? ....
>
> The fact that the victims of this injustice were too timid or ignorant to cry out
> against it was painful in the extreme. It was unacceptable. It had to be
> corrected no matter at what cost. To die fighting to right the wrong would be
> the greatest gift of life! Yes, the gift of life. And I felt better...My spirit would
> not be broken. Never! [p. 18, 19].

Given the earlier news about Saro-Wiwa's tribulations, we were
indeed delighted to have him among us, but as he left soon after receiving
the Folon-Nichols Prize, a prize awarded annually by the ALA to a writer
whose life and work stands as an example in defense of truth and justice
even at the risk of persecution, there were many among us who could not
but fear for his future. Little did we know that in less than two months, he
was to be back in chains and that in time the chains were to be followed by
the hangman's noose.

The example of Ken Saro-Wiwa and the many other writers in Africa
who have been prepared to suffer imprisonment, exile, and indeed death, in
defence of a new life of liberty and fulfillment for their people must stand
as one of the most important guarantees of hope for the future of a
continent so often burdened with misery and despair. However, beyond the
heroic self-sacrifices of these writers and a few others, it is important that
the rest of us see our way clear enough to take a stand on the side of those
who are dedicated to the future prosperity of African people. This was
Saro-Wiwa's final message to us, as contained in his "Closing Statement to
the Military Appointed Tribunal" which sentenced him to death:

> My lord, we all stand before history. I am a man of peace, of ideas.
> Appalled by the denigrating poverty of my people who live on a richly
> endowed land, distressed by their political marginalization and economic
> strangulation, angered by the devastation or their land, their ultimate heritage,
> anxious to preserve their right to life and to a decent living, and determined to
> usher to this country as a whole a fair and just democratic system which
> protects everyone and every ethnic group and gives us all a valid claim to
> human civilization, I have devoted my intellectual and material resources, my
> very life, to a cause in which I have total belief and from which I cannot be
> blackmailed or intimidated. I have no doubt at all about the ultimate success of
> my cause, no matter the trials and tribulations which I and those who believe

with me may encounter on our journey. Nor imprisonment nor death can stop our ultimate victory....I predict that the scene here will be played and replayed by generations yet unborn. Some have already cast themselves in the role of villains, some are tragic victims, some still have a chance to redeem themselves. The choice is for each individual. [ALA *Bulletin* 21, no 4 (Fall 1995): 3-4]

The trouble with Africa, we must lament with Chinua Achebe, is quite simply, the arrogance and abuse of power, in short, the failure of leadership. It is in this connection that we must recall a particularly significant aspect of the conference, the performance of what was to have been the world premiere of *Nkrumah-Ni!...Africa-Ni!*: A Play about Nkrumah's Conakry Years, written and directed by one of Africa's leading current dramatists, Femi Osofisan of the University of Ibadan, Nigeria. Professor Osofisan arrived in Ghana some ten days earlier as a Guest Artist to direct his new play with *Abibigromma*: xResident Theatre Company of the School of Performing Arts, University of Ghana. After a week of rehearsals under the most intense pressure, Osofisan and *Abibigromma* managed to bring the production to what should technically be considered as a dress rehearsal which was presented at the National Theatre to a full house of ALA conference participants and the general public. As a production, there were still too many rough edges that needed to be smoothed out through further rehearsal. Many felt the play was too long, and yet others were critical of Osofisan's deliberate use of long stretches of political debate within the structure of the play. Later performances of this and other productions were to benefit from some of these observations from a critical ALA audience. Despite these comments on the premiere production of the play, the full significance of this particular Osofisan play must not be lost on us, especially in the context of our conference and its chosen theme. Those familiar with Osofisan's work are aware that each play in his corpus stands as a unique experiment in form, dramatic technique, and thematic thrust.

Nkrumah-Ni...Africa-Ni!. is a high-powered historical drama about the complex question of leadership and Africa's abandoned revolutionary agenda. Unusual and full of surprising, even shocking twists in dramatic form and technique, Osofisan's play features three principal characters taken directly from our recent history—Kwame Nkrumah of Ghana, Sekou Toure of Guinea, and Amilcar Cabral of Guinea-Bissau. In a brief Foreword to the text of *Nkrumah-Ni...Africa-Ni!*, the playwright himself recalls for us the unusual significance of the historical circumstances he has chosen to dramatize through these principal characters. As a contribution of symbolic significance to the Accra conference, this play is

represented here in this volume by the following excerpt from Osofisan's
Foreword:

> [Following his overthrow in the 1966 coup in Ghana] Nkrumah received at
> once several invitations from friendly, progressive countries, but chose in the
> end to go to Guinee, where his friend Sekou Toure was in power. It was
> supposed to be a brief stay, but he was to remain in Conakry for the next six
> years!
>
> Toure was himself another African leader who had achieved "notoriety" by
> daring western imperialism. In 1958, he had said a big NO to France's
> General de Gaule, who wanted to retain all the French African countries in a
> seemingly free, but actually servile relationship with France. Acceding to this
> choice of complete autonomy, France had pulled out of Guinee in anger,
> withdrawing all its personnel, its imported equipment, its financial credits.
> Even telephone wires were ripped off the walls!
>
> Thus it was to a country extremely proud of itself, but caught in the grip of
> political and economic turbulence that Nkrumah went. And interestingly also,
> he was to find in Conakry, the headquarters of the PAIGC, the liberation
> movement headed by Amilcar Cabral, and which was engaged then in a bitter
> armed conflict with the Portuguese colonialists next door in Guinea-Bissau.
>
> Thus, by a strange coincidence of history, three of the most radical African
> leaders lived together in this small town of Conakry for six full years!
>
> They met, according to reports, almost every day, to talk and work out the
> strategies for the emancipation of Africa. But sadly, no record of their
> discussions exists...
>
> Think of them however: one, a leader fallen from power; another, struggling to
> remain in power; and the third, his life at stake, in the violent quest for power.
> All the three were men of astounding visionary and oratorical power. All the
> three were gifted with lucidity and courage, cunning and ruthlessness. All the
> three possessed great natural charm and charisma, a hatred of ostentation and
> cant, and all exuded an unmistakable aura of command. Uncannily, their
> speeches read alike in several instances, like different modulations of the same
> voice!...
>
> Nkrumah was the oldest and the most experienced among them however;
> Toure the most cunning, and the most effervescent; Cabral, the youngest, the
> most compassionate, the most urbane, and the most assured. But that may
> simply be my own reading; the facts may have been otherwise.
>
> I am fascinated. What did these three remarkable figures discuss in those
> years? What, in their death, has Africa lost — or gained?

This is the first of a trilogy about these leaders, and its emphasis is on Nkrumah, the first of them to die. Much as I have tried, this is still a play seeking answers..." [Femi Osofisan, in his Foreword to *Nkrumah-Ni...Africa-Ni!*]

Such a drama of high historical significance could not have been written without a diligent excavation and analysis of our history. It is reported that Osofisan spent at least five years doing research into the historical background of his play. His research had taken him to France, to Britain, and to the United States. Beyond the history, Osofisan recalls for us the tragic but inspiring drama of three great leaders in the splendor and contraditions of their full humanity, their extraordinary compassion for dispossessed Africa and her suffering children, their revolutionary courage, and their "unmistakable aura of command." But he also makes sure he catches them-especially Nkrumah and Toure—in moments of despair, frustration, and tendencies toward ruthlessness. The playwright takes care to allow interventions from those who oppose what these men stand for and their human as well as political failures. As the history unfolds in action and word, moments of dramatic glory are constantly invaded by a chorus of masked "ruffians" with a licence to debunk the assumed power and glory to which the central characters lay claim. Something of the contradictions that mark the Osofisan play may be seen in the collection of selected conference papers presented here in this volume.

The contributions fall under five broad headings, beginning with an introductory section featuring three important addresses delivered during the 1994 ALA annual conference in Accra, Ghana, at which most of these papers were first presented, as well as a specially commissioned essay in memory of the late Flora Nwapa, one of Africa's best known pioneer women writers. The four other sections present a total of twenty essays on: "Shifting Paradigms"; "New Life: Language and Artistic Tradition"; "New Life: Language, Literature & National Policy"; and "Resistance Strategies."

The essays under "Shifting Paradigms" focus, among other things, on historical and contemporary reality, drawing particular attention to attempts through literature to imaginatively confront, transform or transcend the more stifling dimensions of such reality. Included in this section is Niyi Osundare's substantial theoretical statement on various ways in which post-structuralist, post-modernist and especially post-colonialist schools of literary criticism are fundamentally flawed by their inability to fully appreciate the fact that they play a part in "the institutionalization and strengthening of the metropole-periphery, centre-margin dichotomy.... a trope which brings memories of gunboats and mortars, conquests and dominations, a trope whose accent is bloodstained.... a terminology whose 'name' and meaning are fraught with the burdens of history and the anxieties of contemporary reality." Something of the burdens of that history is captured for us in Kwadwo Opoku-Agyemang's important opening paper which reminds us of what he terms "the final importance of Equiano's autobiography": "by its embedded silences regarding the people the boy left behind, it brings into focus the fact that the European slave trade left graves without bodies in the lives and minds of surviving kinsfolk of the captured." Between these two papers, and also the papers by Akosua Anyidoho and Edris Makward, there is a strong suggestion that the crippling effects of these burdens of history and of the anxieties of contemporary reality could be substantially mitigated through very vital lessons highlighted for us in such literary texts as Equiano's autobiography. In the words of Opoku-Agyemang, "Equiano was concerned with much more than survival. He was caught in the struggle to give order to chaos, and as Ellison puts it, to rearrange reality to the patterns of his imagination."

The papers under "New Life" address themselves to various ways in which the creative imagination in their chosen authors and texts perform transforming engagements with various contexts of literary production through the power of language and creative strategies developed within artistic tradition and also through the intervention of individual and strategic planning and practice in the face of a crippling history reinforced by unimaginative and sometimes pernicious official policy. Fahamisha Brown's paper, among other things, demonstrates how "By the selection of vernacular expression as the favored poetic language, the Black poet infuses her/his art with a cultural specificity.... asserts a socio-political identification with the group that shares the language." Ezenwa-Ohaeto demonstrates various ways in which two contemporary African poets "effectively portray an enrichment of modern African poetry in terms of craft, and the poets establish that a conscious assimilation of oral traditions could act as both creative inspiration and creative strategy in order to invigorate modern African poetry." Oliver Lovesey draws special attention to a hopeful future orientation in Ngugi's last narratives properly read as allegories of transformation envisioning community survival, novels that use allegory to facilitate "a projection into a tumultuous but ultimately triumphant future." Souley Y. Ousman brings Soyinka's dramaturgy back into a new and revealing focus as he seeks to demonstrate how

> One cannot ultimately talk of the sources of Soyinka's drama without mentioning it's basic projections: language, music and dance. For there is an area of the traditional Yoruba psyche where the metaphysical and mytho-

religious, the natural and supernatural meet, and there create a new being and a new awareness; an area of ecstatic upheaval where the most significant and profound feelings and emotional responses take shape, where the scattered fragments of reality combine with mythopoeic images as a grand matrix in traditional Yoruba memory to produce a synthesis of ordered experience....Soyinka thus fuses the reality of Yoruba linguistic, musical and dance conception to produce a unified ecstasy.

Judith Miller establishes a close connection between Ina Cesaire's theatrical tales and their oral heritage models, and argues that "Told tales and Césaire's theatricalized ones participate in the community's efforts to keep itself (or make itself) healthy by providing a symbolic space for release and celebration." In "Blood, Memory, and Voice," Peter Hitchcock employs certain aspects of the philosophy of language to demonstrate ways in which two important North African writers confront and transcend the silences imposed by French colonial language policy on the cultural and political landscape of their respective societies. The full details of such policy and its devastating consequences and attempts to reverse such consequences, constitute the substance of the papers by Fredric Michaelman and Robert C. Newton.

The section "Resistance Strategies," brings together papers that foreground much more pointedly an undercurrent in many of the earlier papers, the combative and temper that sometimes informs the literary imagination, helping it not only to survive the impositions of a furious history and also to rise above the dehumanizing conditions that define contemporary reality. Don Burness speaks for all the others included in this section, for the entire collection of essays, and indeed for the Accra conference as whole when he asserts that:

Life is not just survival. There is gaiety in the creative process. For social poets like Jacinto and Craveirinha, literature offers a path to a new and better life, a path from colonization to independence, a path from human folly to human fulfillment. Beyond survival there is hope.

In concluding this brief introduction, we must record our deep appreciation to the following institutions for making the conference possible: the W.E.B. DuBois Memorial Centre for Pan African Culture, for hosting this special meeting of the African Literature Association; the University of Ghana and Rutgers University for collaborating with the DuBois Centre as co-hosts; and to the Rockefeller Foundation for making available to the organizers a grant towards various organizational expenses and the participation of our many guest writers and scholars. It is also this grant that has made it possible in part for us to finance the publication of *Beyond Survival: African Literature and the Search for a New Life*. It is a

Salem Academy and College
Winston-Salem, N.C. 27108

matter of deep regret that it has taken us almost four years to pull these papers together and make them ready for publication. Much may have changed since many of these papers were first presented in Accra. Indeed, Africa has gone through some particularly terrifying disasters since then. But, as always, the yearning and the search for a new meaning to life remains as strong as ever, especially as we see a few of our longest-lasting dictators and their regimes of death give in to the inevitable logic of time, of history and of struggle, leaving their people exhausted but ready to begin life all over again.

Kofi Anyidoho
Anne Adams
Abena P.A. Busia

WELCOME ADDRESS

by J. H. Kwabena Nketia

Creative writers and masters of verbal art bring to us an unusually intimate and perceptive understanding of society and the individual, for they are able to see far more in their mind's eye than many of us do as they focus on men and women in action in the past, present or future, as they reflect on the joy of life or its pain and suffering, the achievements or foibles of our leadership, the vision or lack of vision and initiative of those placed in positions of responsibility as well as the hopes and aspirations of ordinary individuals in both rural and urban environments for a better tomorrow as they cope with basic problems of survival, deal with the dialectics of social life or cultural encounters or with the impact on their lives of schemes and reforms that raise more problems than they solve. The programme of this conference indeed reveals a wide range of concerns emerging from the historical, prophetic, futuristic, millennial, moral, tragic or uneasy vision of our creative artists that scholars and critics seem to have vigorously pursued in their research and reflections or their analysis of experience. Literature, whether written or oral, printed or performed, is an art that forces us to think or reflect as it stimulates our imagination and excitement, awakens our sensibility as well as our aesthetic appreciation of language and its surrogates.

Believing like many of us that this art has been with us from time immemorial, Dr. K. A. Busia established a research fellowship in the Department of Sociology so that we could study our traditional heritage. Nkrumah sought, about thirty years ago, to encourage the collection and publication of what he called African classics and invited some of us to think of it as a national project. He was particularly interested in items from the body of oral traditions cultivated throughout Ghana, including oral narratives that would reflect classicism that is Africa's own creation and felt that this would be a major contribution in its own right to world literature. It would lay the foundation for the growth of new modes of literary expression in Ghanaian languages rooted in the art and sensibility of Africa's own traditions. That is why he was fascinated by Okyeame Akuffo's synthesis of *apaeï, amoma* and *ayan* (drum language), and his update of their referential components and so created the position of state linguist so that on important state occasions we may hear new versions of court literature in performance in contemporary contexts.

The idea that African classics of an earlier tradition could be assembled in this manner was not far fetched, for Stuart Wilson, one time President of the International Music Council, once said,

> Folk music is not an embryonic art. It exemplifies the principles of great art and a basis of taste is therefore, cultivated by its practice. (Wilson 1965: 49).

Bela Bartok made a similar comment in the introduction to his collection of Hungarian folk songs. To him folk songs were classical models, for as he put it,

> In their small way, they are as perfect as the grandest masterpieces of musical art. They are indeed classical models of the way in which a musical idea can be expressed in all its freshness and shapeliness...in short, in the very best possible way, in the briefest possible form and with the simplest of means. (Bartok 1981: 3)

One could paraphrase this and say that "Oral art forms are as perfect as the grandest masterpieces of literary art. They are indeed classical models of the way in which a literary idea can be expressed in all its freshness and shapeliness...in short, in the very best possible way, in the briefest possible form and with the simplest of means"—a description that is certainly apt for the proverb.

I believe that it was this idea of a "classical model" that Nkrumah meant by his use of the term African classics. In any case when he used it I was not surprised, for my own work in the Department of Sociology headed by Dr. K. A. Busia, on the Funeral dirges of the Akan people had led me to appreciate and believe in the aesthetic merit of oral forms of the literary art.

Although following Nkrumah's dream of African classics a good start was made with the collection of some oral narratives, the scheme came to an abrupt halt for reasons you are all aware of. Fortunately private and institutional collections now exist in limited quantities in the form of audio tapes in our universities, Ghana Broadcasting House and a few other places. No effort has been made, however, to bring copies of these together in a central archive. Nor has the work of transcribing and translating such material been carried out systematically, for what Nkrumah envisaged was not just recording, the first stage, but the transformation from recording as audio visual documents to paper documents that may be preserved in archives and libraries, and eventual publication of very selective anthologies in a worthy format as treasures of the African personality.

The Ghana Academy of Arts and Sciences that has focused on the collection of oral histories hopes, as a coordinating body, to do something about this in cooperation with interested institutions at home such as the

Language Centre and the International Centre for African Music and Dance at the University of Ghana, the DuBois Centre, the Ghana Folklore Board as well as individuals, organizations and institutions abroad so that one day large organized collections of audio and video tapes of such materials in different Ghanaian languages, suitably transcribed, duly translated, annotated and catalogued would become accessible to writers and students of African literature.

When I was in the United States, I was impressed by the existence of one kind of grant which was not available to non-resident aliens: a Grant for Travel to Sources or rare materials and manuscripts in libraries and archives— generally those in Europe because they were also an integral part of Euroamerican culture. I hope that Africa will provide an alternative grant for travel to sources for members of the African Literature Association and that one day individuals can come and do similar research in our archives of oral literature and also experience such literature in its performance and other cultural contexts, for they will find an interesting referential system that extends from language to dance and the visual arts. Awareness of this will enable them to study such materials on their own terms, to recognize and appreciate similarities and differences, something that the women of Ashanti stressed in 1920 when they sent a gift of a silver stool to Her Royal Highness Princess Mary on the occasion of her wedding. The speech made by Queenmother Serwaa Akoto as she presented the stool is a classic preserved for us in translation in the work of Rattray. She said:

> I place this stool in your hands. It is a gift for the King's child, Princess Mary. Ashanti stool makers have carved it and Ashanti silversmiths have embossed it. All the Queenmothers who dwell here in Ashanti have contributed towards it. I stand as a representative of all the Queenmothers and place it in your hands to send to the King's child (Princess Mary). It may be that the King's child has heard of the Golden Stool of Ashanti. That is the stool which contains the soul of the Ashanti nation. All we women of Ashanti thank the Governor exceedingly because he has declared to us that the English will never ask us to hand over that stool.

> This stool we give gladly. It does not contain our soul as our Golden Stool does, but it contains all the love of us Queenmothers and of our women. The spirit of this love we have bound with silver fetters just as we are accustomed to bind our own spirits to the base of our stools.

> We in Ashanti here have a law which decrees that it is the daughters of a Queen who alone can transmit royal blood, and that the children of a King cannot be heirs to that stool. This law has given us women a power in this land so that we have a saying which runs, "It is the woman who bears the man" (that is the King).

>   We hear that her law is not so, nevertheless we have great joy in
> sending her our congratulations, and we pray that the great God
> Nyankopon, on whom men lean and do not fall, whose day of worship is
> Saturday, and whom the Ashanti serve just as she serves Him, that He
> may give the King's child and her husband long life and happiness and
> finally, when she sits upon this silver stool, which the women of Ashanti
> have made for their Queenmother, may she call us to mind. (Rattray:
> 1923: 294-5)

We wish you a happy stay in Ghana and, as the Queenmothers put it,
when you go back home "may you call us to mind."

References Cited

Bartok, Bela. *The Hungarian Folk Song*. Albany: State University of New York
    Press. 1981, p.3.

Rattray, R.S. *Ashanti*. Oxford: Clarendon Press. 1923, p.294-5.

Wilson, Stuart. "The Role of Folk Music in Education." *Music Education*. Paris:
    UNESCO. 1956: 49.

OPENING ADDRESS

by Abena P. A. Busia
President

It is indeed, an honour to be here, and to respond to this welcome on behalf of my colleagues and friends. Yet at the same time it is a strange, though wonderful experience, because after all, this is my home. This is, after so many years, a homecoming. Yet, I speak on behalf of a foreign-based association which has claimed me as its own in my sojourn among familiar strangers. Or perhaps it is my strange familiars. In the dissonance between these two phrases lies the world of our being. In thinking about what I could or should say as a vote of thanks for being received as one amongst my peers who have travelled so far to be here, I could not help but think of the multiple meanings of that simple word. Home. This is for us as an Association indeed another homecoming.

When we first met on African soil at our 15th annual meeting in Dakar, Senegal in 1989, we resolved to return every five years. The kind invitation from the DuBois Centre and the University of Ghana has made that possible, and for us, this is an exciting confirmation of the art of the possible. Yet, I cannot but confess the wry irony of the situation for me and I suspect for many of you with me here.

For so many of us we think of home with, if you like, a small 'h' and a capital 'H' and its location changes according to time, place and context and yet somehow its meaning seems to stay the same. For my successor to this office, our distinguished elder statesman Prof. Edris Makward, the gentleman who first took us to Dakar, that word 'home' has for example meant Banjul in the Gambia, Dakar in Senegal, Paris in France and Madison Wisconsin amongst many other places. For me, it has meant the corner of 125th Street and Riverside Drive in Harlem, the small town of Highland Park on the Banks of the Raritan River New Jersey, the even smaller village of Standlake on the river Windrush just outside Oxford.

I too have known rivers. We have all known rivers. And some of mine flows through this land. But where my other references are specific, the ones here seem far less tangible. A few years ago I remember hearing Njabulo Ndebele, the South African writer, speak of his first return home after the opening up that followed the release of Nelson Mandela. He told the story of his years of exile which he had spent telling his children stories of the place he where grew up; vivid descriptions of open places, of specific street corners, billboards, the sounds and smells and colors of his youth. On his first opportunity he loaded his children into a car and drove them home to show them this place so rich and full of memories. He could not find it. I always remember the power of his language and the emotion of his voice as he described the landscape gliding by as he looked for a loved and familiar crossroads that he never come to.

Last Sunday I understood how he must have felt. Driving West along the Winneba road from Kaneshie towards Weija, I looked South searching for a left turn. I knew that at one point if you took a once untarred road you saw it rise up in front of you at a particular bend in the road where the frogs used to nocturne. Odorkor. My father's house. I have not been there in a while. I never dared approach it since I was marched out of it at gunpoint twenty years ago and more. And I could not find the turning.

I felt as if someone had shifted the road and cluttered it up, just to disturb me, and make the neighbourhood half familiar but not my own. Bigger, denser, brasher, bolder, much, much more exciting than when I had been there but not mine. It seems only the soldiers remained the same. I was seized with a sudden and rising sense of panic.

This one small old road had become a dual carriage way and the approach to it went by somewhere, somewhere other than where I thought it should be. I felt old. Bypasses bypass old familiar paths and in the end remove them from the memory of the young. With such memories, I felt no longer young. To be able to mark the site of something you can remember you have forgotten, is to have memories that will not accommodate themselves in time. This is the condition of exile. It is the sorrow of migrants, outcasts, all displaced oppositional forces long out of power or away from home. All of us, stolen souls. We are time's ancient children. Accumulating memories and biding our stories in the silence of separation. Yet at the same time, we are all of us individuals, associations, communities, nations in search of new life. This is our theme for this week and we must claim it.

Home means so many things and for so many of my colleagues, this is a spiritual homecoming. Many of the people who have come with me have waited their lifetime to come to Ghana. Yet this spiritual home has no fixed reference point present or disappeared. For the African-Americans and Afro-Caribbeans amongst us, who have for the past decade or more welcomed me to their home, histories of separation are not quite so visible as a missed left turn. What marks their lives is their own presences. The fact of their very being when seen from the opposite shores of the Atlantic.

Over here on these shores, what we contend with is the meaning of their absences. But in truth, not always and not all the time. So we must all of us, myself included, challenge nostalgia. And, also, it is a very heavy business to walk with ghosts. Not simply memories, but ghosts. The Beloved.

We do not today walk solely with ghosts. Our very past gives us the untold stories of our tomorrows. Today may bring uncertainties, terrors, internments, and new hungers but we are surviving all that. Today we walk with the power of convictions, we are to go beyond, and we re-figure time and meaning to shape our world through poetry and story into myth. Something we can hold, which creates the visions of our tomorrows as well as it survives and sustains all our yesterdays.

I speak here on behalf of an Association of writers and scholars. For some of us, Africa is indeed home. For others she is a metaphor for home. For all of us, Africa is a vocation and an avocation. We are passionate about what we do. And we have with us this week, for the first time in our twenty year history, over twenty African writers whose works we read, study, teach, laugh with, quarrel with and above all share. We are missionaries in a little caring world, but we don't stop. There is no *one* new life. Only many lives renewed and it is our writers who make our world an exciting place.

They remind us that the distance from Africa Square at 125th Street and Lenox, is not so far after all from Bukom Square, if you have walked through both places. We live in shared cultural spaces. And though not identical, we can trace the ties from Africa through Afro-America to the popular culture of the Americas, back here to Africa through food, dress, music, dance and the shifting language which is the substance of our lives.

Over the next few days not all of our words will be visionary or all recording the same lost memories or shared dreams. But it is not our individualities that keep us whole, but our whole that keeps us. This is our twentieth year. We have survived. We seek what is beyond and we are overjoyed to start that here. On behalf of my colleagues, I thank you. We have been gone. We have come back. We will return again.

EDRIS MAKWARD'S

INAUGURAL ADDRESS

Yes! Brothers and Sisters! Colleagues, students, friends, relatives and distinguished guests! This is indeed an important date in the history of our organization, the African Literature Association and, I, for one, am very proud to be its incoming President at the time of its coming of age: Yes! 20 years since that cold Fall of 1974 in Chicago, Illinois, at the ASA (African Studies Association) annual meeting, when a group of us, mostly college and university teachers of African literature in the U.S., with the warm support of colleagues from African universities, agreed, after an open, and at times heated debate to form yet another organization, the African Literature Association, which would subsequently hold its first annual meeting in Austin, Texas, with big brother and mentor, Dennis Brutus, as its first President.

We have come a long way, indeed! Five Nobel Prizes have honored three of our writers from the Continent and two from the Diaspora: Wole Soyinka, Naguib Mahfouz, Nadine Gordimer, Derek Walcott and Toni Morrison. More and more universities in the U.S. and North America are including works of our authors in their curricula. The same is happening in Africa, Europe and elsewhere.

But Accra, 1994, in addition to being a celebration of our coming of age, will also be remembered as our second annual meeting on the continent, following in the footsteps of Dakar, Senegal, 1989; and I would like to take the opportunity here to express a very warm thank-you, on my behalf and on behalf of our Association, to the very dynamic co-conveners of this convention, Kofi Anyidoho, Abena Busia, and all those who helped in turning this our second African dream into a reality, and a very successful and memorable reality at that. I will not forget that it was in Dakar, exactly five years ago that Kofi and others pledged that the ALA should hold its annual meeting in Africa every four or five years. Well! We can congratulate ourselves for having done very well indeed, for here we are, five years later on African soil again, with, in between, last year's unforgettable meeting in Guadeloupe.

Once again a million thanks to Kofi, Abena and their colleagues, to Ambassador Way for Accra 94, and to Aliko Songolo, Eileen Julien, Micheline Rice-Maximin and Susan Andrade for Pointe-à-Pitre 93.

Meeting here in Accra is for me a unique opportunity for personal reminiscences, for it was here in Accra, and exactly at the University the University of Ghana-Legon, that I had the unforgettable honor and pleasure of meeting and shaking the hand of one illustrious elder of our Diaspora, W.E.B. DuBois himself, after the formal opening of the First International Africanist Congress, which he presided over. This was in 1963, exactly 31 years ago. The old man died here in Accra a few months later, on August 27, 1963, at the age of 95. He was born on February 23, 1868, in Massachusetts.

Over and beyond my own idiosyncrasies and personal reminiscences, and in relation to the theme of our meeting, "Beyond Survival: Aftican Literature and the Search for New Life," it stands to reason to evoke here, even if briefly, the life of this great elder of whom we can say, symbolically, that he crossed the waters twice, but that his crossings were more than symbolic! Only the utterly ignorant amongst us, or the bigoted, would deny that the passage of W.E.B. DuBois through our planet and our continent left us all the richer and wiser. A Massachusetts native, DuBois received a Ph.D. degree from Harvard in 1895 and was, the following year, the author of the first monograph published in the Harvard Historical Series: "The Suppression of the Slave-Trade to America." He spent a lifetime career as a professor of economics and history (1897-1910), and as head of the Department of Sociology (1932-1944) at Atlanta University, an historically black university. There was at that time and for several more decades to come, a requirement, a qualification, that neither he nor, for that matter, a number of us gathered here today, could fulfill satisfactorily to deserve an invitation to join the faculty of Harvard, Yale, Columbia, Ohio State or the University of Wisconsin!

One of my favorite lines from Ousmane Sembène's masterpiece *Les bouts de bois de Dieu* (*God's Bits of Wood*) is when the French Railway Company foreman responds to Doudou's complaint about European workers having the right to a 10-minute break for a snack, and not the Africans, with these words: "Va te faire blanchir et tu auras tes dix minutes!" (Sembène, 1960, p. 234) (Go and make yourself white, then you will have your ten minute break!). Doudou will naturally remember this line, and not without bitterness, when, at the beginning of the Railway workers' strike, Isnard now tries to bribe him with 3 million francs ($12,000 at the time, 1947): "Trois millions, ça ne blanchit pas un Nègre. Garde-les et dis à Dejean que nous sommes à sa disposition pour discuter," (Sembène, 1960, p. 238) (Three million does not make a black man white. Keep the millions but tell Dejean [the Railway Company director] that we are ready to discuss matters with him.)

The experience of Jim Crow laws and more did not stifle or paralyze DuBois. On the contrary, an indefatigable and true believer in himself, and a genuine activist, he founded, in 1905, the Niagara Movement, which would later lead to the foundation of the NAACP (National Association for the Advancement of Colored People), an important non-partisan interracial organization whose principal goals included stamping out lynching and lynch law, eliminating racial injustice, discrimination and segregation, and assuring Black people their constitutional civil rights. From 1910 to 1932, DuBois became the dynamic and eloquent editor of *The Crisis*, the monthly organ of the NAACP, with a circulation, at its peak, of 140,000. He was also instrumental in organizing the First Pan-African Conference in London, in 1900, where he urged the liberation of African colonies. He led four subsequent Pan-African Congresses, in 1919, 1921, 1923, and 1927, and he co-chaired, with Kwame Nknunah, the Fifth Pan-African Congress, in 1945, in Manchester, England. DuBois, a prolific journalist and scholarly writer, was the author of many books, among which I would single out his influential and superb *The Souls of Black Folk* (1903), *The World and Africa* (1947), and *The Battle for Peace* (1952). He moved to Accra in 1962 and started work as editor of The Encyclopaedia Africana Project and became a citizen of Ghana before his death in 1963.

All his life, DuBois worked with energy, confidence and unassailable faith in his people, almost until the last day of his life. His move to Ghana at the age of 93 was definitely not to be construed by him, his family, or his friends, as a journey to a final resting place—far from it. His life was indeed a true and most eloquent personification of the theme of our 20th annual meeting, i.e. "Beyond Survival: African Literature and the Search for New Life."

I could not suppress a chuckle on re-reading recently the *Encyclopaedia Britannica* article on DuBois, that he "was an authentic American radical until the 1940s, when he espoused pro-Soviet doctrines." I chuckle at reading such statements about individuals whose stature and whose real *raison de vivre* are too high and too complex for even relatively knowledgeable encyclopaedia article authors to begin to fathom. DuBois was indeed a man for whom the quest for life, a meaningful life, was a continuous endeavor, a journey indeed, a journey that did not end, or even slow down, with age or with the lashes of bigotry and ignorance, a man in perpetual search for a new life, for a better life for himself, his family and his people.

Words such as arrogance, bitterness, wit, and sense of humor have also been used to describe DuBois. Only the imbecile and the moron would fail to recognize in such combinations, a sound and effective recipe for survival and beyond in that era when even Léopold Sédar Senghor, on a U.S. visit with a group of French parliamentarians, was not allowed to eat dinner with his colleagues in the main ballroom of the Waldorf Astoria Hotel, in New York.

It is in the process of this search for productive survival that DuBois wrote, at the dawn of this century, his landmark work, *The Souls of Black Folk* (1903). Almost a century after its first publication, this book remains highly relevant and full of thought-provoking pointers for the dawn of another century, another millennium, which interestingly, coincides with another dawn, that of the third decade of our Association.

In 1903 DuBois wrote of a world which yielded the Black American:

> ...no true self-consciousness, but only [let] him see himself through the revelation of the other world. It is a peculiar sensation, this double-consciousness, this sense of always looking at one's self through the eyes of others, of measuring one's soul by the tape of a world that looks on in amused contempt and pity. One ever feels his two-ness,—an American, a Negro; two souls, two thoughts, two unreconciled strivings; two warring ideals in one dark body, whose dogged strength alone keeps it from being torn asunder.[1]

These truthful lines still carry a worthy message, a helpful message for our youth, from either side of the ocean, from the diaspora and from the mother continent. I would also add that the relevance of these words remains for those of our generation who have not yet reflected sufficiently and taken action towards the resolution of this dilemma of "being two." And this brings to mind a session of an ASA annual meeting of a few years ago, when several very young brothers and sisters—they must have been undergraduates—joined the discussion on this same question of "double consciousness," and expressed with a touching sincerity, their own sense of loss and bewilderment in their various college environments, surrounded by two sets of demands that they could not comfortably reconcile. What was at the same time most moving and disconcerting for me, was that one

---

[1] W.E.B. DuBois. *The Souls of Black Folk* (1903), in W.E.B. DuBois: *Writings.* Library of America. New York, 1986, p. 364-5.

of these very articulate young students, addressed directly the African professors in the audience, including myself, seeking from us answers to their crippling dilemma.

Naturally, my own personal response to these young people was that we Africans—professors and all!—did not have ready-made answers for this dilemma, which existed and still exists in our midst as well; and that the resolution of this dilemma had to come as the result of personal reflection, hard work and resolve. And, of course, I have a multitude of personal anecdotes and experiences to draw from a life of several decades, as an African growing up, working, studying and travelling in Africa, in Europe, in North America, the Caribbean and elsewhere, to illustrate and bring home, in no abstract way, my meaning and my understanding of the far-reaching implications of that dilemma. In this particular instance, two will suffice:

One took place in up-country Gambia, my birth place, where I was conducting a tape-recording session one night in a remote Wolof village. In the middle of a very exciting three-hour session, the informant, a very knowledgeable elderly man, suddenly worried about the money that had been agreed upon before the beginning of the session, asked one of the young villagers in the audience to remind the toubab not to forget about the deal that had been struck and agreed upon beforehand, by all the parties concerned, pointing to the only toubab in the room, my "little" 20 year-old French brother-in-law, Jo Perrin, who was, at that particular time in his life, trapped in a web of uncertainties about choices and the future; and my way of helping him resolve his own dilemma was to have him join us in Dakar and travel with me in the Senegambian brousse (bush), as my research assistant. Needless to say that the venerable patriarch's question brought an irresistible smile to the faces of at least three members of the audience: Jo, the young villager who was supposed to translate to the toubab but whose services were not needed in that particular circumstance, and myself. This was 20 years ago.

The second anecdote took place more recently, about ten years later, in southeastern Nigeria, in Cross Rivers State, in the town of Uyo, in Ibibio country. I had just driven from Calabar to the Uyo College to perform the functions of an external examiner in the Department of Modern Languages there. On arrival I was taken to the local motel by my Uyo College colleague, Head of the Department of Modern Languages, an Ibibio sister who had lived and studied in Cameroon and France, and who held at the time, the unflinching position that Nigerians, in particular, and Anglophone Africans, in general, had not suffered as much as Francophone Africans from the colonial brainwashing that Franz Fanon so aptly described as "l'intériorisation du complexe d'infériorité" (the interaction of the complex of inferiority) (Fanon: *Peau noire, masques blancs*, Seuil, Paris, 1952). It goes without saying that my own position was different, based on the conviction that the result of colonial brainwashing was basically the same everywhere, with naturally a variety of nuances. But I could not convince my colleagues. I was naturally happy that an incident at the Uyo motel did seem to shake her staunch certitude, somewhat: Confronted with difficulties at the registration desk, we had asked the clerk to call the motel manager. The clerk then ordered a messenger to go and tell the manager that two "expatriates" wanted to see him! Needless to elaborate here on my triumphant grin and my colleague's genuine bewilderment at the clerk's spontaneous explanation that his use of the word "expatriate" meaning white or European, or *Mbakara* in Ibibio and Efik country, *Oyinbo* in Yoruba country, *Toubab* in Senegal *Mzungu* in East Africa ... etc... etc ... was the best way to convince the manager that there were two "important" people asking to see him and thus get him out of his office without undue delay!

DuBois' formula, "to be a co-worker in the kingdom of culture, to escape both death and isolation" is, in my opinion, still most valid for us, as we move into our 21st year of existence as an association of teachers, critics and students of African literature and culture.

While I would be the last person to want to exaggerate the importance of the recognition represented by the winning of Nobel Prizes, Booker Prizes and Pulitzer Prizes or Goncourt Prizes, for that matter, by our writers, I am, and I believe that we should all be, elated by such events, because they do indeed help make our writers move away from forced isolation to the attention of a broader readership, as well as gain more overdue deserved recognition within the academy of which we are an integral part. However, we, in the ALA, have not waited and will not wait for these recognitions, to do our own reckoning and to honor our writers and artists through our serious and thorough studies, through the expanded insertion of their works within the curricula of our institutions and beyond.

After a separation of over a quarter of a century, I recently reestablished contact with an old colleague and friend from my early years at the University of Ibadan, in Nigeria, more than thirty years ago. He was anxious to know whether I believed that Wole Soyinka *really* deserved The Nobel Prize for Literature which he won in 1986. My response was that he deserved it at least as much as one of his predecessors to the same prize, the American novelist Saul Bellow, who once asked with provocative arrogance: "Who is the Tolstoy of the Zulus? The Proust of the Papuans ... I'd be glad to read them!"

Alan Bloom, author of the best-selling *The Closing of the American Mind* (Simon and Schuster, NY, 1987 with a Forward by Saul Bellow) deplored what he saw as the descent of contemporary American culture into mediocrity, and pointed his finger at the culprit, i.e. cultural relativism or the so-called notion that "all societies, all cultures are equal."

While we, as members of this Association, scholars, teachers, writers, critics and artists committed to the dissemination of ideas, concerns and forms that are enriching for the whole community of man and woman, can but agree with Alan Bloom, Saul Bellow, Susan Sontag and the like, that the "real community of man [and woman] is the community of those who seek the truth, of the potential knowers, that is, in principle, of all men to the extent they desire to know"[2] or that "Literature is not an equal opportunity employer,"[3] we however, should continue to reject vehemently the tendency to reserve membership to this "community of seekers of truth" only to one's "own kind" and only, in accordance with one's own set of arbitrary criteria.

When Chinua Achebe visited my campus last Spring, I brought to his attention a March 1991 *COMMENTARY* article by a certain Carol Iannone, entitled "Literature by Quota." The author, then a candidate for Director of NEH (National Endowment for the Humanities) from the far conservative end of the American intellectual establishment, was embarking on a righteous crusade against what she deplored forcefully as a signal of the new order of things in literature and the arts, in the United States of America, when writers of the calibre of Alice Walker, Gloria Naylor, Joyce Carol Oates, Charles Johnson and Toni Morrison were honored more for "who they were" than for their literary achievements. It was both ironic and disturbing that as a launching premise for her diatribe against what was, in her view, the poor quality of such literary works as *Beloved, The Women of Brewster Place*, or *The Color Purple*, Ms. Iannone would choose a passage from Achebe's *Anthills of the Savannah*, the delectable scene where Ikem Osodi, the journalist and writer in the novel, castigates vigorously the young pseudo socialist university students of the fictitious country of Kangaan, i.e. contemporary Nigeria, and urges them to drop

[2] Alan Bloom, quoted in *The New York Times Magazine* article of January 3, 1988, p. 15 "Chicago's Grumpy Guru. Best-selling Professor Alan Bloom and the Chicago Intellectuals."

[3] Susan Sontag's words at a 1986 international PEN conference in response to a protest by a group of participants against the under-representation of women writers on PEN Conference panels, quoted by Carol Iannone in March 1991 *COMMENTARY* article "Literature by Quota," p. 51.

their procrastinating, their posturing and their self-indulgence, and make better use of the meager educational resources that are squandered on them: "Yes you prefer academic tariff walls behind which you can potter around in mediocrity. And you are asking me to agree to hand over my life to a democratic dictatorship of mediocrity? No way..." (Achebe 1987, p. 160).

Within the context of the African writer's mission as perceived by Chinua Achebe, Ousmane Sembène, Wole Soyinka, Ngugi wa Thiong'o, and, in view of the reality of Africa today, the weight and meaning of the above passage are unmistakable. However, the off-context use of the passage by Ms. Iannone to sustain a discourse that most of us in this gathering, and Achebe himself, would not even begin to condone, while misleading, is unavoidable. It is the price to pay for exposure, for being part of a global world, and we, as lovers of good literature—and *Anthills of the Savannah* is indeed good literature—we prefer exposure, recognition and equal treatment to "isolation and death," to paraphrase W.E.B. DuBois.

I would now like to conclude and end the torture which you all seem to have voluntarily accepted so graciously, with an invitation to pay attention to the passionate plea that Ngugi wa Thiong'o makes in his recent collection of essays, *Moving the Centre*[4] regarding our national African languages. His plea is not just words; it is an invitation to an action into which he himself has already plunged, for more than a decade and a half now, through the writing and publication of creative pieces, as well as essays and children's books. And he is fully aware of the frustrations involved in fighting what he calls "the present conditions of a continent's disbelief in itself" (Ngugi 1993, p. xiv). Fortunately, Ngugi's invitation to move the center of our literary engagements from European languages to "a multiplicity of locations in our languages" (Ngugi 1993, p. xiv) is not a lone voice in the wilderness.

Some of you may remember the inaugural speech of our Dakar Conference in 1989, when the Minister of Culture, Professor Saxiir Caam, a mathematician, recited some of his own poetry in Wolof. Also in Senegal, a poet, playwright and novelist, Cheikh Aliou Ndao, a widely published author in French, is now producing work, mostly poetry, in Wolof. There are also other younger voices emerging from different backgrounds and presenting different outlooks, such as Thierno Seydou Sall and his *Kir doff* or *The Mad House*.

---

[4] Ngugi wa Thiong'o, *Moving the Centre. The Struggle for Cultural Freedoms*, Heinemann, 1993.

It is high time we listened, and listened actively.

I will illustrate what I see as progress in this area, with a final anecdote and a quote from a Wolof poem by Cheikh Ndao. Slow progress to be sure! But progress all the same.

In 1963, some 31 years ago, at the historical meeting on "The Teaching of African Literature in African Universities" in Dakar, Senegal, Ousmane Sembène walked to the podium and stated that there would be no true African literature as long as African writers persisted in writing only in French, English, Portuguese. The late Birago Diop, author of *Les Contes d'Amadou Koumba*, feeling the brunt of the provocation, challenged Sembène in his turn by inviting him to return to the podium and repeat his eloquent speech in Wolof or in any other Afiican language. Needless to say that at the time, Sembène chose not to oblige. Nevertheless, he did get involved later, and for a number of years, in the publication venture of *Kaddu*, a cultural and literary magazine in Wolof together with other Senegalese intellectuals and scholars. He also endeavored to write a number of his subsequent film scripts in Wolof or in other Senegalese languages.

It is notably important to point out that not only has Ngugi published novels (*Devil on the Cross*, Heinemann 1980; *Matigari*, Heinemann 1987), a play (*I Will Marry When I Want*, Heinemann 1980) in Gikuyu, but he went even further in his commitment to assuring a place in the future to our African languages, by writing two of the essays included in his collection *Moving the Centre*: "English, a Language of the World?" and "Welcome Home Mandela," initially in Gikuyu. However, only the first one (Kiingeretha: Ruthiomi rwa Thi Yoothe? Kaba Giithwarri!) has so far been published (in the *Yale Journal of Criticism*, Fall 1990) in the original African language.

As we look to the future of our Association and our continent it is appropriate and envigorating to look beyond the waters, for linkages, exchanges and stimulation with our Diaspora. It is equally stimulating to look both to our South and to our North for inspiration and assurance. I will therefore end my presentation with a few lines from a poem in Wolof by my Senegalese brother Séex Ndaw and another in French, by my Moroccan brother Abdellatif Laâbi.

The poem from Cheikh Aliou Ndao (Sèex Aliyu NDAW's collection *Toalaon (woy)* 1990) is titled "Mandela ken du yow" (Mandela you are One (Dakar, 1985)[5]

---

[5] Séex Aliou NDAO, *Lolli Taataan*, IFAN, Univ. Ch. A. Diop, Dakar 1990, p. 32.

Ma ne ken du yow Mandela borooom jalóore
Dingana Citewayo ak Tchaka teew
Di la jàngal gar sa bakken ci sam réew
Ma ne ken du yow Mandela boroom jalóore
(I say, there is only one Mandela, the hero
Dingane, Cetshwayo, Chaka are your witnesses
They taught you the sacrifice of life for country
I say there is no equal to Mandela the hero.)

It should be noted that these lines were written five years before Mandela's
historic release from prison in 1990.

The Laâbi lines are from his 1992 volume *Le Soleil se meurt* (The
Sun is Dying) (Edit. de la Différence, Paris, 1992, pp. 71-72).

Non!
le temps n'est pas au rêve
C'est impudique un rêve
et inutile
comme les larines du poète
It n'y a de monde
que ce monde-ci
A lui nous appartenons
et à lui nous retournons
Que sa raison soit sanctifiée
Que son règne demeure
Il y a tout dans ce monde
tant décrié
Le soleil, la lune
les vaches, les cochons
la mer, la glèbe
l'amour, la haine
la joie, la tristesse
la paix, la guerre
les hauts et les bas
Que voulez-vous donc de plus?
Ce monde n'est pas parfait
mais c'est le seul qui existe
Trouvez-nous-en donc un autre!
Si j'avais des réponses
je ne me brûlerais pas aux questions
(No!
The time is not for dreams.
Dreaming is immodest and useless
like the poet's tears.
There is no world
but this our world
To it we belong
and to it we return

May its reason be hallowed
May its reign endure.
There is everything in this world
so often disparaged
the sun, the moon
the cows, the pigs
the sea, the earth
love, hate
joy, sadness
peace, war
the ups and downs
what else do you want?
this world is not perfect
but it is the only one we have
I dare you find us another one!
If I had answers
I would not burn myself with questions.)[6]

This closing message is the same as Achebe's to his fictional African student audience when the protagonist Ikem Osodi tells them that "Writers don't give prescriptions....They give headaches!"

Yes, Sisters and Brothers, colleagues, students, friends, relatives and distinguished guests! Let us ponder over these points, at the beginning our 21st year of existence and almost at the dawn of a new century and millennium, let us endeavor to act, however modestly, in our creative, in our academic and in our administrative activities, on these words of Ngugi wa Thiong'o:

> The growth of writing in African languages will need a community of scholars and readers in those very languages, who will bring into the languages the wealth of literature on modern technology, arts and sciences. For they need platforms. It is a vicious circle.[7]

Above all, brothers and sisters, ladies and gentlemen, let us continue relentlessly to build bridges across all barriers, real and fictitious, across the seas and across the deserts, from North to South, and from East to

---

[6] My translation.

[7] Ngugi wa Thiong'o, *Moving the Centre: The Struggle for Cultural Freedorns*, Heinemann, 1993.

WesT Yes! "No prescriptions! Only headaches!" Sorry, I did not bring any Tylenol or Advil with me on this trip!

March 1994,

Accra, Ghana

IVORY BEFITS HER ANKLES:
In Celebration of
Flora Nwanzuruahu Nwapa
and Her Legacy

by Marie Umeh
John Jay College

Our struggle is also the struggle of memory against forgetting.

bell hooks

If we stand tall it is because we stand on the backs of those who came before us.

Yoruba proverb

Ogbuide, the Queen of Women, comes from the Moon. She is good; the woman is beautiful, an invisible leader of the group. She helps the poor. When a poor person is hungry and comes to the water side, Ogbuide will give the person food.

Mrs. Onyemuru, ferrywoman at Oguta Lake.[1]

In the Southeastern part of Nigeria, women who have honored the community and distinguished themselves by accomplishing unusual feats, similar to Flora Nwapa, the mother of African women's literature, are given the title, "Lolo." Many Igbo women who take the title "Lolo" wear ivory anklets, which represent their great achievements. These women walk with pride and dignity throughout the community. They are highly recognized and respected.

Flora Nwanzuruahu Nwapa, Africa's first published female writer in the English language of international repute, was also known as Chief (Mrs.) Flora Nwapa Nwakuche. Certainly, "ivory befits her ankles." Her life's commitment to create realistic literary representations of Oguta women paved the way for other African writers, both female and male, to portray women in African literature outside the stereotypical images of

---

[1] This is how Mrs. Onyemuru, an indigene and griotte, describes the awesome water goddess Ogbuide, who dwells in Oguta Lake. See her oral testimony in Jell–Bahlsen's film *MammyWater: In Search of the Water Spirits in Nigeria*.

women as either *femmes fatales* or ne'er–do–wells. Her adult and children's books consistently reveal her commitment to the cause of women and her concern for their freedom from all practices and beliefs which distort their socio–cultural realities. Her creative works, especially those based on Igbo traditional life, show the illusory nature of the claim of superiority of man over woman.

Undoubtedly, in traditional African societies, women are highly visible and influential as the custodians and transmitters of the group's cultural heritage. That is why the Africans say that the language given to us at birth is the mother's tongue. The mores and values of the community are passed on to us through our elders, especially women. Their use of prayers, lullabies, proverbs, riddles, folksongs, and life stories has been effectively didactic and highly instrumental in molding the African personality. It is through the oral tradition that members of the group learn their place in the world.

The study of Flora Nwapa's creative works gives credence to Amanor Dseagu's statement that "the African novel has been influenced by the oral traditions of Africa" (589). Flora Nwapa's major literary motifs, in her novels *Efuru, Idu, Never Again, Women Are Different*, and *The Lake Goddess* (forthcoming) are linked to the creativity embedded in Oguta oral traditions, which are dominated by women. One finds, for example, that the mythical figure of Ogbuide (also known as Eze/Nne Mmiri and Uhamiri), the divine Woman of the Lake, is woven into her novels. The creativity shared by the Oguta griottes and Nwapa has prompted Gay Wilentz to define her *oeuvres* as "woman–centered oraliterature"[2] (10).

There is no doubt that the predominant realism of Ogbuide, the Mother of the Lake, in Oguta lore and life is the central unifying device in the fiction of Flora Nwapa. As Henry Louis Gates, Jr. puts it: . . . the vernacular informs and becomes the foundation for formal black literature . . . black writers, both explicitly and implicitly, turn to the vernacular in various formal ways to inform their creation of written fictions. (xxii)

By extension, the griotte Mrs. Onyemuru and Flora Nwapa are both cultural progeny of Oguta myth and lore. Their shared oral heritage in Nwapa's last novel, *The Lake Goddess,* is gender specific, with both artists pointing to a female deity revered by the Oguta community. In Mrs. Onyemuru's oral rendition of Ogbuide, the Lake Goddess is described as "the Queen of Women" who "comes from the moon," one who is "beautiful, an invisible leader of the group."

---

[2] This is Gay Wilentz's term and spelling.

Another Oguta storyteller, Mrs. Nwammetu Okoroafor, extols the mythical powers of Ogbuide: "Uhamiri, the Goddess of the Lake, goes to the market. You will not know her. You can see her in the form of a beautiful woman. You cannot tell that she is from the water. She comes, buys and goes back. Before coming to the market, she ties her hair. After that she disappears and you don't know who she really is ... ."[3]

Both storytellers celebrate the Goddess for her beauty and greatness. The supernatural and beneficial attributes of Ogbuide as examined and extended by Nwapa, especially in her novel, *The Lake Goddess*, illustrate a conscious manipulation of these Oguta oral traditions. Gates calls this a "double–voiced relationship," wherein one speech act determines the internal structure of another, the second affecting the voice of the first by repetition and difference, signifyin(g) (xxv). Nwapa's rhetorical strategy, her creation of a "speakerly text," is a form of signification.

Ona, the protagonist in *The Lake Goddess*, is born into a Christian family in the town of Oguta, located in the southeastern part of Nigeria. From all appearances, Ona from the outset has been destined to serve Ogbuide as a priestess. As a child she is gifted and beautiful, born with supernatural powers such as the ability to prophesy. However, her parents, Mgbada and Akpe, attempt to thwart their daughter's call to serve the water goddess. They send Ona to a mission school and see to it that she marries a prosperous businessman who is a member of the church. Ona and her husband, Mr. Sylvester, have three children. Despite Ona's fellowship in the Christian community, however, Ogbuide continues to haunt her chosen disciple in dreams and visions. At the end of the novel, Ona leaves her husband and children and successfully takes up the full–time role of diviner and spiritual healer of the community. Obedience to Ogbuide confers status and power. As expressed by Jell–Bahlsen in "Female Power: Water Priestesses of the Oru–Igbo," Ogbuide provides her devotees with a special space, with recognition, and with a freedom that is accepted within their own society, transcending ordinary constraints (15).

The song which Ona sings at the end of *The Lake Goddess*, when she finally embraces her natural gift, gives glory to Ogbuide for her magnificence and kindness similar to that exhibited by the griottes Onyemuru and Okoroafor. Nwapa's creative use of the Oguta griottes' own creations establishes the art form Gates identifies as rhetorical naming (52). Nwapa's formal revision, elaboration, and amplification represent both the group mind and her conscious artistic synthesis of her own life

---

[3] Mrs. Nwammetu Okoroafor's oral testimony also appears in Jell–Bahlsen's film *MammyWater*.

experiences with Oguta oral traditions. Ona's song demonstrates the interplay of Nwapa's art with those of Onyemuru and Okoroafor and reveals an intertextual relationship of ideas and feelings of the artists:

Supreme God
The creator of
Water
Land
Air
The Lake goddess
Water goddess
You are water
Without water
We die

Without water
We are nothing
Ogbuide
You taught me
From my mother's womb
To worship you
To use your water
To cure
All diseases
Because water is life
Without water
The fishes of the lake
Would die
Without water
The plants in the forest
Would die
Without water
We humans
Would die
Great goddess
The supreme God
Made you great
By making you
The water goddess
Ogbuide, the Lake goddess
You chose me
From my mother's womb
To serve you and
To be your priestess
Therefore
Ogbuide
I must be your priestess

Until I die. (227–28).

The attribution of life to water is realistic and at the same time carries mythological implications. Ordinarily, water is essential to life, but its symbolic source of strength through the beneficial activities of Ogbuide makes it a mystical essence in the life of the Oguta people. In effect the Lake Goddess becomes the kind and powerful mother of the Oguta community, and this feminine presence is Nwapa's way of asserting and highlighting the feminine principle as a distinct cultural factor in Oguta life. The mystique of the Lake Goddess also asserts the centrality of the feminine essence in the society. In addition, the words of the song take on a wider meaning when the novelist writes: "Without water/ we humans/ would die," thereby portraying the manner in which natural elements have become part of the human element and presence.

Nwapa's technique, as illustrated above, displays her conscious manipulation of Oguta oral traditions to achieve an individual creative alchemy. This technique does not falter even when she adopts the multiple character approach whereby the story is presented from the perspectives and views of several individuals. Generally, the characters who emerge from her novels are strong, individualized women who are not burdened with the baggage of patriarchal societies. These women often make decisions and act in ways that question the general assumptions and social practices that restrict womanhood. In the creation of Efuru in the novel of the same name, Amaka in *One Is Enough* and Ona in *The Lake Goddess*, for example, Nwapa presents the female characters as decisive in stepping beyond the institution of marriage. And while Nwapa may not be insisting that marriage itself is an institution that is obsolete, she gives considerable emphasis to the idea that such institutions should not be seen as insurmountable barriers to female self–actualization.

The novels of Flora Nwapa examine and revise the prevalent notions of marriage, social responsibility, self–sacrifice, and service to society and humanity. Ona's decision to serve Ogbuide, the Lake Goddess, is part of this service to society, for she no longer functions as a mother to three children but as a mother–priestess to all the men, women, and children of the community, who are all children of the water. This is obviously a higher responsibility since it signifies an ennobling duty and calls for Ona to devote her time and energies both to act as spokesperson for the Lake Goddess and to mediate between the Lake Goddess and the people.

Another factor which emerges from Nwapa's feminine perspective is that the actions of her female characters catalyze events, and furthermore, the fates of other characters depend upon those actions. This revisionist stance is deliberate, for it stresses the realism of daily interactions in the

Oguta society where the women are easily perceived as industrious, successful, and socially important in business as well as in religious and cultural activities. The revisionist aspect of Nwapa's novels becomes even more prominent when one notes that in divine activities the Goddess of the Lake is given much respect in the Oguta community, which means that the women who become her priestesses have a large measure of that respect and dignified reverence attached to them. In Chinua Achebe's *Things Fall Apart*, Chielo, the Priestess of Ogbala, is glimpsed only occasionally, but in *The Lake Goddess*, Ona the Priestess of Oguta Lake is just as much the center of consciousness as the character of Ezeulu is in Chinua Achebe's *Arrow of God*. Like Achebe, Wole Soyinka focuses on male figures. In his plays, especially *The Strong Breed*, the famous priests and particularly the "carriers" on which the society depends for survival are male, with all the attendant patriarchal implications. In Nwapa's novels, short stories, and children's books, on the other hand, the "carriers," those characters who make sacrifices in the interest of the rest of the people, are female. Thus, the magnificence of the female essence of priesthood in Flora Nwapa's fiction subverts the literary tradition of patriarchy in Nigerian modern literature.

Nwapa gave African women an authentic identity in literature by introducing a female literary tradition at a time when little or nothing of a realistic nature had been written about African women. For the most part, Nigerian male authors such as Chinua Achebe, Wole Soyinka, and Cyprian Ekwensi depicted women living under a rigid sex–role segregation system, with no individuality, personhood, or power. However, Nwapa's women take center stage by exerting their industry, ingenuity, and resilience. They often wield power and protect themselves from humiliation and dehumanization, unlike many of Buchi Emecheta's and Mariama Bâ's fictional heroines.

One critic, Chidi Ikonné, contends that Nwapa's womenfolk are imbued with beliefs that mirror Oguta society. He goes on to say that her women passively accept the idea that "woman is basically inferior to the man, a concept which underlies the folk attitude to, and treatment of women" (102). While it may be true that Nwapa records traditional practices which oppress women such as clitoridectomy, polygamy, wife inheritance, and property disinheritance, she also challenges some of the fundamental assumptions concerning Igbo women passively accepting retrogressive cultural norms. For example, Idu, in the novel *Idu*, rejects the cultural ethics of wife inheritance, male dominance, and the primacy of the child. After years of yearning for an offspring, Idu finally gives birth to a son. But when her husband dies prematurely, she wills herself to die rather than permit herself to become the wife of Ishiodu, her husband's younger brother. Idu had had an ideal, loving relationship with Adiewere that another husband would find impossible to live up to. Her death shortly after her spouse's demise therefore unequivocally professes her deep affection for her husband who could not be replaced by someone else. In defense of Idu's final act, and of Nwapa's unconventional ending, Ernest Emenyonu, in "Who Does Flora Nwapa Write For?" says: Too fantastic? Not if you have been listening to the voices in the novel. Too unrealistic? Not if you have been close enough to the Igbo culture and life–ways. Too remote? Not if you understand that even among the Igbo, love between two individuals can be such that one cannot die without the other. (30)

Thus Nwapa in this novel writes off the effacement, marginality, and misrepresentation of women with subtlety and grace, contending that a woman is not an inanimate object without brains, feelings, emotions, and desires. In challenging male perceptions of what women want and need, Nwapa gives the female point of view. In her "woman–centered oraliterature," she emphatically asserts that the so–called passive, passionless, unimaginative, powerless, and irresponsible African woman is a figment of the male's imagination which she has set out to correct. It is for this reason that Susan Andrade calls Nwapa's creation of strong, intelligent protagonists an act of rebellion against a Nigerian literary tradition dominated by male writers (105).

Indeed, Nwapa unleashed a vibrant creative energy and began a female tradition in African letters that successfully confronted the one–dimensional, stereotypical portrayal of women as *femmes fatales* and ne'er–do–wells. The year 1966 can therefore be considered the beginning of the female "oraliterature" renaissance in African letters, with Flora Nwapa as the first Nigerian female novelist and its primary exponent.

With Nwapa's picture of the community of Oguta women, a positive, multi–dimensional, complex, and realistic vocabulary describing women was introduced into African letters. For example, in Nwapa's pathbreaking novel *Efuru*, the word "female" represents a wealthy trader, a sharp business entrepreneur, a decision–maker, an independent thinker, a powerful, respected priestess, and a deity, Ogbuide. The idea of women as *femmes fatales* and ne'er–do– wells is nonexistent in Nwapa's texts. Efuru, the main character in the novel, is deliberately drawn as a character noted for her business acumen, wealth, and resilience.

Another erroneous conception that Nwapa challenges in her *oeuvres* is the idea that African women are not property owners. It may be true that in some African communities women do not inherit property and are never heirs to their husband's wealth. Only sons are heirs. However, Nwapa points to the fact that in Oguta many of the "upstairs" (a two–three storey [*sic*] building) in the township were erected and owned by women, whose sons inherit their wealth! One character in *Efuru* says, "[L]ook around this town, nearly all the storey [*sic*] buildings you find are built by women who at one time or another have been worshippers of Uhamiri" (192). Priestess or not, having economic independence is part of an Oguta woman's self–esteem. Hence, Nwapa's fiction provides authentic glimpses of Oguta women achieving economic power and exalted positions through participation in religious, business, and political activities.[4]

In *The Lake Goddess* Nwapa gives women a voice of their own in her literary explorations of the depth and meaning of female bonding.[5] Female bonding is female solidarity and woman–centered networking. Women have always depended upon the positive voices and healing powers of an extended family of sisters—women who instruct, assist, and protect other women—for understanding, compassion, empathy, and truth in order to transcend threatening situations and achieve liberation from oppressive forces in their lives. The two fish sellers in *The Lake Goddess*, Mgbeke and Ekecha, epitomize female friendship without eroticized bonds. They reflect the ideal in companionship: they nurture and comfort each other, and they think alike. They cohere as partners in trade and again as friends in the private space of their homes. For example, in the business of finding husbands for their daughters, their cooperation differentiates their relationship from the largely negative picture in literature of women competing with one another for the attention of a male. Mgbeke and Ekecha independently decide to seek the services of Mgbada, Ona's father, a diviner with mythical powers to solve their problems. When Mgbeke thinks aloud on the subject, Ekecha replies, "I have already made up my mind to see him about my daughter" (198). The next episode shows them together in consultation with the renowned *dibia*, Mgbada.

Almost ten years before publication of *The Lake Goddess*, Nwapa presented a paper at the Second International Feminist Book Fair in Oslo, Norway, in which she said that sisterhood would survive "if we as women pay less attention to men and marriage . . . I am married and I have children. But I do not live for my husband alone. I live for him, for my children and for my profession" (6). The close relationship between

---

[4] In her short story "The Campaigner," Nwapa has her female protagonist, Chief Mrs. Deide, influence the outcome of an election by means of her political prowess.

[5] Female bonding is also an important motif in *Efuru*, *One Is Enough*, and *Women Are Different*.

Mgbeke and Ekecha reflects Nwapa's belief that sisterhood is very much alive in Nigeria today.

In addition to mirroring positive African traditions that still exist in Oguta society despite colonial intrusion, Nwapa's creative works are rich in Igbo proverbs, folkways, and linguistic syntax that gracefully flow into her narratives to strengthen her plots and add color to her characters' speech. It is Nwapa's accurate portrayal of Igbo thought patterns, imagery, humor, and philosophies that prompted Ernest Emenyonu, in his essay "Who Does Flora Nwapa Write For?" to say that "the realism of her themes and her ever–increasing sensitive use of language are two of Flora Nwapa's most enduring qualities as a novelist" (32). Her characters' speech authentically represents Oguta parlance. The heroine, Amaka, in *One Is Enough*, is a case in point. Disappointed in her marriage to Obiora, which was one of deception, sexist domination, and exploitation, she returns the bride price. She subsequently has twins by Father McLaid but decides *not* to marry him. To make her point to her mother and sister that one husband is enough and she will stick to her initial decision not to marry the father of her twins, she employs an Igbo idiomatic expression:

> You heard me. *I didn't have water in my mouth* when I spoke to you. I don't want to be a wife anymore, a mistress yes, with a lover, yes of course, but not a wife. (127, emphasis mine)

"I didn't have water in my mouth" is an idiomatic folk expression that captures Igbo figurative language. Amaka makes herself unequivocally clear when Father McLaid proposes that the single life suits her. She declares, "As a wife I am never free. . . I am almost impotent. I am in prison, unable to advance in body and soul" (127). Amaka's use of colloquialism here reflects the influence of a traditional art form that Nwapa consciously taps, identifying women as "carriers" of Oguta verbal art.

Good "oraliterature" is also distinctive for its use of proverbs. As Chinua Achebe says, "Proverbs are the palm–oil with which words are eaten" (6). Just as palm–oil is an essential ingredient found in most Igbo cuisine, proverbs add spice and flavor to Igbo verbal art. Igbo proverbs also reflect the Igbo community's outlook and philosophies of life. Nwapa's novels are enriched with proverbs that comment on the moral and ethical life of her characters. An exemplary use of the proverb is found in *The Lake Goddess*. When Ona's husband, Mr. Sylvester, learns that his wife, and the mother of his children, is called by Ogbuide, the Mother of the Lake, to be her priestess, he cries, "The spirit has killed me" (216).

Mgbada, the diviner, replies with the proverb, "When the gods give us craw–craw, they also give us the nails with which to scratch."[6]

The position of this saying toward the end of the novel when the nagging problem arises of whether or not to allow Ona to serve Eze Mmiri, the Lake Goddess, is quite appropriate and effectively demonstrates the skill of the author. Proverbs can sum up a situation, pass judgment, or recommend a course of action; they give advice as well as recall traditional wisdom to clarify a given situation. In this case, the proverb recommends a course of action and foreshadows a positive ending, the resolution of the conflict in the novel. At the family meeting that follows Ona's acceptance of her divine calling, it is decided that Ona will relinquish her role as wife and mother and serve the Lake Goddess, instead of thwarting the will of the deity and her destiny. The family's wise decision to find another wife for Mr. Sylvester and have Ona's parents care for her three children while she serves Ogbuide—a decision that captures the wisdom of the ancients— brings peace to Ona and every member of her family after years of resistance and psychological disorientation.

Rhonda Cobham, in her "Introduction" to the special issue of *Research in African Literatures* on women's writing, called for the recognition of images/traditions of female strength and transcendence from which African women writers draw (139). Certainly, Nwapa's novels address Cobham's plea for a more realistic picture of African women in literature. Her *oeuvres* counteract the distorted and largely pejorative images of women in Nigerian literature depicted by her male compatriots and acknowledges female empowerment in an African community. Her "oraliterature" is a celebration of positive female archetypes, such as the water spirit Ogbuide and the earth goddess Ala, as well as the griottes who form a vibrant part of African life and culture even today (Arinze 14). In fact, Nwapa's theory of female independence is based on the female models she witnessed as an active participant in the Oguta age–grade network from childhood to adulthood. Coming from a culture where women are no strangers to self–actualization and industry, her womanist perspective is rooted in Oguta cultural dynamics. Additionally, her *noire vision du monde* supports Ester Boserup's statement that the women traders of West Africa are famous for their enterprising spirit and account for over half of the labor force in trade (87–88).

African women have a voice not only as griottes in the artistic realm and as traders in the economic structure of their respective communities but also as priestesses in the religious sector. In her essay "Female Status

---

[6] Craw–craw is an itching disease similar to chicken pox.

in the Public Domain," Peggy Sanday asserts: "It is the existence of positive female deities who have general powers in the community that provides women with opportunities for activity outside the domestic realm" (206). Ogbuide, as the spiritual and mythical female figure to Oguta indigenes, is the revolutionary symbol that gives Oguta women autonomy and honor in the face of phallocratic imperatives that lay claim to women's bodies and beauty.

Nwapa's role in the Nigerian literary canon has been to initiate the womanization of Nigerian letters. Her originality of vision and rich "oraliterature" set the stage for her literary followers, Buchi Emecheta, Zulu Sofola, Mabel Segun, Tess Onwueme, Ifeoma Okoye, Zaynab Alkali, and Eno Obong, to name only a few contemporary female authors who revised and expanded her authentic characterization of African womanhood. As Kamene Okonjo points out, African women have a vital place in the scheme of things within the African world order. She goes on to say: The African woman has not been inactive, irrelevant and silent. Rather, African tradition has seen the wisdom of a healthy social organization where all its citizens are seen to be vital channels for a healthy and harmonious society. Hence the establishment of a dual–sex power structure which is lacking in European and Arab cultures. (46)

Most African women work both inside and outside the compound in order to take care of themselves, their children, their husbands, and their relatives. Hence, more often than not African women writers qualify the term "feminist" since it does not adequately describe their socio–cultural realities. Nwapa prefers to identify with Alice Walker's term "womanist" to show her allegiance to the struggle of black women in Africa and the Diaspora against racism, sexism, and ageism (Perry 1262). Womanist poetics in general celebrates male–female relationships, family stability, and the healing of black nations torn asunder by colonialism, ethnicity, corruption, individualism, and innumerable social ills. Womanist poetics, as adapted by Nwapa, is similar to Walker's ideology, involving as it does the coming together of males and females on issues of gender asymmetry such as polygamy, wife inheritance, and son preference. Nwapa's attempt through her art to transform her society into a more humane community is recognized in the ending of *The Lake Goddess*. All minds, both male and female, join together in coming to the decision that Ona should follow the will of Ogbuide, the merciful and kind water spirit, who protects her children from evil. As Chikwenye Okonjo Ogunyemi points out,

"Womanism is a philosophy that celebrates black roots, the ideas of black life, while giving a balanced presentation of black womandom" (240).[7]

A complex figure and a private, dignified individual, Flora Nwapa labored against many odds to surmount obstacles that would have defeated a lesser person. Not content with the mere publication of adult novels, she went on to write children's books, plays, and essays. Additionally, she actively marketed her books at international conferences and book fairs to disseminate her "woman–centered" perspective to academic and grassroots communities all over the globe. In 1977 she established Tana Press Limited to ensure that her books would continue to circulate throughout Africa, as well as Europe, Asia, and the United States. In 1992 she successfully launched her publishing debut with Africa World Press in the United States, which reprinted and distributed her *oeuvres*. And, according to her son, Uzoma Gogo Nwakuche, he and his sisters, Ejine and Amede, are committed to seeing that their late mother's dream becomes a reality. In an interview with Mr. Nwakuche, this writer was informed that just before Nwapa was to begin a teaching appointment as a Visiting Professor at East Carolina University in North Carolina, she marked off a tract of land for a Flora Nwapa Foundation to be built in Oguta as a center of learning.[8] The Flora Nwapa Foundation will enable scholars and students of African literature and African studies to read and study her published and unpublished manuscripts, short stories, plays, and essays as well as Oguta lore and culture.

Toni Morrison, the first African–American woman to receive the Nobel Prize for literature in 1993, stated in an interview–essay, "Rootedness: The Ancestor as Foundation": "If you kill the ancestor you kill yourself" (344). We must stand tall knowing the power, strength and wisdom of the ancestor is as close as a breath. All that we ever need to be, to do, to know, to have, is available. All we need to do is to take a stand and not forget to remember. Flora Nwapa, the mother of African women's literature, must be remembered. Our ancestor has passed on as part of the evolution of the race. She died so that her force would be shifted into the invisible, untouchable force that sustains us and our children. Let us continue to keep Flora Nwapa, our ancestor, alive by disseminating her ideas and her philosophy with the same energy that her own artistic life radiated. This tribute then, is a kind of praisesong, honoring our literary

---

[7] Chikwenye Okonjo Ogunyemi identifies a womanist streak in Black women's writing in "Womanism: The Dynamics of the Contemporary Black Female Novel in English."

[8] Uzoma Gogo Nwakuche, personal interview, 13 July 1994.

foremother, Flora Nwapa, for her foresight and forthrightness, her inspiration to all of her children on earth to work for greater self-actualization and happiness.

WORKS CITED

Achebe, Chinua. *Things Fall Apart*. London: Heinemann, 1958.

Andrade, Susan Z. "Rewriting History, Motherhood, and Rebellion: Naming an African Woman's Literary Tradition." *Research in African Literatures* 21.1 (1990): 91–110.

Arinze, Cardinal Francis. *Sacrifice in Ibo Religion*. Ibadan: Ibadan UP, 1970.

Boserup, Ester. *Women's Role in Economic Development*. New York: St. Martin's, 1970.

Cobham, Rhonda. "Introduction." Spec. Issue on Women's Writing. *Research in African Literature* 19.2 (1988): 137–42.

Dseagu, Amanor S. "The Influence of Folklore Techniques on the Form of the Novel." *New Literary History* 23.3 (1992): 583–605.

Ekwensi, Cyprian. *Jagua Nana*. London: Hutchinson, 1961.

Emenyonu, Ernest. *The Rise of the Igbo Novel*. Ibadan: Oxford UP, 1978.

_____. "Who Does Flora Nwapa Write For?" *African Literature Today* 7 (1975): 28–33.

Gates, Henry Louis, Jr. *The Signifying Monkey: A Theory of African–American Literary Criticism*. New York: Oxford UP, 1988.

Ikonné, Chidi. "The Folk Roots of Flora Nwapa's Early Novels." *African Literature Today* 18 (1992): 96–104.

Jell–Bahlsen, Sabine. "Female Power: Water Priestesses of the Oru–Igbo." *Sisterhood, Feminisms and Power*. Ed. Obioma Nnaemeka. Lawrenceville, NJ: Africa World P. (Forthcoming, 1995).

_____. *MammyWater: In Search of the Water Spirits in Nigeria*. Berkeley: University of California Media Center, 1991.

Mojola, Yemi. "Flora Nwapa." *Perspectives on Nigerian Literature: 1700 to the Present. Volume II*. Ed. Yemi Ogunbiyi. Lagos: Guardian, 1988, 122–127.

Morrison, Toni. "Rootedness: The Ancestor as Foundation." *Black Women Writers (1950–80): A Critical Evaluation*. Ed. Mari Evans. New York: Doubleday, 1984.

Nwakuche, Uzoma Gogo. Personal interview. With Marie Umeh. 13 July 1994.

Nwapa, Flora. "The Campaigner." *The Insider: Stories of War and Peace from Nigeria*. Ed. Chinua Achebe et al. Enugu: Nwankwo–Ifejika, 1971. 75–88.

_____. *Cassava Song and Rice Song*. Enugu: Tana, 1986.

_____. *Efuru*. London: Heinemann, 1966.

_____. *Idu*. London: Heinemann, 1970.

_____. *The Lake Goddess*. (Unpublished manuscript)

_____. *Never Again*. Trenton, NJ: Africa World P, 1992.

_____. *One Is Enough*. Enugu: Tana, 1981.

_____. "Sisterhood and Survival: The Nigerian Experience." Paper presented at the Second International Feminist Book Fair. Oslo, Norway, 1986.

_____. *This Is Lagos and Other Stories*. Trenton, NJ: Africa World P, 1992.

_____. *Wives at War and Other Stories*. Trenton, NJ: Africa World P, 1992.

_____. *Women Are Different*. Trenton, NJ: Africa World P, 1992.

Ogunyemi, Chikwenye Okonjo. "Womanism: The Dynamics of the Contemporary Black Female Novel in English." *Revising the Word and the World: Essays in Feminist Literary Criticism*. Ed. Vèvè A. Clark, Ruth–Ellen B. Joeres, and Madelon Sprengneter. Chicago: Chicago UP, 1993. 231–48.

Okonjo, Kamene. "The Dual–Sex Political System in Operation: Igbo Women and Community Politics in Midwestern Nigeria." *Women in Africa: Studies in Social and Economic Change*. Ed. Nancy J. Hafkin and Edna G. Bay. Stanford, CA: Stanford UP. 1976. 45–58.

Perry, Alison. "Meeting Flora Nwapa." *West Africa* (18 June 1984): 1262.

Sanday, Peggy. "Female Status in Public Domain." *Woman, Culture, and Society*. Ed. Michelle Zimbalist Rosaldo and Louise Lamphere. Stanford, CA: Stanford UP, 1974. 189–206.

Vanzant, Iyanla. *Acts of Faith: Daily Meditations for People of Color*. New York: Simon & Schuster, 1993.

Wilentz, Gay. *Binding Cultures: Black Women Writers in Africa and the Diaspora*. Bloomington: Indiana UP, 1992.

SECTION B:

Shifting Paradigms

GRAVES WITHOUT BODIES:

The Mnemonic Importance Of Equiano's Autobiography

by Kwadwo Opoku-Agyemang
University of Cape Coast, Ghana

Celebrating Equiano: The Triumph Of An Interesting African
American Literature makes available to us direct autobiographical knowledge about life in American slavery from the point of view of the enslaved. This achievement is related directly to the New England Anti-Slavery Society which was founded in 1831 and went on to become a major force in American social and political history. In the thirty years between 1830 and 1860, an age that nearly encompasses the grand Romantic Period in American literary history, a number of autobiographical accounts about life in slavery by escaped slaves appeared as a part of the abolition movement. This body of work is recognized in the literature today by the term "slave narratives." Slave narratives became the popular reading of the time, and many former slaves such as Charles Ball, Moses Roper, Josiah Henson, Solomon Northrup, Sojourner Truth and William Wells Brown, who was also the first American novelist (Holman and Harmon 1986: 560) wrote their stories. The most representative and best achieved specimen of these important historical and literary documents is Frederick Douglass' eponymous *A Narrative of the Life of Frederick Douglass, An American Slave* (1845). Douglass's personal account dramatizes his quest to escape enslavement and to shape an identity for himself outside the caste and strictures of slavery.

The story Douglass tells is detailed enough to give a clear insider's view of life in slavery in America: the diurnal activities on Colonel Lloyd's plantation in Maryland; the quality of the white overseers—not always, but often enough atrocious; the desperate need of slaves like himself to escape up north to freedom; the equally urgent desire for an education, which is seen as the gateway to freedom; and the utterly dehumanizing impact of slavery on both the victim and those who enjoy its profits. The most interesting sections of the autobiography occur, however, when Douglass stands back from the details to reflect on the significance of his life and experiences. For example, early in his life, while living in Baltimore with the Auld family, he came to see a crucial connection between slavery, freedom and education. Slavery and freedom are two opposite conditions of life mediated by education, for the knowledge that comes with education intensifies awareness of the intolerable condition of slavery. He became dedicated, therefore, to acquiring the ability and habit of literacy so that, as Mr. Auld predicted, he would make himself unsuitable for slavery.

Douglass offers some other interesting insights into life in slavery, one of which is worth noting here. Indeed his comment that there is no joy without sadness in the songs one heard on the plantation is a valid and accurate description of Blues music. In a fine book on African-American culture, *Stomping the Blues*, Albert Murray (1976) has elaborated on the subject by making a distinction between Blues as music, and blues as such:

> The blues as such are synonymous with low spirits. Blues music is not ... With all its preoccupations with the most disturbing aspects of life Blues music is something contrived specifically to be performed as entertainment. (Murray: 45)

Albert Murray's optimistic interpretation of Blues music is qualified by "the most disturbing aspects of life"; this gives the music its quality of *discordia concors*, abject melancholia that simultaneously transforms itself into harmony, release and joy, or what Frederick Douglass identified as "no joy without sadness."

Douglass's autobiography epitomizes the many stories of hardship, escape, and the dignity of self-discovery common to the slave narratives. These narratives are interesting as both history and literature, but in a more specific sense their major appeal lies in the fact that together they are the considered reflections and historical evidence of one of the three moving forces in the history of slavery, the other two being the African on one hand, and the European and the American of European descent on the other. In other words they are important as literature.

The verdict is not unanimous regarding the literary status and acceptable definition of autobiography (Roy Pascal 1960; James Olney 1972; Stephen Butterfield 1974; Estelle Jelinek 1980; Paul Eakin 1985). In the view of some scholars, however, autobiography occurs in a formal sense when there is coincidence between author, protagonist and narrator in a prose narrative (Philippe Lejeune 1982).

As autobiography the slave narrative cannot by definition be duplicated for the reason that each specimen of the genre is the unique representation of a life. It is a self-reflexive, imaginative activity in which the autobiographer must decide, within the given facts, the proper way to imagine and present the individual self. Whereas the autobiographer may not imagine the facts of the life, he or she is at liberty to formulate the voice of the persona and the personality of the protagonist in the direction of predilection. Another reason why each text of autobiography stands alone is the unique and individual interpretation it gives of the life experiences which forms its subject. Even when distorted by suppressed or half-truths the autobiography remains valuable in what that unfaithful allegiance to facts shows of character. Thus even when an autobiographer clearly lies about the facts of his or her life this should not affect the value of the work in any major way: it may merely reveal to us the writer's attitude to those facts, and that revelation should help us in forming our picture of the character. Frank Harris (1963), the Victorian philanderer, exaggerated his sexual exploits beyond belief, but the value of *My Life and Love* remains intact, if only because it privileges entry into Harris' frenetic world of sexual fantasies. Autobiography as a whole rests on historical accuracy but our attention is claimed first and foremost by the perceptions, the quality and selection of material, and the exercise of judgement by the writer. The successful autobiography is one that shows a mind reflecting upon, sifting and relating to events; it must display a person changing and being changed by life's experiences, and sometimes even by the very process of writing the autobiography.

Thus, in the slave narratives we get unique eye-witness accounts of life in slavery in North America, but even more important, we discover in them the mind and judgement of the enslaved African in America.

* * *

African literature does not possess a comparable body of writing, but there are a few important examples of autobiographical reflection on the slave experience to dramatize the absence. The most prominent, because most complete and best achieved, is Olaudah Equiano's *The Interesting Narrative of the Life of Olaudah Equiano or Gustavus Vassa, the African*. The work was first published in two volumes in 1789, an apparently auspicious year for literature since the same year saw the publication of the first American novel, William Hill Brown's *The Power of Sympathy*, and William Blake's *Songs of Innocence*. 1789 was also a good year for politics, for that was when the American Federal Government was established; and of course, the Bastille was stormed that very year to herald the French Revolution.

It is interesting to consider what the year meant to two contemporaries of the age, William Wordsworth and Olaudah Equiano. The budding English poet, Wordsworth, was nineteen years old in 1789 and in school in Cambridge when the Revolution broke. The promise of the new excited him. Two years later he went to France, clearly taken by the fresh dawn in European political history. Reminiscing later in his life about the euphoria of the period, he was to write in his autobiographical account of the development of a poet's mind, *The Prelude*, written between 1798 and 1805, that it was bliss then to be alive, but to be young was very heaven. The year was also full of new promise for Equiano the African, but for a different reason. Formerly a slave, he had worked for his freedom and had now reached a point where he could see in print the story of his life, and in it the story of a continent racked to the limit of endurance under bondage. The publication of his work is perhaps equal in import to that great revolution in terms of what it meant to the idea of freedom.

Olaudah Equiano was born in 1745, forty-four years earlier, in present-day Nigeria in a village probably to the east of the Niger river. At the age of eleven, he and his only sister were abducted by slave-raiders and sold into slavery. He was taken to the coast then across the Atlantic to Barbados in the Caribbean, and from there to Virginia in the United States where he was bought by the owner of a trade ship. For the next thirty years he worked on many naval and trading ships. One of his many owners allowed him to trade on the side and by hard work and sheer frugality he was able to save the forty pounds sterling necessary to buy his freedom. This was in 1766. He was twenty-one.

As a free man, Equiano continued to make his living as a sailor and saw a great deal of the world as a result. He visited the Mediterranean and was part of an ill-starred expedition to the Arctic in 1773. He maintained an active interest in the British anti-slavery movement, and grew to become one of the acknowledged leaders of the African community in London. It is known that in 1787 he was deeply involved in the first expedition of freed Africans to settle in Sierra Leone. A year after that, in 1788, and twenty years after achieving his own freedom, he presented the queen of England with a petition on behalf of the enslaved in the Caribbean.

Equiano published his autobiography in 1789 at age forty-four. He focused on the first thirty-two years of his life. It was well received. In the first thirty-six years of its publication the book saw seventeen editions in Britain and the United States alone. In 1967 Paul Edwards abridged and edited the two-volume work into a compact 200-page edition for Heinemann's African Writers Series. The year of Equiano's death remains uncertain, and has been variously given as 1797 and 1801.

The year 1989, marks the 200th anniversary of the publication of Equiano's autobiography. This is an important occasion in modern African letters for many reasons. First, the work is perhaps the first example in English of modern African autobiography. There is no full text of the genre of equal vintage. But even more important it remains the earliest and fullest literary statement by an African about the European slave-trade and the experience of slavery. There were other Africans before Equiano to write about their life in slavery and to express their views about their experiences. For example, two years before Equiano, in 1787, Ottobah Cuguano's *Thoughts and Sentiments on the Evil and Wicked Traffic of Slavery* appeared. Cuguano's book is interesting in what it reveals of its writer's strong feelings about slavery; and for that reason it remains an important document of the period. But the work shows little of Cuguano's life, except for his capture off the coast of present-day Ghana, probably near the village of Ajumako in the Central Region. Another work from the same period is Ignatius Sancho's letters of 1782. Sancho was a contemporary of Equiano and Cuguano, but his work does not refer directly to Africa, and it has no working memory of life there because he was born on board a slave ship in 1729. Thus, Equiano's is most likely the first true autobiography that provides a finished testimony by an African and gives a clear, first-hand account of the total range of the slave experience.

The range of Equiano's autobiography is total because it shows the life of the protagonist before his enslavement, during enslavement, and after enslavement, when he succeeded in buying away his freedom. Until his kidnapping by slavers, Equiano lived with his parents and family in the Ibo village of his birth. The early chapters of the book give an account of life in 18th century eastern Nigeria; they reveal a society whose inner workings rest finally on a finely-wrought system of checks and balances that place co-operation over competition, a society that possesses an intricate and well-developed aesthetic sense.

Between his capture when he was eleven years old and his freedom ten years later Equiano was a slave. He was owned and controlled by various "masters," and rights over his own productive powers were severely limited. But even though in his autobiography Equiano illustrates the horrors of enslavement with all the sharpness of an intelligent eyewitness, he places his greatest concern elsewhere in telling his story. He finds himself suddenly plucked from his birthplace and deposited with equal speed in a world in which he must learn to survive or die. Without the most basic tool of survival, language, and without knowledge of the environment, he must conjecture his destiny. This difficult ten-year period is characterized by Equiano's attempts to gain an understanding, and thus some control, of this new place and culture which his own have not prepared him for, and which, for the young boy, is so filled with evil he cannot account for. This effort to understand, illustrated by his extraordinary hunger for education, shows that from the very beginning of his captivity Equiano was concerned with much more than survival. He was caught in the struggle to give order to chaos, and as Ellison puts it, to rearrange reality to the patterns of his imagination (Ellison: 238). True that his life was filled with great tragedies, violence, brutalities, defeats and back-breaking work; but his life has to be seen and judged not merely in terms of these conditions. Equiano's life in slavery has to be conceived in terms of his will to challenge the reality imposed by his situation, and judged by the strengths that distinguish him. The autobiography attests that the man is more than the aggregate of the brutalities visited upon him, even in slavery.

Twenty-one years into his life and ten years after he was forcibly removed from his homeland, Equiano again became a free man. He spent the greater part of his active life in this period traveling, but in the last chapter of the autobiography, his tales of travel and adventure give way to a philosophical and scholarly recapitulation of his views on slavery and the European slave trade. For example he proposes as an alternative to enslavement, the conversion of Africa into a market for European goods by which British manufacturers "must and will, in the nature and reason of things, have a full and constant employ by supplying the African markets" (Equiano 159). Aware that the basic moving force of the slave trade is not racial hatred but the attraction of economic profit, Equiano argues that rather than go to the trouble of capturing Africans and inducing labour out of them in a foreign land, Europeans could make the same profit by turning Africans into consumers of manufactured goods in their continent. He envisioned "legitimate trade" as a commercial intercourse between Africa and Europe that would be less harmful to Africa and in which Europe could still make its money. The advantage of hindsight enables us to see this alternative as the standard bourgeois solution of the Abolitionists, the solution of capitalist imperialism and colonialism whose effects we are living with today in Africa. The point, however, is that Equiano comes across in the final chapter of his autobiography as an articulate spokesman for Africa and its predicaments. No longer the young Ibo boy of his mother's village, and no more the slave determined to break his chains by first freeing his mind from ignorance, he is now a mature defender of the destiny of his people. He no longer speaks of Iboland but of Africa; and even though he never got the opportunity to return physically to the lost patria, he reaches across the distance to make an emotional and metaphysical return.

An important feature of Equiano's work, and reason to acknowledge its 200th year of publication, therefore, is that it gives the African viewpoint in a history that has been inadequately constituted in our modern writing. In itself the book is not historiography; it is not a formal presentation that applies the strict techniques and methods of historical research. But it is history in the sense of standing as evidence of the past, a monument and material of the history much as the slave castles that line the coast of West Africa are artifacts of the period, awaiting the historian's insight.

Secondly, Equiano's autobiography is worthy of note because it stands at the aetiological confluence of the modern literatures of both Africa and Africa-America. The work is African because it is written about African issues from a viewpoint that is peculiarly African. But it is also African-American because its subject and thrust describe it as an early example of the slave narratives.

But more than any of these reasons, there is cause to celebrate Equiano's autobiographical achievement because by its eloquence it reaches into those areas of African history that have customarily been invisible in modern writing and shapes them into form. Let me explain what I mean. By virtue of his autobiography we know Equiano's story. At the age of eleven he was kidnapped and taken away:

> One day, when all our people were gone out to their works as usual and only I and my dear sister were left to mind the house, two men and a woman got over our walls, and in a moment seized us both, and without giving us time to cry out or make resistance they stopped our mouths and ran off with us... (Equiano: 16)

From here we follow the details of Equiano's life story and so discover the full geography of his tribulations. His story becomes our story because we possess the text, the *materia critica*. But complete as it is, Equiano's story is not the full story; it is only a part of it. Equiano's mother came home from the farm one day to find her only daughter and youngest son stolen, never to be found or heard from ever again. We do not know her half of the story. Nobody knows the story of her grief.

The final importance of Equiano's autobiography is that by its embedded silences regarding the people the boy left behind, it brings into focus the fact that the European slave trade left graves without bodies in the lives and minds of surviving kinsfolk of the captured. To find the full measure of the impact of slavery and the slave trade on the African victim society we shall have to think of Equiano's mother, her pain and suffering at the sudden loss of her children, the uncertainty and wild fears she carries all her life-long years. We shall have to consider the measures she takes, and the adjustments she will make to her life, her family, and her society. And then we shall have to take this bundle of untamed agonies and multiply it not by one woman, not by one family, not by one fearful community, but by a continent full of people, living hearts of unspoken fear. We shall have to consider what such precarious living does to motherhood, fatherhood, attitudes to child rearing, community organization, education, and culture as a whole. This is a way to enter the story of Africa's culture under siege.

REFERENCES CITED

Butterfield, Stephen (1974). *Black Autobiography in America*. Amherst: University of Massachusetts.

Douglass, Frederick (1845). "Narration of the Life of Frederick Douglass, An American Slave," in *The Norton Anthology of World Masterpieces*. Volume 2. Eds. Mayna Mack et. al., 1985. 649-79. New York: W.W. Norton and Company.

Eakin, Paul (1985). *Fictions in Autobiography: Studies in the Art of Self-Invention*. Princeton University Press.

Equiano, Olaudah (1789). *The Interesting Narrative of the Life of Olaudah Equiano, or Gustavus Vassa the African, Written by Himself*. Abridged and edited by Paul Edwards as: *Equiano's Travels* (1967). London: Heinemann.

Harris, Frank (1963). *My Life and Loves*. New York: Grove Press.

Holman, C. Hugh and William Harmon (1986). *A Handbook to Literature*. 5th Edition. New York: Macmillan Publishing Co.

Jelinke, Estelle ed. (1980). *Women's Autobiography*. Bloomington, Indiana: Indiana University Press.

Lejeune, Philippe (1982) . "The Autobiographical contract." In Tzvetan Todorov, eds. *French Literary Theory Today*. Cambridge: Cambridge University Press.

Murray, Albert (1976). *Stomping the Blues*. New York: McGraw Hill.

Olney, James (1972). *Metaphors of the Self: The Meaning of Autobiography*. Princeton: Princeton University Press.

Pascal, Roy (1960). *Design and Truth in Autobiography*. Cambridge: Cambridge University Press.

African Literature and the

CRISIS OF POST-STRUCTURALIST THEORISING

by Niyi Osundare
University of Ibadan, Nigeria

Interrogating the Interrogators

Let me begin by confessing to a nagging unease about the 'post-ness' tagged on to contemporary theorising in general: post-structural, post-modernist, post-colonial; post-Marxist, post-industrial, etc. There is also talk about the 'posthumanist' era, though we hope in all earnestness that the 'post-human' society will never arrive! This innocuous-looking prefix, 'post,' kicks up temporal, spatial, even epistemological problems, operates most times on a set of fallacies which seduce us into a false consciousness that human thoughts, ideas, actions, experiences, and the significant events they generate are arrangeable in a linear, x—before—y; y—after—x framework, very much like a series of temporal scenarios in an overdeterministic succession.

Implicit in this linear arrangement is a suggestion of misleading chronology, a temporo-ideational fiction which constructs progression as a process in which ideas are used and discarded, then superseded and supplanted by new ones. This method hardly looks back except for self-justification and self-authentication;[1] it is so full of contemporaneist bravado about the relative (at times absolute) superiority of its own perceptual ideology, theoretical re-categorization and analytical methodology.

---

[1] See Biodun Jeyifo, "Decolonizing Theory: Reconceptualizing the New English Leteratures," paper presented at the 1990 MLA annual conference, Chicago, USA, p.2.

However, the prefix 'post' raises issues of a fundamentally philosophical nature. When used with a temporal signifier, it acquires a clearer, more originary power than when yoked up with the ideational. Compare 'post-1945' and 'post structuralist.' While it is possible to point to January 1946 as the specific, immediate commencement of 'post 1945,' we would be hard put to it to tell specifically when 'post-structuralism' began—the time and place it was born, its progenitors, its birth-weight, the attending midwives, etc. This is why, despite the several claimants to its originary authorship, we still find it difficult to say in unmistakable terms who the 'founders' of post-structuralism were or are. There is an inevitable fuzziness, even indeterminacy, about these things which theories of the "post" variety are often too hasty to admit.

It is an irony that a theoretical theology such as post-structuralism whose principal tenet is the deconstruction of dichotomy should have its own temple erected on a similar binarism: structuralism versus post-structuralism, modernism versus post-modernism, etc. For one of the abiding concerns of the New Historicism is the reconstruction of our view of history not as a progressional, evolutionary inevitability, but as a multidirectional network of ruptured continuities in which cause may be effect, effect cause, a complex, supratemporal artifact in which the present derives its force from the unpastness of the past.

Post-structuralist practice understands this temporal and ideational fluidity, even if its theory appears to negate it. More than any other literary theory in recent times, post-structuralism derives a great number of its paradigms from the 'unpastness of the past.' In a rarely eclectic case of archaeology and necromancy, deconstructionists have exhumed the sagacious bones of Plato, Nietzsche, Schlegel, Hegel, Schopenhaur, Heidegger, Marx, Sartre, Bakhtin, etc. For critical and analytical terminologies (and methods) they have dug deep into the catacombs of classical and medieval rhetoric: tropes, topos, metaphor, metonymy, hypostasis, aporia, polysemy, etc. have all been dusted up and sent on 'new' post-structuralist errands.

There is thus a significant 'bending over backwards' in post-structuralism, a rummage through the jungle of primeval epochs. How really self-assuredly new, then, are these terminologies, these methods, even in their new significations and functions, when their very origination interrogates the 'post-ness' of their 'structuralism'? Most times the old-new wine of post-structuralist analytical idioms feel quite ill at ease in the old wine-skin of their theory. Contemporary literary discourse is thus clogged with mongrel jargon, cultic, overprofessionalized, trapped in hermetic closures. The newer things appear to be, the older they really are.

How "post-colonial" is post-colonial discourse?

The world is shaped—and frequently determined—by the words we use for expressing it. In naming the world we also name ourselves, evoking a recognizable, tangible construct of that panoply of realities which constitute what we call the human experience. Names serve as the door to the house of experience, a guide to hidden meanings in the shadowy nooks of time and place. Names tell stories, liberate or imprison; they may also serve as self-fulfilling prophecies. Names commit ... which is why the Yoruba say that it is only mad people who do not mind the names they are called, or who refuse to see the difference between the names they choose to bear and the ones the world prefers to call them by. The negative policies of 'representation' so famous in contemporary literary discourse is very much the product of misapprehension as it is of mis-naming and mis-verbalization. There are times people do not need to call a dog a bad name to hang it. The bad name does the hanging itself.

Conscious of the politics of naming, many African writers have expressed profound apprehension about the term 'post-colonial' as applied to the African situation in general and African writing in particular. For instance, speaking at a Commonwealth conference in London in 1991, Ama Ata Aidoo, playwright and novelist, challenged her audience in these words: "Ask any village woman how post-colonial her life is." "Colonialism," she added, "has not been 'posted' anywhere at all."[2] Most appropriately, the paper from which these words emerged was titled 'Collective Amnesia and the Role of the African Writer.'

First let us collectively remember to ask a few questions: whose invention or re-invention is the term 'post-colonial'? Who was the first to apply it to the writings of Africa and other parts of the 'developing world'? Since when has it become fashionable, theoretically and critically correct, to refer to these parts of the world by this term? What social and cultural constructions are thrust up by this concept? How are we committed by this term, having so profoundly naturalized its meaning without pausing to think about its implications? To re-echo our former trope, this terminology names us, but do we know the meaning of its own name and the origin and giver of that name?

It is pertinent to ask these questions, for the term 'post- colonial' is not just another literary-critical construct to be used with the same

2 Cited In Firinne Chreachain, "'Post-Colonialism' or Second Independence?," *African Literature Association Bulletin*, Vol. 17, No 3, 1991 pp. 5-6.

terminological certitude and blissful complacency with which we employ its counterparts such as 'post-structural' 'post-modernist,' etc. More than other terminologies of the 'post-' variety, 'post-colonial' is a highly sensitive historical and geographical trope which calls into significant attention a whole epoch in the relationship between the West and the developing world, an epoch which played a vital role in the institutionalization and strengthening of the metropole-periphery, centre-margin dichotomy. We are talking about a trope which brings memories of gunboats and mortars, conquests and dominations, a trope whose accent is bloodstained. We are talking about a terminology whose 'name' and meaning are fraught with the burdens of history and the anxieties of contemporary reality.

The first of these burdens concerns the politics of the genealogy of the term 'post-colonial.' Like many other phrases and concepts which define the African reality, this terminology owes its origination to foreign Adams. It is yet another instance of a 'name' invented for the African experience from outside, a name which finds little or no acceptance among its African objects. It is undoubtedly this conflict between the African reality and the exogeneist determination and representation of it that led Firinne N. Chreachain to this conclusion about the Commonwealth conference mentioned earlier on in this essay: "It is obvious to anyone familiar with British Africanist circles that a vast gulf exists between critical perspectives within Africa and those prevalent among British Africanists"[3] (For 'British' substitute 'Western').

Chreachain's views here possess a thrust similar to that of Biodun Jeyifo in his critique of the "exclusively and prescriptively *Western* monument of High Theory." Jeyifo observes further:

> the contemporary understanding of theory not only renders it an exclusively Western phenomenon of a very specialised activity, but also implicitly (and explicitly) inscribes the view that theory does not exist, cannot exist outside of this High Canonical Western orbit.[4]

This apprehension about the imperialism of theory is by no means an exclusively African concern. In an interview with Gayatri Spivak in New Delhi, Rashmi Bhatnager, Lola Chatterzee and Rajeshwari Sunder Rajan took their learned guest to task on the use of 'First World elite theory' for the literatures of the 'colonies':

---

[3] Ibid, p.5.

[4] Biodun Jeyifo, op. cit., p.2.

Now there is a certain uneasiness here about the ideological contamination of theory by the specific historical origins which produce it and therefore about the implications of employing it in our own context. Would you defend the post-colonial intellectual dependence upon Western models as historical necessity?.[5]

It is instructive to note that Spivak's short, cryptic, and evasive answer to this very important question indeed ends up in another question counter-posed to her interviewers: "What is an indigenous theory?"

For ideological and intellectual reasons, it must be stressed here that what is really at issue in this argument is not simply the provenance of theories, but the ease and complacency with which Western theories take over the global literary and intellectual arena, the way they inscribe themselves as though the other parts of the world were a *tabula rasa*. There is something ethnocentric about this 'universalism,' an attitude and behaviour which constitute the world's literary discourse into a monumental Western monologue. In several ways, this totalises literary experience and the way people relate to it. So rigidly located in one place, how can we see the Great Mask of the world from different angles?

The second problem with the. term 'post-colonial' is its denotative and descriptive inadequacy. What are the semantic and sociosemiotic designations of this compounded word; beyond—colonial; anti-colonial, or simply not-colonial? In other words, is 'post-colonial' a qualitative tag or a mere *temporal phase marker?*

Bill Ashcroft, Gareth Griffiths, and Helen Tiffin (1989) wrestle bravely with the monster sprung up by this term when they declare in *The Empire Writes Back,* a very valuable even if controversial book:

> We use the term 'post-colonial'—to cover all the cultures affected by the
> imperial process from the moment of colonization to the present day."[6]

This declaration gives the prefix morpheme 'post' a new and baffling meaning. At work here is an aberrant one, one-catch-all metonymy in which the part is too small for the whole it is used to represent. The logic of this definition puts works as far apart *as When Love Whispers* (1947),

---

[5] Rashimi Bhatnager, Lola Chatterzee and Rajeshwari Sunder Rajan, "The Post-Colonial Critic" (Interview with Gayatri Spivak) in Sarah Harasym (ed.), *The Post-colonial Critics Interviews, Strategies, Dialogues* (New York and London: Routledge), p. 69.

[6] Bill Ashcroft, Gareth Griffiths, and Helen Tiffin, *The Empire Writes Back: Theory and Practice in Post-Colonial Literatures* (London-New York; Routledge, 1989), p.2.

The Palmwine Drinkard (1952), *Fragments* (1969), and *I Will Marry When I Want* (1982) in the same 'post-colonial' bag. There is no doubt that this container is also large enough to swallow the works of D. 0. Fagunwa, or the poetry of Shaaban Robert!

Further down the page, attention shifts from 'culture' to place, and the authors disclose the enormous assortedness of the fishes in the post-colonial net: Africa, Australia, Bangladesh, Canada, the Caribbean, India, Malaysia, Malta, New Zealand, Pakistan, Singapore, South Pacific, Sri Lanka—and the U.S.A. Needless to say, what we have here is an unconscionably mixed bag whose constitutive items are so gross and so general that very little room is left for the crucial specificities of individual parts. And what's more, to so liberally apply the 'post-colonial' label to places such as Africa and Australia, the Caribbean and Canada—places whose colonial pasts are so fundamentally different—is tantamount to mocking the real wounds of the Colonial infliction where they are deepest and most enduring. We certainly need to distinguish formal and superficial coloniality in places like Canada, Australia and New Zealand from the systematic, exploitative—and, above all, racist—coloniality in the rest of the countries in the list.

Colonialism is a complex, protean monster with various levels, degrees, and complexions. Its intricate mutations defy a simple, short-hand name; its continuities make a mockery of a totalising, comprehensive nomenclature. Thus, Ashcroft *et al's* submission that "The idea of 'post-colonial' literary theory emerges from the inability of European theory to deal adequately with the complexities and varied cultural provenance of post-colonial writing"[7] sounds ironical in the face of the inadequacy of the emergent 'ideal' itself.

And besides, who needs this adumbrative tag with its own 'false notions of the universal'? Wasn't this name invented by Western Theory as a convenient nomenclatural handle on their epistemic spheres of influence? To reiterate our earlier point, the tag 'post-colonial' is more useful for those who invented it than it is for those who are supposed to wear it, its *passive signifieds.* It rings truer for those who have 'posted' colonialism in posh conference halls and arcane seminar rooms conveniently far from the real battleground of colonial encounter.

And this explains the problem of misrecognition and the resultant misrepresentation plaguing the term 'post-colonial.' Whether used ideationally or temporally, the term lures us into a false sense of security, a seeming pastness of a past that is still painfully present. It is common

---

[7] Ibid.

knowledge (no longer restricted to social scientists, especially of the political economy persuasion) that to apply the term 'post-colonial' to the real situation in Africa today is to be plainly naive or majestically futuristic, no matter what the degree of metaphoric extension we are prepared to grant that term. We are talking about a continent with very little control over its economy and politics, whose intracontinental interactions are still dominated by the same old colonial languages—a continent so heavily indebted to the finance houses of the advanced industrialized world, that many of its governments are virtually under foreign receiverships. How can we talk so glibly, so confidently about the 'post-coloniality' of a place so *neo*-colonial? Shouldn't we distinguish 'flag postcoloniality' from its genuine, purposive namesake? We need a new dictionary of contemporary literary terms.

The term 'post-colonial' is thus more loaded, more polysemic, more positional than its inventors and users are readily aware of. It even carries an (unintended) taint. The word 'post-colonial' endows its principal morpheme 'colonial' with an originary privilege. 'Colonial' carries the voice of the beginning; it is the moving force, the significant point of departure.

African literature, oral or written, in whatever language and style, is presented as having no identity, no name except in reference to it. However, history frequently intervenes with its intriguing fluidity. Consider the example of Ayi Kwei Armah's *Two Thousand Seasons* written in the 'post-colonial' period, but whose content and politics are so aggressively pre-colonial; or Achebe's *Things Fall Apart* written in the colonial period, but whose narrative thrust straddles both pre-colonial and colonial epochs. What name, relative to 'colonial' shall we call those epics which thrived in many parts of Africa when history was once-upon-a-time and the white man had not made his momentous entry? What makes a work 'post-colonial': the time and place of its author or its own intrinsic subject?

Lastly, the phatic import of that term. How does it sound, how does *it feel* to be called a 'post-colonial' writer? Should Ngugi wa Thiong'o, Achebe, Aidoo, etc. feel happy for having attained the 'post-colonial' status? When you meet me in the corridors tomorrow would you congratulate me on my 'post-colonial' poetry? Is there anything worth talking about outside 'coloniality'? In brief, is there life besides 'coloniality'?

Undeconstructed Silences

All theories leak. Old assumptions give way to new ones. Pre-existing platitudes get spruced up in new raiment, and what used to be called 'six' receives a brave new baptism of 'half-dozen.' Post-structuralism in its various mutations and manifestations is, no doubt, *a grand ambitions project.* Its grounding in history, philosophy, and linguistics certainly gave it a rigorous, even radical head-start. Its interrogative methods have provoked answers from shadowy silences, or gingered those answers into further questions.

But like Oedipus, post-structuralism's swollen foot emanated from its origins. As an "exclusively and prescriptively Western"[8] theory, post-structuralism has erected the West into a monumental metonym for the world, another instance of that part which considers itself larger than the whole. Because Africa (and the rest of the developing world) is absent or absenced from the post-structuralist Master Theory, most of its theoretical and conceptual projects have proved grossly inadequate in the analysis and apprehension of issues and developments outside the Western orbit. Literary space is inundated by a plethora of 'new' terminologies, methods and discursive practices, but hardly are these matched by a new consciousness about the world outside Europe and the United States, by a new grasp of the social, political, economic and cultural specificities of those parts of the universe pushed to the fringe.

In no aspect is this exclusivist ideology more palpable than the dialect of the celebrated practitioners of contemporary theorising, their preoccupation with Western topoi and exempla, their cultivation of impenetrable jargon, their demonstration of utter lack of awareness about places and peoples outside their own locales. In fact, many aspects of post-structuralist theorising have made the humanization of discourse impossible, as a result of their fetishization of the text and its theory. The *over-abstract, reified* processes of contemporary theorising have hitherto not shown any efficient medium of recognizing, analysing and representing the urgent, concrete specificities of the so-called developing world. Old prejudices, myths, fallacies, and misconceptions have not been deconstructed; on the contrary, they have been reconstructed into faddish frameworks couched in new-fangled lingo. The interrogative power of contemporary theories has been severely selective.

---

[8] Biodun Jeyifo, op. cit., p.2.

Let us illustrate some of the points above by examining a new book on Conrad: *Heart of Darkness: Case Study in Contemporary Criticism.*[9] It must be said to the credit of this book that it provides a potentially solid pedagogical tool for the study of Conrad's most famous book. It is compact, well-researched, informative, a long-overdue attempt at bridging the gap between post-structuralist theorising and post-structuralist literary analysis. And it takes Conrad through the diversity of contemporary projects: a chapter each on Psychoanalytic Criticism; Reader-response Criticism; Feminist Criticism, Deconstruction; and the New Historicism.

I grabbed this book with effusive enthusiasm, eager to see Conrad's archetypal silence and ambivalences unravelled, the gaps in the tale filled in, the old parable interrogated with a revolutionary critical weapon in this last quarter of the 20th century. I was anxious to see which theoretical practice would be able to engage the story, enter the text, initiate a *humane* dialogue with Conrad, ask him why there are no African *human beings* in a 'yarn' whose setting is Africa. I was expecting a post-structuralist open surgery on Conrad's *Heart of Darkness* but what I got is a complex series of evasions, open-eyed blindness, willful forgetfulness, or simply, an intellectual and racial connivance with the European novelist.

Instead of a set of new, vigorous perspectives, what hit my eye were the same old critical shibboleths in tinsel post-structuralist phraseology: the chinese box narrative structure; the dangerously thin divide between civilization (Europe) and barbarism (Africa); the ordeal of the civilized European mind when thrown in the heart of Africa's darkness, and one or two suppressed murmurs about Conrad's view of imperialism. In none of these chapters is Conrad's systematic and pervasive dehumanization of Africans discussed, talk less of interrogated. Our critics simply join Conrad in a 'post-structuralist,' 'postcolonialist' voyage down the Congo, they too being 'wanderers on a prehistoric earth' (*HOD* p. 50) surrounded by 'black shadows' (*HOD* p. 3), 'black bones' (*HOD* p. 31), cannibals splashing around and pushing (*HOD* p.49), appalled by the 'smelly mud' (*HOD* p. 35) of the Congo—several miles, several centuries away from 'the tranquil dignity '(*HOD* p. 18) of the Thames. To them, too, Africa is nothing more than a "wild and passionate-uproar" (*HOD* p. 51).[10]

And yet, one of the most significant chapters in this book is on a 'reader-response' approach to *The Heart of Darkness.* Now, reader-

---

[9] Ross Murfin (ed.), *Joseph Conrad, Heart of Darkness: A Case Study in Contemporary Criticism* (New York: St Martin's Press, 1989).

[10] All page references to the Ross Murfin's edition of *Heart of Darkness* abbreviated here as H.O.D.

response criticism operates through an empowerment of the reader, making her/him "an active, necessary, and often self-conscious participant in the making of a text's meaning."[11] Meaning becomes an event through which the reader comes to a deeper, fuller understanding of art and the persons it fabricates. The reader, too, is expected to live through the text, probe its absences, fill in its gaps. The act of reading thus becomes an art in itself, a conscious, dynamic process of unravelling. This process functions through collaboration or confrontation with the text and its originary spirit.

It goes without saying that this chapter has opted for collaboration with Conrad and his vision, or rather, with the Western reader of Conrad and her/his vision. How else could Adena Rosemarin have arrived at this "reading" of Conrad's colour code:

> While it is true that dark men in this tale tend to behave in ways more moral and more civilized than do white men virtually every critic notes, for example, that the near-starving cannibals on board keep their hungry eyes off their masters—darkness remains the place and mode of Mario's terminal struggle with Kurtz.[12]

So much then for noble savages and benevolent cannibals and their missionary restraint! Rejoice, oh black anthropophagi! You are "more moral *and* more civilized" than white men in Africa. And you have the magnanimity of Conrad and the naivety of his critic to thank for this! And for this piece of unmatchable wisdom Rosemarin has the authority of "virtually every critic"[13] as source of ready appeal. Need we ask who such critics are, and what their intellectual and racial identity is?

On page 156 of this book, Rosemarin asks a crucial question: "What is the experience of reading *Heart of Darkness* like?" How I wish she had included the African in her group of respondents. But as is customary in most Western discourse on *Heart of Darkness,* the African is conspicuous by her/his very absence. After all, in Conrad's tale, it is the forests, the shrubs, the river which possess the active, transitive impulse; not the Africans who, in any way, are nothing more than a swarm of "naked breasts, arms, legs, *and* glaring eyes."[14] The African response can only matter if you agree that she/he is a human being in the first place. But if,

---

11
    Adena Rosemarin, "Darkening the Reader: Reader-Response Criticism and *Heart of Darkness"* in Murfin (ed.), *Joseph Conrad, Heart of Darkness: A case study in contemporary criticism,"* p. 155.

12
    Adena Rosemarin, *Ibid., p.* 15.

13
    Adena Rosemarin, *Ibid.*

14
    Heart of Darkness (Ross Murfin Edition), p. 60.

like Conrad, you believe she/he is not, why should you waste precious time seeking the response of a savage beast?

Rosemarin's reader-response criticism of *Heart of Darkness* is a clear demonstration of the fundamental ethnocentrism of most post-structuralist theorising, its several blindnesses and pitfalls; and, in particular, of the new metaphysics of readerly power and authority. For the questions which are left perpetually unanswered include: Who is the reader? What kind of pre-text—social, cultural, ideological, epistemic, etc.—is she/he importing into the text? What are the reader's primal, unconscious, or subconscious conspiracies with the text? Is or isn't the text really what the reader means it to mean?

The chapter on "The New Historicism and *Heart of Darkness*" begins with a cautions, dubitative concession (the only such concession in the whole book): "It *(H.O.D).* tells us little, *perhaps,* about Congolese peoples" (my emphasis)."[15] But earlier on in the paragraph Ross Murfin has hit the reader with this magisterial 'new historicist' proclamation:

> A work of art, it *(HOD)* is at the same time a kind of historical document. It *undoubtedly* presents as *accurate* a picture of a colonized Africa as many other supposedly non-fictional accounts written during the same period.[16] (my emphasis).

By the impeccable logic of this assertion, Conrad's jaundiced fiction is Africa's historical fact, a European novel 'about' Africa becomes an 'accurate' chronicle of Africa by some other name. But there is some method in the madness of the above proclamation: the 'non-fictional accounts' mentioned as parallel text here are, indeed, most likely to contain the same 'history,' being invariably the accounts of colonial functionaries, European missionaries, or various 'discoverers' and 'explorers' of the African 'darkness.' But some information about modern African historiography would have instructed Murfin on the kind of 'history' in such accounts. However, this is not the place to ask how much or what kind of African history our author knows. We can only wonder how seriously to take those critics who embark upon a 'new historicist' analysis without a thorough and comprehensive apprehension of the text and its context; critics who practice 'historicism' without history.

---

[15] Ross Murfin, in Ross Murfin (ed.), *Joseph Conrad, Heart of Darkness: A Case Study in Contemporary Criticism.* p. 226

[16] Ross Murfin, Ibid.

In fairness to Brook Thomas[17] his new historicist analysis is the one that shows the most prominent awareness of the African in *Heart of Darkness*. Unfortunately this awareness only comes in brief, pale flickers, the analytical channel having got thoroughly clogged by mountains of received critical baggage.

For instance, Thomas follows in the old beaten path. Conrad remains for him the chronicler of human experience.[18] Africans, even of the late 19th century, "exist in a state prior to history."[19] A journey to Africa is both a physical and temporal journey into darkness; African savagery is the context in which European civilization finds its truth, Africa remains the abode of the unconscious, contrasting sharply with Europe's triumphant rationality.

Most times Thomas's interrogative reading leads to further perversity. Like Rosemarin mentioned earlier on, he too awards Africans who accompany Marlow up the river a medal for restraint for not "killing and eating the whites"[20] despite their lingering starvation. Even more intriguing is Thomas's reading of the following passage which is Conrad's clearest summative testament to the African's sub-humanity:

> The earth seemed unearthly. We are accustomed to look upon the shackled form of a conquered monster but there—there you could look at a thing monstrous and free. It was unearthly, and the men were—no, they were not inhuman. Well, you know, that was the worst of it—this suspicion of their not being inhuman.[21]

Note here the complex dubitabilities, the stalking, stammering syntax of a mind which puts the African's claim to humanity to a monologic European debate. Note the tortuous indirectness which finds expression in the choice of double negatives: "their *not* being *inhuman*." The word 'human' occurs twice in this passage, undermined each time by the negative prefix 'in-.' In the final analysis, the African's humanity is a mere 'thought,' a 'suspicion,' her/his relationship to the world dims into a 'remote kinship' from 'the night of first ages.' Conrad's Africans "howled and leaped, and spun, and made horrid faces;" engaged in a 'wild and passionate uproar;'

---

[17] Brook Thomas, "Preserving and Keeping Order by Killing Time in *Heart of Darkness*" in Ross Murfin (ed.), *Ibid.* pp. 237—258.

[18] Brook Thomas, *Ibid.,* p. 337.

[19] Brook Thomas, *Ibid.,* p. 248.

[20] Brook Thomas, *Ibid.,* p. 251.

[21] Quoted by Brook Thomas, Ibid. p.242.

they were 'ugly.' In spite of these and several other implicit and explicit textual signals so prevalent in the novel, Thomas comes up with the conclusion that Conrad's narrative 'disrupts' commonplace racial prejudices. He seems to have been misled by the jejune chinese box narrative trickery which outs those rabidly racist words and thoughts in the mouth of a distant narrator while granting Conrad their creator an absolute indemnity.

Even so, Thomas reinforces rather than deconstructs the ontological binarism which confirms Conrad's studied Manichaeism:

the West	vs	Africa
Future	vs	Prehistory
European civilization	vs	African savagery
Rational	vs	Unconscious
Language	vs	Silence
Light	vs	Darkness
European Self	vs	African Other

The last pair in the series is particularly important here. For although Thomas makes some attempt at critiquing the 'Eurocentric perspective'[22] which constructs itself into a Self that constantly distances 'the Other,' he himself demonstrates a Eurocentric inability to recognize that 'Other,' to apprehend her/his misrepresentation. This is partly so because, like Conrad and his critics, Thomas neither knows nor understands the African 'Other,' and therefore cannot sympathize with her/him as a victim of a Eurocentric discursive and cognitive violence. For in actual fact, Conrad's construction of the African in *Heart of Darkness* is other than the 'Other.' The sense of complementarity which shores up the relationship between the Self and the Other cannot exist in a situation of an absolute negation of that Other. It would be enormously charitable to picture Conrad's African as the true Other of the European, for what does not exist cannot, except by some liberal metaphoric license, aspire to the *alter ego* of what does. In Conrad's Africa, the real absent factor is the African.

A practical, incontestable demonstration of this dehumanization and absencing is Conrad's denial to his African that most supremely human of all attributes; language. Africans 'howled' and 'shrieked'; these beings are so rudimentarized by the novelist that their "wild and passionate uproar" never rises to the level of linguistic sublimity. There is sound and noise all right, but no language, no articulatory competence, no discursive command. A pathological silence entraps the 'natives' as they become, in

---

[22] Brook Thomas, *Ibid.*, p. 245.

Toni Morrison's words, "Conrad's unspeaking."[23] Any wonder then that
for a definition and articulation of the African's world-view (if she/he is
ever credited with any such thing in the novel) we have to rely on the
pronouncements of a new Prospero, of another "bud of the nobler race"?

But the real pathology here is Conrad's, a victim of a chronic
ethnocentric malaise which springs instant hostility to, and denigration of,
what he does not *understand*. To such afflicted souls, difference (on the
other side) is defect, variance is abnormality. Since Conrad never
understood, and never considered worth understanding, the linguistic
'peculiarities' of his Africans, whatever language they possessed could not
have been anything more than "a violent babble of uncouth sounds." After
all, his Africans spoke no Polish nor French nor English.

And yet a prevalent, perplexing blindness/silence has fallen on this
aspect of Conrad's ethnocentrism in Western criticism. For instance, Brook
Thomas makes the very important point that "language is humanity's only
access to truth,"[24] but his 'new historicist' project at no time interrogates
the denial of that 'access' to Conrad's Africans.

This combination of silence and blindness has characterized Conrad
scholarship in the West since the debut of *Heart of Darkness*. Ross
Murfin's case study, despite its post-structuralist aspirations, is no
exception. It is noteworthy, for instance, that apart from Brook Thomas
who cited Chinua Achebe's thoughtful and seminal eassy[25] in his
reference, no other contributor to this book showed any awareness of an
African response. Even Thomas's magnanimity is limited: although
Achebe's essay is listed under "Recent Historical Studies of Conrad,"[26] his
own new historicist study does not betray even the slightest trace of the
content of Achebe's essay. With this process of 'unfair selectivity' and
'preferred visions'[27] late 20th century Western critics have continued
Conrad's silencing and negation of Africans. Contemporary Western

---

[23] Toni Morrison, "Unspeakable Things Unspoken: The Afro-American Presence
in American Literature," *Michigan Quarterly Review*, Vol. XXVIII, No. 1, 1989,
p. 9.

[24] Brook Thomas, *op. cit.*, p. 250.

[25] Chinua Achebe, "An Image of Africa: Racism in Conrad's *Heart of Darkness*, in
Hopes and Impediments: Selected Essays (New York: Doubleday 1989), pp. 1-20.

[26] Brook Thomas, *op. cit.*, p. 257.

[27] Biodun Jeyifo, "For Chinua Achebe: The Resilience and Predicament of
Obierika," manuscript, 1990, p. 10.

critics are still co-pilgrims in the steamer up the Congo; for them, the African's humanity still remains a 'thought,' a fragile 'suspicion.'[28]

Either as a result of the politics of their provenance or an inherent crisis in their modes and methods of analysis and application (or both), 'mainstream' Western post-structuralist theories have demonstrated little or no adequacy in the apprehension, analysis, and articulation of African writing and its long and troubled context. This essay is not intended to push an exclusivist, essentialist viewpoint that 'our' literature cannot be apprehended by 'their' theory. But it is the case that the ethnocentric universalism of contemporary theoretical practice, its reification of theory into some oracular Western canonical monologue, its fetishization of text and disregard for the deeper reaches of referentiality, its replacement of theory itself with masochistic theoreticism—all these crises have produced a kind of radical conservatism, an anti-hegemonic hegemony which distances Western theory from the fundamental peculiarities of non-Western people.

In many ways, the post-structuralist method and tool of analysis lack the depth of perception, cogency of insight, and the clarity of procedure displayed by other theories.[29] Deconstruction, for instance, confuses rather than explains, pontificates instead of interpreting. Its treatment of African literature has demonstrated that 'new' is not necessarily better, and that a project which sounds 'post-colonialist' in intent may turn out to be neo-colonialist, even 're-colonialist' in practice.

The preceding submissions are not another 'anti-theory,' anti-rigor campaign, and should not be misconstrued as such. Theories matter. They provide a neat, handy background aid to methodological and analytical procedures. They foster and enhance a reflective globality on issues while sharpening that predictive and speculative capability which facilitates the marriage of imagination and knowledge. So a critique of one type of theory (in this case the post-structuralist variety) should not be mistaken for a negation and rejection of all theories. As post-structuralist theories are beginning to accept, thanks to the New Historicism, all theories are positional, contingent, connected, even partisan. In their originary, epistemological, and analytical presumptions, the 'major' literary theories in the world today are exclusivistically Western and oracular. They have

---

[28] Niyi Osundare, "An Empty Technology of the Text?: Deconstruction and African Literature," *Critical Currents in African Literature* (forthcoming).

[29] Niyi Osundare, "An Empty Technology of the Text?: Deconstruction and African Literature," *Critical Currents in African Literature* (forthcoming).

yet to demonstrate adequate capability for coping with issues and events in other parts of the world.

TEXT WORSHIP

(Or the deconstructed passport of Travelling Theory)

Did you see the text pass this way
In coat and collar and pompous sway
A wizened Canon with the cutest creed
With a temple full of the bravest breed
Did you see the Text on the conference table
Talkative giant of a faddish fable
Pounding the podium, a moustached tyrant
How holy his sin-tax, stupendously brilliant!'
When I woke up this morning the Text was in my room
I aimed at its shadow, it held my broom
It jumped into my wardrobe, turned into a hat,
Now I strut the streets with a trendy heart
It opens the door to the fattest jobs
The prettiest journals up for grabs
Arrange your jargon on a glittering rack
Your feet are firm on the tenure track
      Post-day post-night
      Post-history post-reason
      Post-humanist post-human
      Show me the post of your post-coloniality
      Aporia comporia catachresis
      Totalizing razmatizzing
      Meto nym nym nym logocentr tri tri tri
      Show me the structure of your post-structurality
      Oh for a gram of Grammatology!
      A sample sperm of Disseminations
      The Discourse tree with fruits of Discord
      And the New His-story-cism, New Her-story-cism
The madder the smatter, the harder the better
Make it new, make it arcane
The clumsier the code the sweeter the pain
It's the brave new era of the gaudy patter
Signs are here, the Word is dead:
The funeral of meaning a tropical debt
Paid in the surface of an idle game
In the dim-lit abyss of pedantic fame
War may rage, Hunger may spread
The river may die in its lowly bed
Chains may descend from every sky

The price of Freedom raised so high
Count your tropes, praise the Text
The meaningless meaning is a grand pretext
'Oppression' is merely undecidable reference
'Poverty' is slave to metaphysics of presence
The Author is dead, in unmarked grave dumped
The Reader to power with crown has rumped
The Text writes itself with a magic hand
In the curious way its priests can stand
It shouts in French, in English it whispers
It murmurs in German in gasps and whimpers
A Kingly silence in other tongues
The youngest heir to older wrongs
I bend my knee, oh mighty Text
Spare my days of your nightly test
Assure my path to your Temple of Awe
Let me rant while my listeners snore
                              —Niyi Osundare

Acknowledgement:

The topic of this essay was originally presented in the Brown Bag Seminar Series of the University of New Orleans, U.S.A., in April 1992. I am grateful to my colleagues there for their valuable observations.

OUSMANE SEMBENE:
Griot of Modern Times and Advocate of a Casteless African Society

by Edris Makward
University of Wisconsin, Madison

Ousmane Sembène as a writer and filmmaker, is undeniably a towering figure among contemporary African writers and intellectuals. His name has been associated with many labels and often, without much protest on his part: "Marxist," "revolutionary," "man of the people," "anti-intellectual," "ceddo" (pagan, unbeliever), "griot of modern times" among other things. Françoise Pfaff quotes Sembène himself as saying that "the African filmmaker is the griot of modern times" and that he is above all "a storyteller" (Pfaff 1984, p. 40).

For Sembène, the griot is essentially an artist who uses his/her talent to mirror his society. He wrote in 1978 that:

> The artist must, in many ways, be the mouth and the ears of his people. In the modern sense, this corresponds to the role of the griot in traditional African culture. The artist is like a mirror. His work reflects and synthesizes the problems, the struggles, and the hopes of his people. (Pfaff, 1984, p. 29).

In this paper, I wish to examine Sembène's concern with social transformation, with a specific emphasis on prejudice and contempt in contemporary Senegalese society on the basis of caste. My contention is that this concern is not new in Sembène's work, but permeates it from the very beginning. The same constant concern for an open world where there is consideration, respect and equality for all people, regardless of race, ethnic origin or gender is also a central theme in his work from the very beginning. Thus, in *O Pays, mon beau peuple!*,[1] his second novel, published in 1957, Oumar Faye, the central character and a prototype of Bakayoko, the quintessential Sembenian hero, and in many ways, the alter-ego of the author, disregards his ancestral family tradition of professional

---

[1] Ousmane Sembène. *O Pays, mon beau peuple*, Le Livre Contemporain, Paris, 1957.

fishermen, and strives to become a farmer to organize the local farmers into a farmers' cooperative, against the exploitative French entrepreneurs. His mother, the old kind-hearted and loving Rokhaya, wonders why he wants to become a farmer against the tradition of his family:

> Pourquoi, veux-tu devenir cultivateur? ... Ton père, le père de ton père, tous ètaient des pécheurs, mais toi, le toubab, tu veux la terre? Je n'y comprends rien.[2] (Sembène, 1957, p. 87).

Oumar Faye "fils de l'homme des eaux" (son of the man of the waters), as he is referred to by one of the elders among the peasants, admits the truth of her statement regarding the ancestral family tradition of fishing, but his decision of becoming a farmer in order to fight colonial exploitation, is unshakable.

Likewise, in this same early novel, Sembène's denunciation of polygamy and the mistreatment of women, makes its appearance in a forceful manner, through actions such as the generalized fist fight between the dock workers and the outnumbered sailors and militiamen, triggered by Oumar Faye's indignation at the sight of women painfully loading a ship in the port of Ziguinchor in Casamance in southern Senegal:

> Des femmes chargeaient l'un des trois bateaux qui se trouvait à l'extrémité du môle. Faye les regardait travailler. Ce spectacle n'était pas nouveau pour lui, mais il sentit un pincement au coeur. C'était mal, c'était odieux que des femmes besognent de la sorte! Le fait que personne ne réagissait devant cet état de choses lui donnait un espèce de malaise. Il se savait responsable en partie de la somnolence du pays; lui non plus ne faisait rien.[3] (Sembène, 1957, p. 89).

Even in his description of the women's song, Sembène becomes very explicit about their plight of endless misery and pain. His equating the sadness of these songs with the joyless songs of excision is indicative of the

---

[2]
(Why do you want to become a farmer? ... Your father, your father's father, all of them were fishermen, but you, the "toubab" (white man), you want to work the land. Don't you? This is beyond my understanding.) This and following translations by E. Makward.

[3]
(Women were loading one of three ships which were at the end of the pier. Faye was watching them work. This spectacle was not new to him; he had witnessed such scenes since his childhood. All the same, he felt a pinch in his heart. it was bad, it was horrid to have women working this way! The fact that no one would react to this state of things made him feel nauseous. He knew he was partly responsible for the inertia of his country; he too was to blame for doing nothing about it.)

author's unequivocal position almost four decades ago, regarding this
ultimately feminine or feminist concern of the 1990's in Africa and
elsewhere (cf. Alice Walker's recent video and text (*Possessing the Secret
of Joy*: *Warrior Marks*):

> En chœur, ces femmes chantaient comme on étouffe un sanglot—pour ne pas
> sentir la fatigue. Elles chantaient comme au moment des excisions et c'était
> une chanson qui n'exprimait pas la joie, mais la douleur; elle commençait là
> où elle finissait, car elle incarnait la misère... et leur misère ne finissait
> jamais.[4] (Sembène, 1957, p. 90).

That it is an educated Christian woman who makes the most
passionate but objective social plea against polygamy as an obstacle to
social progress, and not a Muslim man or woman, is again indicative of
Sembène's unequivocal condemnation of polygamy or its justification
through religion:

> —La polygamie a existé dans toutes les nations. Mais vous, tant que vous ne
> considérerez pas la femme comme un être humain et non comme un
> instrument de vos viles passions, vous piétinerez. Les femmes constituent la
> majeure partie du peuple. Il n'y a pas de plus puissant obstacle que la
> polygamie en ce qui concerne l,'évolution.[5] (Sembène, 1957, p. 98).

As regards social discrimination and even contempt and repugnance
on the basis of caste, Sembène brings it up in most of his works, but it is in
his more recent novel, *Le dernier de l'Empire* (L'Harmattan, Paris, 1981)[6]
that his concern and position on this question are most compelling.

The Senegalese sociologist Abdoulaye-Bara Diop discusses at length
the caste system and its foundations among the Wolof people in his
seminal work, *La société Wolof. Traditions et changement. Les systèmes
d'inégalité et de domination* (Karthala, Paris, 1981). He states initially that
there are among the Wolof, groupings that are characterized by heredity,
endogamy and the specific professional activities of their members. These
groupings are hierarchically ordered and entertain among themselves

---

[4] (in chorus, these women sang as if to choke down a sob—in order to beguile their
weariness. They sang as they would during excision rituals; and it was not a song
of joy but of pain; it began where it ended, for it was the incarnation of misery ...
and their misery was never ending.)

[5] (Polygamy has existed in all nations. But, as for you, as long as you will continue
treating women not as human beings but as objects of your base passions, you will
be merely marking time. Women are the majority of our people. There is no
greater obstacle to progress than polygamy.)

[6] Ousmane Sembène: *The Last of the Empire*, Heinemann, London, 1983.

relationships of interdependence (Diop, 1981, p. 33). However, in Diop's view, one must distinguish between two such systems that have often been mistaken as one, that is, the caste system which is closely linked to the division of labor, and the system of orders which is more intimately linked to the political structure of society (Diop, 1981, p. 33).

Diop discusses also at length, the various distinctions between castes and sub-castes and the reasons why slaves (or jamm) should more accurately be classified within the order system (political) rather than within the caste system (professional).

For the purpose of this paper, we will retain only the binary distinction of *géér* as the so-called superior caste and ñeeño as the inferior caste. Diop's refusal to translate *géér* by *noblemen* or *freeborn* as is frequently done, is quite logical, and in line with his distinction between the caste system and the order system. It is indeed more accurate to define the ñeeño as artisans, including the smiths or *tëgg,* the *udde* or leatherworkers, the *sees* or woodworkers, the *ràbb* or weavers, the *géwël* or griots, that is, the traditional masters of language, bards, poets, oral historians, genealogists, and the *géér,* as non-artisans, defined negatively so to speak, as they are not allowed traditionally to be artisans. Traditionally, the *géér* were basically farmers but they could also often be fishermen or cattle herders.

While Abdoulaye-Bara Diop insists often in his work on the relative insignificance of the caste system in contemporary postcolonial Wolof and Senegalese society (Diop, 1981, pp. 44, 94, 343), he also admits that the beliefs and attitudes of untouchability referred to in the famous "Cahiers de Yoro Dyâo"[7] at the turn of the century, are far from having completely disappeared from the Wolof psyche, in spite of the often professed opinion by marabouts (Muslim leaders) and taalibes (disciples) alike, that Islam is essentially based on an ideology of equality and brotherhood.

Thus, Diop reveals that his research trips have led him to traditional villages—not many—where:

> ... les ñeeño, et particulièrement les griots, ne peuvent résider ni même passer la nuit. Jusqu'à ces dernières années, des villages refusaient l'enterrement des griots et, dans un certain nombre, ils ont encore leur cimitière propre. On évite toujours le contact étroit—direct ou indirect—avec le forgeron: toucher sa sueur, porter son boubou, s'asseoir sur son lit, monter sur son cheval. Du

---

7
   R. Rousseau: "Le Sénégal d'autrefois. Etude sur le Oualo Cahiers de Yoro Dyâo." *Bull du com. d'et. Hist. Sc. de l'A.O.F.* no. 1-2, 1929, pp. 133-211.

moins, la croyance relative aux méfaits de ce contact demeure; elle est connue de nos jours de tous les Wolof.[8] (A. Diop, 1981, p. 39).

It is the persistence of such prejudiced beliefs and practices in contemporary Senegalese society that Sembène combats in a number of his works of fiction. For him, these beliefs are both irrational and unacceptable in the context of a modern Senegal.

Thus in his masterpiece, *Les bouts de bois de Dieu* (Le Livre Contemporain, Paris, 1960), Bassirou, the office worker ("le bureaucrat") makes a contemptuous oblique remark, clearly directed at Boubacar the blacksmith, with reference to people of low caste extraction. Boubacar's reaction is immediate and quite indicative of Sembène's strong belief in and commitment to a modern society based on total freedom and equality and an unequivocal rejection of all forms of slavery, dependency or patronage:

—Tu crois donc que j'en suis, moi? Je suis forgeron de naissance et de métier et si, par la force des choses, mes parents ont dû accepter d'être de basse condition, moi je ne serai jamais l'esclave de personne.[9] (Sembène, 1960, p. 46).

In fact, this rejection of the traditional stratification of society by Sembène, arises from his strong belief that all inequalities or differences in status or consideration based on anything but competence and actual achievements, are without foundation and ought to be combated vigorously.

Thus, in his confrontation with M. Dejean, the Director of the Railway Company, Bakayoko, the central character and hero of *Les bouts de bois de Dieu*, insists on equality between men, between workers: ..".

---

[8] (... the ñeeño, and particularly the griots, can neither reside nor even stay overnight. Until a few years ago, some villages would refuse to bury griots and, in some of them, they [the griots] still have their own cemetery. Intimate contact—direct or indirect—with smiths is still to be avoided: touching his sweat, wearing his gown (boubou), sitting on his/her bed, riding on his/her horse. At least, the belief relative to the evil effect of such contacts still persists; All Wolof people are aware of this today.)

[9] Sembène: *Les bouts de bois de Dieu*, Le Livre Contemporain, Paris, 1960, p. 46: (—You think that I am one! [a member of an inferior caste] I am a blacksmith by birth and by profession and if, owing to the force of circumstances, my parents had to accept a lower place in society, I for one, will never be anybody's slave.)

nous sommes ici pour discuter entre égaux, et nous n'avons que faire de vos menaces."[10] (Sembène, 1960, 277).

But for Dejean, it is very important to maintain the inequality between blacks and whites. Thus, in his eyes, a line must be drawn between a compromise on salaries to end the strike and satisfy the industrials, the businessmen, the Railway Company share holders, on the one hand, and, on the other, the award of family allowances. Indeed such an award would amount, in Dejean's and his colleagues, view, to "a recognition of the customs and culture of members of an inferior race," and he could not submit to such a capitulation:

> céder sur la question des allocations familiales, c'était beaucoup plus que d'agréer un compromis avec des ouvriers en grève, c'était reconnaître pour valable une manifestation raciale, entériner les coutumes d'êtres inférieurs, céder non à des travailleurs mais a des Nègres et cela Dejean ne le pouvait pas.[11] Sembène, 1960, p. 280).

And, in his anger, Dejean becomes even more explicit: ..".vous insultez une nation, une race qui vaut cent fois la vôtre!" (... and you are insulting a nation, a race that is a hundred times better than yours). (Sembène, 1960, p. 281).

For Bakayoko and for his colleague, Lahbib, the distinction between race and class is essential, just as is for Sembène, the distinction between caste and class. Thus, for Sembène, racial discrimination in a colonial setting is indeed synonymous with caste discrimination and prejudice, in a traditional or in a modern context, and neither has a convincing foundation in his view:

> —Monsieur le directeur, vous ne représentez ici ni une nation, ni une race: une classe. Et nous aussi nous représentons une classe dont les intérêts sont différents de ceux de la vôtre. Nous cherchons un terrain d'entente et c'est tout![12] (Sembène, 1960, p. 281).

---

[10] (... we are here to discuss matters among equals; you cankeep your threats to yourself.)

[11] (... to give in on the question of family allowances was more than agreeing to a compromise with striking workers; it would amount to recognizing as valid and respectable one cultural feature of a racial group, to accepting as respectable the customs of inferior beings; this would indeed mean giving in, not to workers but to a bunch of Blacks; and that Dejean could not do.)

[12] (Sir. You represent here, neither a nation nor a race; a class, yes. And we too do represent a class whose interests are different from your own. We should be looking for a ground for mutual understanding; that is all!)

This distinction in the mind of Sembène permeates also the memorable scene in the novel when the white foreman, Isnard, tries unsuccessfully to bribe Doudou, the secretary-general of the Railway Workers' Union, with the tempting amount of 3 million CFA francs (US $12,000 at the time, 1948). Doudou's outright rejection of this astounding offer flies in the face of "everything Isnard had believed in for many years, and on which he had built his life" (Sembène, 1960, p. 237):

> —Trois millions, c'est une somme pour un nègre, pour un ajusteur-tourneur nègre, mais je préfère rester nègre car les trois millions ne pourront pas me blanchir. J'aime mieux les dix minutes de casse-croûte.[13] (Sembène, 1960, p. 236).

Doudou is alluding here to an earlier encounter with the foreman who responded in front of all the workers, to Doudou's reported complaint about the African workers being denied a tea break which was allowed the white workers, with the humiliating words: "Va te faire blanchir et tu auras tes dix minutes" (go and make yourself white, then you can have your ten minutes!)

As indicated earlier in this paper, it is in his 1981 novel *Le dernier de l'empire* (*The Last of the Empire* 1983) that Ousmane Sembène treats the theme of the caste system and states his advocacy of a casteless Senegal in the most compelling fashion. It is undeniable that in this novel, Sembène is far from espousing the position that prejudices and considerations related to the old caste system are disappearing, or in the process of disappearing rapidly from the contemporary Senegalese political, social and cultural scene.

To begin with, early in the novel, Daouda, who is the only central character in the novel whose family name is never given, is advised by his father Gorgui Massamba, griot of the Ayane dynasty, the princely family of his political rival Mam Lat Soukabé, the Finance Minister, that "quel que puisse être ton avenir, Daouda, tu dois savoir tenir ton rang" (Sembène, 1981, p. 33: Whatever the future may hold for you, Daouda, you must keep to your station in life).

The truth of his father's words hit home soon enough, when he is turned down by the family of his Christian Senegalese bride-to-be, Madeleine, on account of his lower caste origins. After completing a brilliant college record in France, which is not just remotely reminiscent of

---

[13] (Three million is a lot for a Black man, for a Black lathe operator, but I would rather remain a Black man because three million francs will not make me white. I would rather have the ten minutes' tea break.)

current Senegalese President Abdou Diouf's own record,[14] he is called to
service by President Léon Mignane who is also in many ways, only a
slightly fictionalized version of the first president of independent Sénégal,
poet Léopold Sédar Senghor.

He then marries Guylène, a West Indian who, while adjusting well to
life in Africa, has also been able to pick up the intricacies of the caste
system among the Wolof, the Manding and the Pulaar of Senegal
(Sembène, 1981, p. 175). As the political crisis which is the central plot of
the novel, unrolls around her husband and other figures of the élite,
Sembène reveals the reality of a conflicting relationship between Guylène
and her sister-in-law Coumba based on cultural misunderstandings.

Sembène also points out the fact that even when the Senegalese élite
appears to be more preoccupied with the problems of present-day Africa,
"as if the dead hand of irrelevant traditions such as caste distinction and
prejudice has been overthrown for good," this is only a simulated and
feigned attitude.

Thus, while the old man of Senegalese politics in the novel, Doyen
Cheick Tidiane Sall, another slightly fictionalized version of the real life
"dean" of contemporary Senegalese politics, the late Lamine Guèye, is
decidedly against caste distinctions as a vestige of the past that has no
place in modern Africa, his two sons Dioulde and Badou are clearly
divided on the subject. Dioulde, the older son, who is a political wheeler-
dealer, causes outrage to his father when he says without any hesitation
whatsoever that regardless of competence, Daouda is unfit for the
presidency, following President Léon Mignane's disappearance, because of
his caste origins:

> Doyen Cheikh Tidiane Sall had risen early as usual, this Saturday morning.
> What his elder son Dioulde had said last night remained stuck in a corner of
> his mind. He had served under Daouda without reservations; the question of
> caste hadn't come into it. (Sembène. *The Last of the Empire*, Heinemann,
> 1983, p. 83).

Discussing the subject with the young journalist Kad, the old man confirms
the incapacity of both monotheistic religions, Christianity and Islam, to
affect the persistence of caste prejudice:

> 'Religions are only superstructures. They are the summit, not the source of our
> culture. The Catholic minority is influenced by our common culture. They

---

[14] "Major de sa promotion, muni de tous ses diplomas et de deux licences..."
Sembène, 1981, p. 33. (The top of his class, with all his degrees and diplomas and
two B.A.'s ...)

belong to the same tradition as the Muslim majority. There have been Catholic girls who have turned down highly qualified men, because of their lineage ... They didn't turn them down for religious reasons, but for fear of what people would say. It is difficult to deny the permanence and power of tradition.'

This statement echoes convincingly the conclusion of sociologist Abdoulaye-Bara Diop on the subject of Islam and caste:

> L'Islam, quelle que soit son importance, ne pouvait par sa seule force idéologique bouleverser le système des castes, le réduire. Les grands marabouts, issus dans leur immense majorité de la caste supérieure des géér, ne se sont pas mobilisés pour faire prévaloir le principe égalitaire; ils avaient même intérêt au maintien du système des castes—avec les transformations mineures qu'il avait subies—dans la mesure où ils créaient un système d'ordres avec une hiérarchie qui, malgré sa noveauté dans son fondement et ses principes, se reproduit en instituant, á son tour, une hérédité des fonctions religieuses.[15] (Diop, 1981, p. 98).

It is interesting to note how the conversation in the old couple's living room, between Cheikh Tidiane Sall, his wife Djia Umrel Ba and the journalist Kad, which started on the thorny topic of the caste system, moves to the choice between having a First Lady in Senegal who is a foreigner and a President who is of a lower caste, then poses a rhetorical question about the people of Washington, of Moscow, Peking, London, Tokyo, Rome, Paris ... accepting a Black First Lady, a woman from an African country, and finally the conversation moves back home, so to speak, to bring up a modern, or to be more accurate, a colonial version of "caste" distinction, with reference to the new arrogance of Africans against other Africans, on the basis of who had gotten closer to the European model:

> Look at the inhabitants of the towns, Saint-Louis, Dakar, Rufisque, Gorée ... Because of their long period of contact with Europeans, they thought themselves more "civilized" than the other bush Africans living in forest or savanna. This arrogance grew when they alone were given the vote and considered French citizens. People from these four communes, and their descendants, were proud of being the equals of Europeans. They began to

---

[15] (Whatever its importance, Islam could not, by its sole ideological force, overturn or reduce the caste system. The powerful marabouts, emerging in most cases from the higher caste of the *géérs*, did not mobilize themselves to bring the egalitarian principle of Islam to prevail; they were even more interested in maintaining the caste system—with the minor transformations that it had undergone—as long as they were able to establish a system of orders with a hierarchy which, in spite of the novelty in its foundation and in its principles, was reproducing itself by instituting, in its turn, hereditary religious functions.)

parody them, and acquired a pretentious mentality ... How many times have we heard a man from Dakar, Gorée, Rufisque or Ndar (Saint-Louis) say contemptuously to his country cousin: "I was civilized before you were." These alienated, rootless people, enslaved from within—of whom I was and still am one—were unconsciously the most faithful and devoted servants of the then prevailing system of occupation...(Sembène, 1981, pp. 134-5).

It is clear from this passage that as far as Sembène is concerned, caste, caste distinctions, and prejudice on the basis of caste, should be seen primarily as a tendency to divide society and categorize human beings in a hierarchical manner, granting the greatest privileges, respect and consideration to those at the top and leaving only contempt and oppression to those at the bottom. Thus, while Sembène does not equate race with class in this novel or in any of his works, he seems to consider that their ultimate effect on people and society is the same and consequently considers them as practically the same as caste distinctions. And here, Frantz Fanon's statement about the second phase of colonialism when the "natives" internalize "the complex of inferiority" (Fanon: *Black Skin, White Masks*, 1961) applies also, as in many instances during the action of the novel, to Daouda-David, the Prime Minister of griot caste, who, appointed by the Catholic President in spite of disapproving rumblings from many quarters, cannot conceal his timidity, his inhibitions, his "complex of inferiority." This is true of his own sister Coumba as well. And it is this "internalized inferiority complex" that his West Indian born wife Guylène is referring to, when she protests that she "was not brought up in this humiliating mentality," and that she did not want her children to inherit that "inferiority complex" (Sembène, 1983, p. 176).

In conclusion, Ousmane Sembène, Griot of Modern Africa and advocate of a truly egalitarian society, has one feature among many in common with many a traditional griot, in that he is proud of his place in society and remains more than ever, a staunch defender of that place and role within a classless, casteless society, where consideration, respect and position are bestowed upon people in accordance with their competence, the quality of their contributions to society and their achievements rather than on the basis of birth or genealogy.

Influence of Socio-Political Changes

on

Akan Royal Praise Poetry

by Akosua Anyidoho
University of Ghana, Legon

Introduction

The paper examines different contexts in which *apaeɛ* (royal appellation poetry of the Akan of Ghana) is performed in order to demonstrate how performers situated in time and space employ it to "reflect on their conditions, define and\or re-invent themselves and their social world, and either re-enforce, resist, or subvert prevailing orders" (Drewal 1991: 2). To achieve this objective, I shall discuss the conventional and non-conventional contexts of *apaeɛ* and the disparate functions it serves in those contexts. I shall argue that while *apaeɛ* is used in conventional contexts to promote, sustain and legitimize the authority of traditional Akan rulers, in the modern state of Ghana, it may be used to subvert the authority of the traditional rulers for whom *apaeɛ* pieces were originally composed.

Before I begin the analysis, I would like to observe that *apaeɛ* has received some attention from other scholars. Akuffo (1975) and Nketia (1978) are compilations of *apaeɛ* texts dedicated to various Akan rulers. Yankah (1976) examines several oral art forms of the Akan and devotes a section to performance features, content and form of the genre. Yankah (1983) also uses *apaeɛ* to argue that what has been designated as "praise poetry" in African oral literature might not always articulate the laudatory achievements of rulers. In that paper, Yankah makes a cursory remark about one of the functions of *apaeɛ*: "The object or the referent of the performed appellation is individuated and depicted primarily as deserving the attention of society from among a paradigm of peers and co-equals" (p. 382). However, he does not dwell on the utilitarian aspects of the genre. It is the task of this paper to explore that issue.

Conceptual Framework

In her review of the state of research on performance in Africa, Drewal (1991) underscores a different research orientation that emphasizes the dynamics of African performance practices. She observes:

> Performance challenges the notion of an objective social reality as well as the notion that society and human beings are products. Not only is performance production, but both society and human beings are performative, always already processually under construction... As restored behavior, both performance and research entails repetition—not as reproduction, but as transformational process involving acts of representation with critical difference. (p.4)

I would like to observe that much of the discussion of Akan oral literature has dwelt on the conventional aspects, as researchers tend to look "for regularity, pattern, and convention" in oral performance. One of the few studies of Akan verbal art that depart from this orientation is Aning (1969) which focuses on the continuities and discontinuities in nnwonkorɔ, an Akan female song tradition. If we agree with Drewal that performance is "the practical application of embodied skills and knowledge to the task of taking action in everyday social life," then we may also concur that creativity and variation are inevitable in performance. I shall highlight the ways in which contemporary performers employ *apaeɛ* to meet the changing needs of their society.

Apaeɛ in Akan royal courts

Apaeɛ involves a solo performance in which the roles of the performer and audience are clearly demarcated. The performer claims competence in the art and is "licensed", after a long period of training, to recite pieces of appellations in honor of a particular king or chief. Consequently, he is expected to demonstrate exceptional skills of oratory, and he takes an enormous risk in the performance situation. If he is able to perform competently according to the standards of his audience (as he usually does), he gains both royal and social approval. Bauman's (1986) definition of "performance" as far as the roles of artists are concerned holds true for *apaeɛ*:

> I understand performance as a mode of communication, a way of speaking, the essence of which resides in the assumption of responsibility to an audience to a display of communicative skill, highlighting the way in which communication is carried out, above and beyond its referential content. From the point of view of the audience, the act of expression on

the part of the performer is thus laid open to evaluation for the way it is done, for the relative skill and effectiveness of the performer's display. (p. 3)

Apaeε is performed in Akan courts when a king sits in state to receive homage from his people during ceremonial events. At the court, the critics comprise court elders, councillors and attendants, who evaluate the artist's oratorical skills, memory acuity, spontaneity in recalling and performing a series of poems, and agility in the performing arena.

The Akan royal court is the original or conventional context for *apaeε*. In such situations, performers wear leopard skin caps and carry silver and gold-hilted knives called *sepɔ*, formerly used for execution purposes and which also symbolize performers' traditional role in the court. Secondly, the artists carry bayonets and swords, frequently brandishing them. Their costume, weapons and gestures symbolize the ferocity and military valor of the rulers whom they serve and are intended to send signals to opponents. The artists' external appearance, coupled with the content of the texts—couched in a language which exaggerates the social, political, economic and military power of the rulers—portray the referents as superhuman against whom no recalcitrant subject or individual can stand. This seems to be one of the major functions of *apaeε* in the socio-political life of the Akan—to legitimize the ruler's status and to foster a strong awareness among members of the community of his authority and importance.

Information gathered during my field research indicates that for several decades now there have been very few new compositions of *apaeε* texts as far as royal court performances are concerned. A performer at the Manhyia Palace in Kumasi, who claimed to have served in that court for over sixty years, emphasized that he learnt all the pieces in his repertoire before he was admitted to the court. He could not recall having to learn any new ones during that period. This eminent performer agreed with several court elders I talked to on the point that the composition of many of the pieces was motivated by actual historical events. Based on this information, one could conjecture that the Akan composed *apaeε* texts in order to preserve some aspects of their historical experience. This is not to say that composers were concerned only with the representation of historical facts. As Tonkin (1992: 121) has pointed out, representation of what actually happened in the past is a small portion of historical action and discourse in any community. Usually, writers or narrators take a stance on their subjects and audience; they are influenced by past experiences as well as the social, economic and political ideologies of their time. These factors in turn motivate selectivity with regard to aspects of events that are accentuated and the genres chosen for their rendition.

The preceding comments are true for *apaeɛ*; though each piece might
have been inspired by specific historical events, *apaeɛ* only alludes to
actual historical facts in order to extol its referent. I use the word "allude"
for several reasons. First, historical information embodied in the texts is
rarely explicitly conveyed; it is rather expressed through figurative
language. The result is that it is almost impossible to have a full
understanding of particular events by listening to a performance of *apaeɛ*.
One could hypothesize that the difficulty in deciphering historical
information embedded in *apaeɛ* is partly due to the genre itself and partly to
what the composers perceive as its function(s).

The second point which emanates from the preceding one is that
apaeɛ does not often develop themes chronologically or logically. Rather,
the genre concentrates on various types of name—proper names,
appellations and place names that relate to the royal family and prominent
people who have shown tenacity and military prowess. With this feature in
mind, I would like to suggest that historical experiences are restructured in
apaeɛ with the intent of enhancing the political, military and spiritual status
of rulers. Consequently, the genre may be considered a reconstruction of
the past with the main emphasis on the political past; everything else
remains unsaid though, to use Barber et al's. (1989: 6) words, "the unsaid is
always a partner in the discourse."

Another characteristic feature of *apaeɛ* which suggests that it is a
reconstruction of selected aspects of the political past is that proper names,
appellations and place names that are highlighted are usually those
associated with laudatory achievements of royal ancestors. While the
pieces often paint a glorious picture of the ancestors of the leader being
honored, they emphasize their opponents' lack of military and political
power. The focus of the following piece taken from Akuffo (1975: 31), for
example, concerns origins: ancestors, historical places, and achievements of
the referent. In contrast to example 1, example 2, recorded during a festival
at Manhyia Palace, dwells on the incompetence of a rival army.

Example 1:

    Ɔno no

    Mamponten, Adu Ampofo Antwi, Nnyedua-anan-ase

    Adu Akorowa, bɔ wo konkon ma yɛnkɔ ɛ

    Ɔkyerewaa Akenten Siaboɔ

5   Ɔyoko Sakyiampoma nana Kokofuni

    Saasi Ayeboafo ne Akora Bruku nana firi Amanseɛ

    Adu Otu Birempɔn

Ɔko-ma-ahene firi Kɔtɔkɔ
Kagya Agyeman Koforoboɔ Birempɔn a Kagyaa   Tiaa wɔ no
10 Ɔhemmaa Kɔtɔkɔ wo-ahene
Agyeman
Kagya kumanini Nana Owusu Akyaa
Berempɔn Aduomirihene .

That is him
Adu Ampoforo Antwi, who hails from Mamponten,
a town built under the shade of four acacia trees
Adu Akorowa, the vanguard, go before us
Okyerewa Akenten, who is as tough as a rock
5 Grandchild of Sakyiamapoma, a member of the Oyoko clan,
who hails from Kokofu
Grandchild of Saasi Ayeboafo and the deity Bruku, who hails
from Amansee
Adu Otu, the noble one
The great fighter from Kotoko
The unconquerable Agyeman, the victorious one, the owner of
Kagyaa Tiaa
10 The Queen Mother of Kotoko, the mother of kings
Agyeman*
Owusu Akyaa, the indestructible one who executes strong men
The noble one, the king of Aduomiri

Several images in this piece convey the point that the forefathers of the referent, Agyeman, were the founders of the town over which their descendant rules. For example, line 2 mentions landmarks found at the place where Mamponten was built in order to emhasize that there were no occupants of the land before the arrival of the Oyoko clan of the Kumasi royal family. A similar metaphor occurs in line 6 "the old man Bruku who hails from Amansee." The word Amansee can be literally translate as "the origin of nations," a way of saying that Bruku, an ancestor of the referent, was a founder of the town. Note also that most of the names and their epithets in this text point to the royal ancestry of the referent. For example, the recipient is called "Grandchild of Sakyiamapoma," "Grandchild of Saasi

Ayeboafo" (lines 5 and 6), people who are unanimously accepted as true ancestors of the throne. As the text shows, these progenitors are described as the founders of the political unit now under the authority of their descendant. These genealogical references become meaningful when it is understood that in traditional Akan society, political leadership is not achieved but ascribed; therefore, blood relationship is a prerequisite to any claim to political status and social superiority. It is also through genealogy that a chief acquires the right to be honored through certain *apaeɛ* texts.

Another function of *apaeɛ* is related to the people in the communities under the rule of chiefs and kings who are the main recipients of *apaeɛ*. By authenticating rulers' claims to power and authority, *apaeɛ* also serves to validate the community members' claim to property and lands which fall under the jurisdiction of their rulers. Though I was unable to find the exact historical periods when the pieces were created, it is probable that they were produced when traditional state boundaries were not clearly established, a period when there was frequent inter-group warfare, which in turn determined ownership of territories. By legitimizing a political leader's ownership to lands as well as to power and prestige, apaeɛ enables people in the community to gain a sense of belonging and of political authority over members of competing states. Using oral tradition to lay claim to property is not unique to the Akan, for as Diawara (1989: 116) has observed, "oral traditions often serve to legitimize and defend the economic, social and political acquisitions of their authors."

Furthermore, in the attempt to authenticate kings and chiefs as true descendants of the royal stool, *apaeɛ* becomes a tool for intimidating opponents and for mobilizing public support for political rulers. I would like to suggest that the paraphernalia, costume and gestures used by performers are means of waging a psychological warfare against both rebellious subjects and rival states. For example, the frequent simulation of the execution process during performance is a way of giving the audience a visual image of what might happen to enemies or subjects who rebel against the status quo. One could say that this function of apaeɛ is comparable to the modern situation where states and nations conduct military maneuvers and parades to display their potential for destructive military power. The following text may illustrate this point:

Example 2:
    Ɔno no
    Bɛyɛɛ-dɛn ee?
    Bɛyɛɛ-dɛn ee?

Opoku Ware, woakum Bɛyɛɛ-dɛn
5   Woakum deɛ ɔde mmofra baɛ
Woakum "merensom-wo"
Woakum Booman Kwadwo Wea
Woakum Adumankaase Yaw Nwanwa
Woakum Amanseɛ Barima-yɛ-na
10 Woakum werekyerɛwerekyerɛ ama ɔkwan ho adwo
Woako ama ɔforoteɛ ate atɔ pata ama konturomfi ase "oohoo"

That is him
What-did-he-come-here-for?
What-did-he-come-here-for?
Opoku Ware you have slain "What-did-he-come-here-for?"
5   You have slain the one who brought children
You have slain the one who said: "I will not serve you"
You have slain Kwadwo Wea from Booman
You have slain Yaw, the extraordinary one from   Adwumankese
You have slain the strong man revered in Amansee
10 You have slain the nuisance and restored peace
You have fought and defeated the stag, and has caused the
chimpanzee to applaud.

In example 2, the military might of the ruler is conveyed through
enumeration of the people the referent or his ancestors are supposed to have
defeated in battle, rival kings who are considered gallant fighters according
to the standards of their own states. Lines 2 and 3 refer to the object of line
4, one of the powerful leaders supposed to have been conquered by the
referent, Opoku Ware. In the Akan text, the idiophone *ee* at the end of lines
2 and 3 is used in colloquial language when someone shouts out the name
of a person he is searching for. Shouting the name of *Bɛyɛɛ-dɛn* in these
lines is intended to show that the so-called strong one could not be found
because he had been eliminated by a more powerful ruler. Note that the
nominal *bɛyɛɛ-dɛn* literally means "the one called 'what-did-he-come-here-
for'"; the performer seems to question the sense in an opponent's decision
to challenge a particular ruler since the former was no match for the latter.
In line 5, "one who brought children" means the enemy's army comprised
children, indicating inexperience and folly on the apart of the opposing

army. Thus, line 5 reinforces the content of lines 2, 3 and 4. Also, *Booman* in line 7 is derived form *oboo* "stone" and man, "town;" this line therefore implies that the king being honored is able to conquer the strongest of states.

An important point I would like to make from the foregoing analysis is that apaeɛ portrays strong, fearful and powerful rulers in contrast to how adversaries are depicted. As Diawara (1989: 125) observes in his analysis of *tanbasire*, an oral narrative of the Soninke of Mali, at the same time as the performer praises his chief, he is also provoking another. One could argue that by highlighting only the commendatory aspects of ones own social, economic and political history and emphasizing only the negative ones of opponents, *apaeɛ* lacks objectivity. However, as far as impartiality is concerned, one can also ask whether there is any political discourse that is not prejudiced. Even in the Western world which seems to cherish objectivity so dearly, the tendency of selecting and emphasizing only negative characteristics of enemies (perceived or real) is deeply entrenched in certain discourse types.

If the interpretation given in the preceding paragraphs is accepted, one may view *apaeɛ* as a mechanism of political and social control; through the genre, rulers display their power—or do they feign power?—and manipulate to their advanatage the psychological frame of their subjects as well as their foes. I would like to suggest that the tight control that the court maintains over this discourse type becomes meaningful when one sees political and social control as a function of *apaeɛ*. It should be noted that *apaeɛ* performance in Akan courts involves accurate memorization and reproduction of texts, giving the performer no opportunity for unauthorized creativity as far as the text is concerned. I would like to submit that one of the main reasons performers are not allowed to modify texts or to create their own in performance situations is that such a move might jeopardize the authority of the ruler since it cannot be guaranteed that when an artist performs extemporaneously, he would not use the forum to subvert the status quo.

While *apaeɛ* may be a genre of political history, it also provides a means of evaluating political leadership. As I pointed out, instead of dwelling on the total political history, there is a great deal of selectivity in the way that history is recounted. Almost invariably, *apaeɛ* pieces emphasize the admirable qualities that the society expects of its leaders. By way of illustration, I would like to examine the following composition taken from Akuffo (1975: 34):

Example 3:
  Ɔno no
  Ɔsaforo Adu Amankwatia
  Amankwa Kronkron, Bagua Kurontiri
  Ɔkyerebea Yirifi Ahoma Asante Kotoko
5 Ɔko-kyere-hene-ma-ohene
  Suntrɛso barima a, odi ɔko mu akoten
  Ohene ba Ohene; ɔko bɛsi a, yɛka ma wote
  Ɔkyerefo daa Kwabrafo a, okum nnipa sii atoprɛ
  Kwabrafo di-tire-mu-hene a, ɔne n'afɛfo kyɛ ade a ɔfa tire
10 Apraku Panyin Birempɔn nana mpapakyikyi a ɔte n'akurogya
  Bediako, ɔkatakyie a ɔmo ntoa kɔda a, na ɔsum atuduro
  Ankaadu Gyan a mmofra kɔ ase a, wotu nneɛ
  Awua, Nkrawiri a, ɔmo nsaa
  Dwoda mmo!
15 Ɔko-awia nana ɔkofoni a, ɔko kyere dɔm
  Ɔsaforo Adu Amankwatia Brempɔn

  That is him
  Osaforo Adu Amankwatia (proper name)
  Authentic Amankwa , the leader of the right wing of the state
  Asante Kotoko, the climbing plant that spreads everywhere
5 The brave warrior who captures kings
  The man from Suntreso, vctorious warrior
  The son of a chief who gets prior information when there is
      going to be war
  The lion who never loses his prey, one who slays his preys after
      using them as play things
  The lion, the chief of skulls, one who takes the head when he
      shares his preys with friends
10 The ancestor of Elder Apraku, noble one, the reargaurd who
      protects the town
  Natural warrior, the valiant one who straps his ammunition to
      his body when he sleeps and uses gunpowder for a pillow
  The great lime tree under which children find fortunes

Awua, the great drum wrapped in rich *nsaa* cloth

Congratulation, Monday child

15 Grandchild of one who fights in broad day light and captures
    multitudes

Osaforo Adu Amankwatia, the nobleman

In this piece, through an appellation or an epithet, each line expresses an
attribute a political leader is (was?) expected to have. The initial nominal is
then expanded in a succeeding subordinate clause. While the connotational
relations between the parallelistic structures, that is, between the initial
nominal and the following adjectival clause, may be varied, similarity
seems to be the predominant one. For example, apart from lines 1, 2 and
14, all the other lines, each of which contains an initial nominal and a
succeeding relative clause, show semantic similarity or content parallelism.
In line 3, the proper name Amankwa is the name of the ruler of a suburb of
Kumasi, the section of the Asante capital which takes the right wing
position in the military formation of the state. Note that this fact is
expressed in the relative clause that follows the proper name. Also, Asante
Kotoko (line 4) is the appellation of the Asante state, the full version of
which goes "Asante Kotoko, slay a thousand; a thousand more shall rise."
This appellation portrays the dynamism, bravery and tenacity of the Asante.
The meaning of this appellation is virtually given in the ensuing clause. It
would appear that bravery, tenacity, military valor and skills, authority,
power and wealth were considered some of the most important attributes of
rulers. One could say that at the time that the texts were composed, an era
when there was frequent inter-ethnic warfare, the major role of rulers was
military defense and/or offense; consequently, those who proved their
mettle were honored through these special pieces. The following provides
another example:

Example 4:

    Ɔno no

    Opoku Ware, wo ho asɛm merete merete

    Wo ho asɛm te sɛ onyinatan mmiɛnsa so ahahan, awisi

    Wo ho asɛm merete merete

5   Owuo na esi aso.

    Mete a, mete no ko so

    Mete no mmarima so

    Mete no akatakyie so

Ɔkyere fa-nim-ako a wannane ko anto mpanyin ne mmofra so
10   Okontokurowi a ɔda amansan kɔn mu
Na mansan nkɔmmɔ a yɛdie ne Opoku Ware

That is he
Opoku Ware, I have great news about you
The things I hear about you are as numerous as the leaves of
three huge silk-cotton trees
I hear a great deal about you
5   It is only the dead who do not hear anything about you
I hear about your exploits in war
I hear about your manly deeds
I hear about your valor
The captor, the diligent warrior who does not relegate his war to
old men and children
10   The rainbow which engulfs a whole community
Opoku Ware, topic of conversation in the whole community.

Lines 5-9 of example 4 clearly list the admirable attributes of the ruler which the whole community is talking about and praising him for.

If *apaeɛ* gives hints of what is expected of Akan rulers, then one could argue that it forms part of the social apparatus that regulates the behavior of rulers as well as other members of the community. In this regard, one could posit that apaeɛ has an educational function. Through its performance, young royal family members are educated about their social and political responsibilities and privileges. Similarly, the community members are socialized to accept their leaders as their superiors who deserve honor and respect in return for protection and good leadership.

Though *apaeɛ* has some serious political and educational functions in the court, the genre also provides entertainment. In some contexts, a performer might recite a poem intended to cause laughter. However, if the ruler (the referent) laughs, he is required by custom to pay a certain sum of money to the performer. Apart from paralinguistic, kinetic features and techniques used to make some *apaeɛ* pieces entertaining, linguistic features such as hyperbole and alliteration are also employed. In many pieces, including example 5, the accomplishments of rulers are so highly exaggerated that the contents become humorous:

Example 5:

Ɔno no

Kuntun-kantan-mmoho ee

Kuntun-kantan-mmoho ee

Opoku Ware, woma onipa yɛ kuntunn

5   Na woama wayɛ bohoo

Na woama yafrɛ no okuntun-kantan-mmoho

That is he

Arrogant-bloated-and-weakened

Arrogant-bloated-and-weakened

Opoku Ware, you wait until someone becomes pompous

5   Then you weaken him

Then you name him "arrogant-bloated-and-weakened"

The humor in this piece derives partly from the combination of the words *kuntun, kantan*, each of which connotes enormous size without substance, and *mmohoo*—inactivity due to severe illness, fatigue or in this case as a result of a fight with a superior warrior. Basically the piece attributes supernatural strength to the referent, Opoku Ware, who is able to subdue people filled with self-importance. Note that in line 6 the image of the individual supposed to have been defeated changes as a result of the encounter with this more powerful ruler; he acquires a new name: 'arrogant-bloated-and-weakened.' The alliteration and assonance in *kuntun-kantan-mohoo* sounds funny to the native ear and makes the lines memorable.

Apaeɛ also has an aesthetic function. The Akan admire eloquence and speech play, and give special respect to those who are adept in language use, especially those who speak metaphorically and intersperse their utterances with proverbs and other figurative expressions. The Akan have several expressions referring to people who display high levels of competence in language use, for example, *n'ano ate*, "her\his mouth is crisp"; *n'ano awo*, "her\his mouth is dry." Yankah (1989: 334) has suggested that the association of dryness with verbal dexterity and wetness with verbal incompetence may derive from the fact that infants, who usually drool, are incapable of verbal communication. However, as they mature and the drooling stops, they gradually acquire competence in their first language. *Apaeɛ* performance provides the opportunity for the enjoyment of refined and sophisticated language.

To conclude this section, I would like to point out that though *apaeɛ* might serve all these functions, a performer might choose to accentuate a particular aspect or a combination of these and minimize all others. This is done through the selections he performs and how he enacts them. For example, performing at an annual festival where the audience might comprise people from different ethnic groups who might not understand the language, the entertainment function might be accentuated. It is also true to say that individuals viewing the same performance might interpret it differently. For instance, while an elder at the court might be reminded of the historical event related to a text and consider the performance as an enactment of history, a young person who has no knowledge of the origin of the texts and who lacks accurate interpretation of the metaphors employed might focus attention on the gestures and therefore see the whole performance as entertaining. For several reasons that cannot be discussed in this paper, in contemporary Akan society, the entertainment function may be more relevant in many performances than the evaluative or educational ones. Suffice it to say that in modern Ghana, Akan chiefs and kings are military generals only in a symbolic sense; they do not have the power to recruit armies and to declare wars. These functions have been taken over by leaders of the larger, modern state. Consequently the duties of traditional rulers no longer centre around military defense/offense, though in times of crisis they might play that role. Nowadays, different criteria are used in evaluating traditional rulers; among them are the level of education and the ability to attract governmental and non-governmental agencies that may help to develop the areas.

Functions of *Apaeɛ* in contemporary Ghana

Traditionally, *apaeɛ* was a sacred genre which was not expected to be performed outside the domain of the court. However, in the sixties, it was introduced into the modern political arena and has since been spreading to several situations. (For information about the motivating factor for this trend, see Anyidoho 1991). Now, *apaeɛ* occurs in several contexts, for example, church, modern state ceremonies, radio and television. Taking into consideration the new performance situations, contemporary performers, have transformed the art form in several ways. I shall highlight some of the variations introduced in these contexts and comment on the intended purposes of those performances.

***Apaeɛ* in the church**

A variation of *apaeɛ* performance has been observed in some Catholic churches during the administration of the Holy Communion. In those churches, before a priest starts the Holy Communion rituals, two men with pieces of cloth tied around their waists and with swords in their right hands walk to the front and stand about a meter away from the priest with their back towards the congregation. They bend down and point the swords towards the alter. When the prelude to the Communion starts, it is interspersed with recitations by the two men. The following is a transcript of the verbal component of one such performance; it includes the words of the priest:

Example 6:
        Onyankopon Tweduampon
        Yɛyi wo ayɛ
        Yɛkanfo wo
        Yɛhyɛ wo animuonyam
5   Nana brɛbrɛ
        Ɔkatakyie, brɛbrɛ
        Wiase agyenkwa brɛbrɛ o

Priest: Efisɛ, ɔno koro yi ara, anadwo a wɔrebeyi no ama no, ɔfaa paanoo, na ɔdaa ase, ohyiraa so, na obubuu mu maa n'asuafoɔ no see wɔn sɛ, mo nyinaa mongye wei, na monni, na wei ne me honam a, mo nti, ayera no

        Ɔno no
        Awurade Nyankopɔn wɔ ha
        Awurade Nyankopɔn
        Ɔkatakyie barima
15   Wo nkwadaa da wo ase
        Yɛma wo mo
        Mo ɔpeafo
        Ototrobonsu
        Nyankopɔn

Priest: Saa nso na bere a wodidi wieɛ no, ɔfaa kuruwa no, ɔdaa ase, hyiraa so, demaa n'asuafoɔ no, see wɔn sɛ, mo nyinaa mɛgye bi, na wei ne me mogya kuruwa no wɔ nyehyɛɛ foforo no mu. Me mogya yi nti na mo ne nipa nyinaa enti, wobeyi mo afi bɔne mu. Monye wei na mode akae me.

Ɔsabarima ne hwan
Ɔsabarima ne Nyame
25 Amanfoɔ nyinaa wura
Asɛm biara mfitiaseɛ ne awieɛ
Wo a wodua a obi ntimu ntu
Wo a woka a obi nka bi
Wanko a obi ntumi nko
30 Awurade Nyame wo ho yɛ hu
Wo yɛ kronkron
Kronkron mu kronkron
Yɛma wo mo
Mo
35 mo, ɔpeafo
Totronbonsu
Nyankopɔn

Ancient God
We give you praise
We adore you
We give you honor
5 Grandfather, come in your majesty
The great fighter, come in your majesty
The savior of the world, come in your majesty

Priest: Because, the night before he was betrayed, he took bread; he gave thanks and blessed it and he broke it and gave to his disciples

and said to them, you all eat this because it is my body which was
given up for your sake.

That is he
Lord God is in our presence
Lord God
The valiant one
15   Your children give you thanks
We congratulate you
Congratulations
Great one
Lord

Priest: In the same manner, when they had finished eating, he took
the cup, he gave thanks, he blessed it and gave it to his disciples
saying: 'All of you drink this, because it is my blood in the new
covenant. It is through my blood that you and all humankind will be
saved. Do this in remembrance of me.'

Who is the great warrior
The great warrior is God
25   The Creator of the whole universe
The beginning and the end of everything
What you plant, no one can uproot
You have the last say in everything
If you do not fight your wars, no one can
30   Lord God, your are fierce
You are holy
The holy of holiest
We congratulate you
Congratulations
35   Congratulations, the great one
The great one
Lord

Though the performance in the church shares several things in common with *apaeɛ* enacted in the conventional context, it differs in certain significant ways. The commonalities include the costume and the paraphernalia used, paralinguistic features, phraseology of the texts and the prosody. However, while traditionally *apaeɛ* is a solo performance, the church situation involves three participants: two recitors and a priest. Second, instead of honoring a visible and a mortal chief, the preceding text honors the invisible and immortal God. Thirdly, the new referent also influences the content of the text; the preponderant use of war imagery found in traditional apaeɛ is minimized and words and expressions related to the Christian faith are preferred although there is a great deal of war imagery in both the Old and New Testaments. Another peculiar feature of the text is that it incorporates features of other Akan genres such as drum language and libation poetry. For example, the phrase Nana *brïbrï*, which means "grandfather, take your time and walk in majesty," (line 5-7) is used in drum poetry when a chief is walking to a gathering area.

It may be appropriate at this point to comment briefly on the factors that have influenced modern poets to draw on other Akan genres in their attempt to create *apaeɛ* texts for the new contexts. One could attribute the changes in the text to incompetence and lack of knowledge of Akan history on the part of contemporary composers. This observation may be justified considering that modern performers do not serve in the royal court where the genre usually occurs; consequently, they lack the rigorous training and exposure that traditional performers obtain, which enable them to differentiate between the various verbal genres and to be finely attuned to the characteristics of each of them. Though this observation may be valid, it cannot be solely responsible for the performance and textual innovations observed in modern compositions. I would like to suggest that the crucial motivating factor is the new contexts in which apaeɛ is performed. In the context of the church, traditional *apaeɛ*, which always glorifies military strength and defines authority and power in terms of military superiority, may be grossly out of place and contrary to Christian principles. It is also important to recognize that the functions of apaeɛ in church contexts differ from those discussed in relation to traditional performances. The use of oral tradition in the church is a means of indigenizing the church environment and breaking down cultural barriers that separate African communities from the Western-fashioned Christian world. My investigation revealed that the inclusion of apaeɛ in the church liturgy was initiated by The Right Reverend Dr. Peter Akwasi Sarpong, the Arch Bishop of Kumasi, a social anthropologist by training, who still finds time to teach the subject in a local college.

Viewing the church performance from another perspective, one may detect some degree of subversion in it. Christians might argue that all power belongs to God; consequently, no mortal being deserves to be accorded so much power and authority as performers attribute to recipient chiefs through *apaeɛ* performance. By appropriating a genre reserved for traditional political rulers, modern performers in Christian worship are indirectly subverting or challenging the authority of earthly rulers.

Apaeɛ on state occasions

In contemporary Ghana, apaeɛ is frequently performed in honor of Western-styled political leaders at festivals and on state ceremonial occasions. For example, on 7th January 1993, during the official ceremony marking Ghana's return to civilian rule after eleven years of military rule, a performer draped in a rich, hand-woven, multicolored kente cloth—one of the key symbols of Ghanaian culture—preceded the democratically elected President's inaugural address with the performance of panegyrics reminiscent of traditional *apaeɛ*.

There are three features of that particular performance that I would like to highlight. First, after each line was delivered verbally, the performer paused for the text to be reproduced on a talking drum by another person. Second, the attire, paraphernalia, movements and gestures that court performers use were absent; modern artists usually stand behind microphones and recite or read their texts. Third, the text was very long and embodied lines from many traditional *apaeɛ* pieces. It is important to emphasize that texts performed in traditional court ceremonies are sacred and fixed; and the lines of each piece are recited in the same sequence. Not only do modern performers draw on several "set pieces," they also cross generic boundaries. I shall exemplify the preceding observations by examining the text performed on the occasion mentioned above:

Example 7:

    Ɔkyerɛma ma mo atenaase

        The master drummer welcomes you

    Ɔman panyin sɔre ɛ

        The President, be ready

    Akwasi e

        Akwasi (proper name)

  J.J.

J. J. (Jerry John)
5 Rawlings
Rawlings
Jerry
Jerry
Pusu anini ne wo ampa
You really shake up strong men
Atɛkyɛ bi yɛ fɛntɛnfrɛm a ɛmene sono
The great bog that swallows elephants
Ah! Jerry
Jerry
10 Woyɛ bɛɛma
You are a man
Ayɛboafo
The great one
Ɔkɔtɔmene
One who swallows the crab
Akwasi a ɔto boɔ mene no no
One who throws up stone and swallows it
Agya nsuro ogya
Father who is not scared of fire
15 Dadeɛ nkɔnsɔnkɔnsɔn
Unbreakable iron chain
Kokuromoti Prempeh
The indespensable thumb, Prempeh
Otumfoɔ ma wo amo
The man of valor congratulates you
Daasebrɛ ma wo amo
The benevolent one congratulates you
Rawlings a worese a ɔnte ee
Rawlings who is not counselled
20 Awora kɛse a yɛkɔ mu akɔtɔbɔ
The great marshy plain where we search for crabs
Odum fɛtɛ

Destroyer of mahogany tree
Odum fɛtɛ
Destroyer of mahogany tree
Dan fɛtɛ
Destroyer of buildings
Frɛdɛ fɛtɛ
Destroyer
25 Naa Konadu Agyeman kunu bɛɛma kɔrɔ
The husband of Nana Konadu Agyeman
Akwasi mo
Akwasi, congratulations
Sɔre e
Arise
Oman panyin
President
Kasa e
Speak
30 Oman panyin
President
Bɔkɔɔ
Slowly
Dwidwa mu
Say it all
Dwidwa mu
Say it all
Ɔresɔre o
He is rising
35 Wasɔre
He has arisen
Wasɔre
He has arisen
Akwasi mo
Akwasi, congratulations
Akwasi mo

Akwasi, congratulations

Obuebue-akwan

The path-finder

40 Akwasi kronkron

Holy One, Akwasi

Akwasi fɛntɛmfrɛ

Akwasi, the bog

Akwasi mo

Akwasi, congratulations

Kasa, kasa, kasa

Speak, speak, speak

Bɔkɔɔ

Gently

In example 7, there are stock phrases that are usually used by court
attendants to alert an audience to the imminent departure of a traditional
ruler from assembly grounds; lines 34-36 are such lines, ɔresɔre o. Lines
32 and 33 are generally uttered as back channel cues by court attendants
when public speeches are being delivered; the lines signal encouragement,
support and agreement. Traditional *apaeɛ* is not accompanied by such back
channel cues. In addition, lines 21-24, 26-29 and 37-38 are generally
produced on the drum. I have combed through all the *apaeɛ* texts in Nketia
(1978), Akuffo (1975) and my own collection, but could not find the use of
these lines in any of them.

I would like to posit that the interaction between the drummer and the
reciter may have motivated some of these changes. In the traditional
contexts of performance, apaeɛ texts are not accompanied by any drum
interpretation and vice versa. The combination of two art forms—drum and
apaeɛ—in a single performance was motivated by the intended purpose of
the performance; it was orchestrated to display the cultural heritage of
Ghanaians and to give an indigenous flavor to an essentially foreign
ceremony, the inauguration of the president of a so-called modern state
modeled after prodominantly western traditions. Consequently, the more
aspects of the culture that could be put on display the better, hence the
employment of an orator and a drummer in a single performance.

Apaeɛ on Radio and Television

Another context in which *apaeɛ* has been performed in contemporary Ghana is on radio and television. Unlike traditional chiefs, who reside in various communities and who have regular face-to-face contacts with their subjects during special ceremonies which necessitate *apaeɛ* performance, modern political leaders rule from the capital and reach the nation largely through radio and television. Consequently, *apaeɛ* has been adapted to suit these communication media. Yankah (1989: 342) provides a brief account of how this practice began.

Apart from state ceremonies and radio and television, *apaeɛ* has also been adapted to occasions honoring academics. In November 1991, the University of Ghana held a special congregation for the conferment of honorary degrees on eleven scholars and public personalities for their contribution to Ghanaian society. Before each of the honorees proceeded to be introduced to the audience, a text based on the style of *apaeɛ* was recited.

In the situations described in the preceding paragraphs, we see the utilization of *apaeɛ* in basically Western-fashioned events such as a presidential inuagural ceremony, scholars' award ceremony as well as on radio and television. This trend is part of an attempt to project Ghanaian culture and identity. In this connection, *apaeɛ* and other verbal genres of the Akan such as libation and drum poetry have ideological funtions in contemporary Ghana. They are used to assert Ghanaian identity and to communicate to the world that Ghana has a rich cultural heritage of which her people must be proud. To promote Ghanaian identity, governments have also found it necessary to inject Western-style events with doses of indigenous Ghanaian flavor in the form of verbal art, drumming and dancing. Consequently, while during colonial era state events were commenced with prayers said by the Christian clergy, in contemporary times traditional "libation " has also become an integral part of such events. What I am arguing here is that *apaeɛ* performance on state occasions is part of a complex process of re-affirming Ghana's independence and cultural identity.

In these new contexts *apaeɛ* also serves to subvert the authority of traditional rulers. While people in the court still insist that the genre be performed for traditional rulers only, modern recitors utilize that verbal resource to honor modern leaders. One might view the use of *apaeɛ* in modern political situations as reflecting the realities of the time; it suggests that traditional rulers are gradually losing their political, military and economic powers to the Western-styled leaders. Consequently, a genre originally reserved for the former could be extended to the latter.

Conclusion

The discussion has highlighted generic instabilities as in the composition and performance of *apaeε*, a consequence of the socio-political changes that are taking place in modern Ghana. I have argued that the functions of *apaeε* in conventioanl contexts of performance differ from those of modern situations where the art form is enacted. Since modern leaders exist side-by-side with traditional rulers, with the former wielding more power than the latter, *apaeε* has crossed its conventional boundaries to other situations where it might even be used to subvert the authority of traditional rulers.

WORKS CITED

Akuffo, Boafo Okyeame. *Kotokohene Dammirifua Due*. Accra-Tema: Ghana Publishing Corporation, 1975.

Aning, Ben A. "Nnwonkoro: A Study of Stability and Change in Traditional Music." M. A. Thesis, University of Ghana, Institute of African Studies at Legon, 1969.

Anyidoho, Akosua.   "Linguistic Parallelism in Traditional Akan Appellation Poetry." *Research in African Literatures*, 22.1 (1991): 67-82.

Barber, Karin. "Interpreting Oriki as History and as Literature." *Discourse and Its Disguises: Interpretation of African Oral Texts*. Eds. Karin Barber and P. F. de Moraes Farias. Birmingham: Centre of West African Studies, University of Birmingham, 1989. 13-23.

Bauman, Richard. *Story, Performance, and Event: Contextual Studies of Oral Narrative*. Cambridge: Cambridge University Press, 1986.

Diawara, M. "Women, Survitude and History: The Oral Historical Tradition of Women of Servile Condition in the Kingdom of Jaara (Mali) from the Fifteenth to the mid-Nineteenth Century." *Discourse and its Disguises: The Interpretation of African Oral Texts*. Eds. Karin Barber and P. F. de Moraes Farias. Burmingham: Centre of West African Studies, Burmingham University, 1989. 109-137.

Drewal, Margaret T. "The State of Research on Performance in Africa." *African Studies Review*, 34. 3 (1991): 1-64.

Nketia, J. H. *Amoma*. Accra-Tema. Ghana Publishing Corporation, 1978.

Tonkin, Elizabeth. *Narrating our Past: The Social Constructing of Oral History*. Cambridge: Cambridge University Press, 1992.

Yankah, Kwesi. To Praise or Not to Praise the King: The Akan *Apae* in the Context of Referential Poetry. *Research in African Literatures*, 14. 3 (1983): 381-400.

_____ Proverbs: The Aesthetics of Traditional Communication. *Research in African Literatures*, 20. 3 (1989): 325-46

SECTION C:

New Life I:

Language & Artistic Tradition

MOTHER TONGUE:

Creoles, Pidgins, Patois and Black English as Poetic Languages

by Fahamisha Patricia Brown
Boston College

When I speak of Black Mother Tongues—the pidgins, patois, creoles, and Black Englishes which comprise Black vernacular speech—I am focusing on several aspects of language use which occur cross-culturally among poets of African descent. The first is the incorporation of spoken vernacular—vocabulary, syntax, idioms, and pronunciations—into written poetry. The poet strives to render in writing the sounds and idioms of Black vernacular speech. Next is the effort to find written equivalents of the rhythms and tonalities of Black vernaculars, what Asante calls "communication styles" (21). Lastly, at least for this paper, is the Black language act or situation as a source for Black poetic language.

It is almost a truism to state that poets of the African world are influenced by vernacular cultures. The languages that Black people speak, the folk vernaculars, constitute a language rendered literary by the artistry of Black poets. What this paper attempts to explore is the ways in which poetry of the African world—that is, poetry by poets from Africa and the Diaspora—is itself an extension of oral culture possessing what Meineke Schipper calls "written orality" (66). This orality is achieved both in the poet's choice of language and in the poet's incorporation of culturally specific language acts.

Linguists and cultural anthropologists have noted the value which Black cultures assign to verbal ability. In a study of "Black English," Geneva Smitherman posits an African American culture "that produced and continues to generate Black language [as] an oral one in which verbal performance is highly esteemed...[one, moreover] like those of West Africa from which Black Americans come...[that places] a high premium on the spoken word" (3). Roger Abrahams and John Szwed explore a similar phenomenon in the English-speaking Caribbean. "Blacks had brought with them [to the Caribbean] a concern for maintaining a wide variety of rhetorical processes and speech activities as well as the highly systematic canons of appropriateness in content, formality and diction during recurrent interactional situations" (78). Schipper also reminds us that in contemporary Africa the oral is simultaneous with the written. The bilingual or multi-lingual nature of spoken discourse thus informs the written.

By the selection of vernacular expression as the favored poetic language, the Black poet infuses her/his art with a cultural specificity. The poet's selection of the mother tongue, moreover, asserts a socio-political identifcation with the group that shares the language. Gordon Rohlehr has posited a kind of language continuum "from which speakers naturally selected registers of the language which were appropriate to particular contexts and situations..." (1). The implications of the existence of such a continuum are many. First, such a language continuum provides a wide range of options from which Black poets might choose. Educated Blacks, a category from which most Black poets are drawn, often speak a variety of Englishes dependent upon time, place and audience or situation. These various Englishes all constitute parts of Rohlehr's "continuum." For while it is true that Black speakers of English speak some variant or offshoot of the Queen's (or King's) English, Standard American or BBC Standard, that is, the English held up as the "correct" or "proper" model, it is equally true that the Englishes spoken by the masses of Black people around the world deviate from that norm sufficiently that they are entitled to the designation of independent language systems. The English language continuums, along which speakers naturally enter as appropriate, account for the wide variety of Englishes in which Black poets, most of whom have been educated to the literary and spoken "standards," write.

It is in the varied uses of language in a community that I situate Black vernacular spoken languages, the mother tongues, and Black poetry, both vehicles of Black cultural expressivity. Paul Laurence Dunbar (1872-1906) achieved fame in the late nineteenth century United States for what he would later characterize as "jingles in a broken tongue." Elsewhere, Marcellus Blount (582-93) has argued that Dunbar subversively reclaims African American plantation vernacular from oppressive conventions of black-face minstrelsy. The Local Color movement of the late nineteenth century gave rise to an increasing amount of regional and dialect poetry in the United States. Thus, Paul Laurence Dunbar actually was in the literary mainstream when he began to write in dialect. Although Dunbar's dialect poetry partakes of some of the elements of the language of the popular stage of his day, Dunbar uses dialect to fill in the warmth, humor, even humanity of the slaves. In doing so, he replicates in writing a culturally specific language practice—double-voicedness or verbal duplicity, indirection. To achieve his goals, he creates a written equivalent for the mother tongue in which he had probably heard tales of life on the plantation. It can also be observed, however, that Dunbar restricts the subject matter he finds appropriate for dialect. Dunbar's dialect poetry evokes the warmth, the humor, the sentiment, the everyday, ordinary people at home and/or at play. When he wants to evoke the sublime—the dignity, the pain, the suffering, the visionary—Dunbar turns to the literary language of his time. An examination of Dunbar's three poems in tribute to the "colored troops" of the Civil War illustrate this point.

"When Dey 'Listed Colored Soldiers" (265) is a dramatic monologue spoken in dialect by a woman whose beloved "Lias" has enlisted in the Union Army.

> Dey was talkin' in de cabin, de was
> talkin in' in de hall;
> But I listened kin' o' keerless, not
> a-t'inkin' 'bout it all;
> An' on Sunday, too, I noticed, dey was
> whisp'rin' mighty much,
> Stan'in' all erroun' de roadside w'en dey
> let us out o' chu'ch.
> But I didn't t'ink erbout it 'twell de mid-
> dle of de week,
> An' my 'Lias come to see me, an' somehow
> he couldn't speak.
> Den I seed all in a minute whut he'd come
> to see me for; —
> Dey had 'listed colo'ed sojers, an my 'Lias
> gwine to wah.

The poem might be described as sentimental, even "pathetic," in its rendering of the pride of the young recruit and the mixed feeling of the woman who shares her beloved 'Lias's pride, but remains on the plantation to worry and wait. What I see and hear in this poem, however, is Dunbar's giving voice to the people behind the symbol.

His Standard English poems, "The Colored Soldiers" (168-171) and "The Unsung Heroes" (278-9), on the other hand, have a different purpose and are rendered in a different language. "If the muse were mine to tempt it," begins "The Colored Soldiers." The poem goes on to praise the "noble sons of Ham" who "were comrades then and brothers,/ Are they more or less to-day?" "When Dey 'Listed Colored Soldiers" gives voice to a speaking subject proclaiming in her own voice a common emotional experience, both complex in its mixture of pride and grief, and universal. It is the language along with the particulars of time and occasion that tells us who is speaking, when and why. In "The Colored Soldiers," on the other

hand, it is the poetic persona who speaks. This is a public song of praise
combined with an argument for racial equality. "The Unsung Heroes" too
is a public hymn of praise:

> A song for the unsung heroes who rose in
>   country's need,
> When the life of the land was threatened
>   by the slaver's cruel greed,
> For the men who came in from the cornfield,
>   who came from the plough and the
>   flail,
> Who rallied round when they heard the
>   sound of the mighty man of the rail.
> They laid them down in the valleys, they
>   laid them down in the wood,
> And the world looked on at the work they
>   did, and whispered, "It is good."
> They fought their way on the hillside, they
>   fought their way in the glen,
> And God looked down on their sinews
>   brown, and said, "I have made them
>   men."
>   *****
> Give, thou, some seer the power to sing
>   them in their might,
> The men who feared the master's whip,
>   but did not fear the fight;
> That he may tell of their virtues as min-
>   strels did of old,
> Till the pride of face and the hate of race
>   grow obsolete and cold.

Both "The Unsung Heroes" and "The Colored Soldiers" are as much
poems about making poetry as they are about the subjects being praised.
They sing in the language of the school room and the public platform in
order to render the appropriate homage. They define one role of the poet—
to remember/record and praise the heroic.

   When James Weldon Johnson (1871-1938) repudiated "Negro
dialect" in his "Prefaces" to his 1922 and 1931 anthologies of Negro poetry
(40-42 and 3-5 respectively) and his own collection, *God's Trombones* (1-
11), Johnson was reacting to what he viewed as the limitations of minstrel
dialect. His oft-cited summary dismissal of dialect as capable of expressing
only humor or pathos was being refuted, though, in a new turn to Black
vernacular as poetic language by such poets as Langston Hughes and
Sterling Brown. Even Johnson himself, in *God's Trombones*, attempted to
replicate the idioms, cadences, metaphors, and rhythms of the mother

tongue as prayed, testified, and preached. (It is significant that many dramatic performances of the poems from *God's Trombones* are spoken in the vernacular pronunciations of "Black English" rather than in the pronunciations that their spellings seem to demand.)

> And as far as the eye of God could see
> Darkness covered everything,
> Blacker than a hundred midnights
> Down in a cypress swamp.

So successful has Johnson been in evoking the preacherly style and the black language situations of folk prayer and sermon, that he evokes the down home pronunciation too. Johnson's distaste for dialect as literary language seems to be rooted in the way it looks on the page—misspelled, mispronounced English. He is overly sensitive to racial outsiders' condemnations of Black people's "bad English" as evidence of racial inferiority. Johnson articulates as well the ambivalent attitude of "the folk" themselves about the relative value of "good" and "bad" English.

Interestingly, much the same criticism has been voiced about the poets who write in Caribbean patois (Louise Bennett, Merle Collins and others), about the New Black Poetry of the late sixties in the the US (Amiri Baraka, Haki Madhubuti, Nikki Giovanni and others), about the Nation poetry of Great Britain (Linton Kwesi Johnson and others) about the effectiveness of West African Pidgin as a literary language (Niyi Osundare's *Songs of the Marketplace* or Ezenwa-Ohaeto's *I wan bi President*) or the Spanglish or Nuyorican of US-based Puerto Rican poets who write in English (such as Felipe Luciano or Martin Espada). Double consciousness, an awareness of the audience from outside the culture who may be judging by a different standard leads to a condemnation or critique rooted in elements of elitism and/or class bias. For the mother tongue is the language of the masses, of the unlettered. (A need for return to the mother tongue seems most urgent and most visible during times of group consciousness or nationalism. The poet speaks/writes to give voice to a group.)

What dialects do afford the poet is the verbal authenticity to his own "folk." When the poetry is read aloud on the radio or on television or on stage, the "folk" recognize their language and are ready to listen and hear. It is necessary to note here that another important usage of "dialects" in periods of struggle is to communicate invective and insult.

Loretto Todd has argued for pidgin English as a national language for a nation, Cameroon, colonized by Germany, Britain, and France (69-82). Similar calls have been issued for Nigeria by Ike Ndolo (679-84). The Ghanaian poet Erasmus Elikplim Forster Senaye turns to West African pidgin when he wants to articulate a man-in-the-street response to the AIDS crisis in Africa (*"Where did Aids come from?"* Anyidoho et al, 101-2).

> You talk say I have aids;
> Na who cause am brother?
> I need aids;
> Monkey too get aids?
> It jumps up and down tree top.
> You talk say I have aids.
> Monkey fit give me aids
> Me I be man;
> Monkey be animal;
> Surgeon examine proper;
> And judge better.
> Why, why, why?
> Too many aids for the North,
> Na who cause am brother?
> Na who cause am brother?
> I need aids

Senaye's sophisticated punning on AIDS the physical disease and aids (both foreign and material) undercuts the apparent folk simplicity evoked by his choice of pidgin as poetic language. The poem's final stanzas introduce still another element.

> Little children write with pencil
> Adults use pens to write with;
> In the matrimony bliss
> The pen is full of ink
> To sweeten the virgin hole surrounded with black strings.
>
> Chastity reigns in the North of our country?
> Are you a surgeon?
> Or what are you?
> A critic?

In the choice of a poetic language, the poet has language as subject as well as an element of structure. Two poems by the Nigerian poet Ezenwa-Ohaeto from his bi-lingual collection*I wan be president* illustrate the ongoing concern of Black poets about language choice. "Na So Poem Carry Me Go"(47-49) illustrates the power of poetic language.

> I read de poem breeze begin de blow
> I read de poem hurricane come start
> *****
> I just dey read poem dey go
> I see soja begin dey run dey come
> My broder

> Before I open mouth finish
> Na so poem carry me just go

Ezenwa-Ohaeato's choice of pidgin for a poem about the incendiary nature of poetry contrasts with his poem "Gone with the Wind" (49-51) which explores the poet's task and art.

> Dancing with ideas and pen
> Weaving with intricate steps with thoughts
> A poem with something in it
> of bullets singing anthems of death
> And our hopes are gone with the wind.
>   *****
> An occasion of verbal feasting
> A kitchen of boiling ideas
>   *****
> Savour the adroitness of language
>   *****
> Distilled into an aesthetic format

Ezenwa-Ohaeto's bi-lingualism illustrates the ways in which an English language continuum from the formal and standard to the vernacular and colloquial provides a multiplicity of poetic options in the marriage of sense and structure.

In addition to uncoventional spellings representing an effort to create an orthography of a spoken language, mother tongue includes language adaptations, usages, and figures such as simile, metaphor and litotes or hyperbole, in ways particular to a culture. It also includes forms or genres particular to the folk. (Folk culture is other folks' or other times' popular culture.) African poets duplicate forms, rhythms and idioms particular to the oral poetry of their "native" mother tongues in English (as do the South African Bennet Leboni Buti Moleko, the Nigerian Tanure Ojaide, or the Ugandan Okot p'Bitek). Caribbean and British "nation" poets write calypso, reggae and dub poems. African American poets write blues stanzas, jazz riffs, and sermons and stories in the language of the folk (as do Langston Hughes or Samuel Allen). Poets who write in English as a second language also creolize their texts through the incorporation of words from their "native" mother languages (as do the Ghanaian Abena Busia and the Puerto Rican Martin Espada).

Language "more often than not is the strongest factor giving identity, harmony, and continuity to [a people]" (Ndolo 679). Language can also be a source for a "sense of national pride, cultural awareness and [group] loyalty" (Ndolo 680). The Black poet's choice of language becomes both an aesthetic and a socio-political act. The Nigerian writer and scholar Isidore Okpewho discusses the relationship between oral and written poetry at length in several works. His anthology *The Heritage of African Poetry* thematically juxtaposes texts of traditional oral poems translated into English with contemporary African poems. These juxtapositions enable the reader to see/hear how "[m]odern African poetry has looked to traditional culture for the *flavour* [emphasis mine] of its language." (21) African poets writing in English, asserts Okpewho, "make conscious efforts to echo the rhythm of the speech of their people and even borrow some indigenous words and sounds." (21) The mother tongue becomes the marker of personal, national, even racial identity.

The editors of *Voiceprint*, an anthology of oral and related poetry from the Caribbean (Longman 1989), include works by published "literary" figures alongside the words of calypsonians, dub poets, nation poets, dialect or patois poets arranged by categories which indicate language practices or language acts within the culture. The section headings constitute their own poem: "Legend, Tale, Narrative and Folk Song; Elegy, Lament; Dreadtalk, Dub, Sermon, Prophesight and Prophsay; Calypso; Pan, Calypso and Rapso Poems; Parang and Hosay; Monologues; Signifying, RobberTalk; Praise Songs, Prayers and Incantations; Tracings, Curses and other Warnings; Political Manifestoes and Satires; Voice Portraits; and Word-Songs." Only the "Calypso" section contains no "literary" authors. Each form or genre represents a language situation specific to particular groups.

The book *Voiceprint* is itself illustrative of Gordon Rohlehr's language "continuum ...exploring the whole range of language and speech registers open to [poets].   The poets also needed to recognize that alternative registers were accessible to them and to liberate, through an openness to all available voices, such word-shapes as these voices suggest." Oral tradition, then, spoken in the mother tongue, offers a "virtually limitless range of prosodic, rhetorical and musical shapes" from which a poet might select. Additionally, it is an almost inexhaustible source for the generation or "creative extension into new poetic forms" (2). Rohlehr posits "a West Indian aesthetic [that] will embrace all ways of saying, all language registers, however different some of these may seem or be"(23).

Language becomes the vehicle of voice.
                    what i be talking about
                    can be said in this language
                    only this tongue
                    be the one that understands
                    what i be talking about
writes Lucille Clifton in her poem "defending my tongue." The "tongue" which Clifton must defend is Caribbean-Canadian Marlene Nourbese Philip's "mother tongue" described in her poem "Discourse on the Logic of Language."

English
is my mother tongue
A mother tongue is not
not a foreign lan lan lang
language
l/anguish
Philip's multi-vocal, multi-lingual poem explores the complexity of the
Black poet's choice of language citing the contradictions of history,
heritage, and personal inclination. The mother tongue is not a "foreign
language" but a product of culture, education and choice, an expression of
intersections of race, culture and history given voice by Black poets cross-
culturally.

WORKS CITED

Anyidoho, Kofi, Peter Porter and Musaemura Zimunya, editors. *The Fate of
    Vultures: New Poets of Africa.* (Heinemann, 1988)

Asante, Molefi Kete. *African and African American Communication Continuities.*
    CIS Special Studies #61 (SUNY Buffalo, 1975)

Blount, Marcellus. "The Preacherly Text: African American Poetry and Vernacular
    Performance." *PMLA* 107: 582-93 (May 1992)

Clifton, Lucille. *Quilting: Poems 1987-1990.* (Boa Editions, 1991)

Dunbar, Paul Laurence. *The Life and Works of Paul Laurence Dunbar.* (Winston-
    Derek, 1992)

Ezenwa-Ohaeto.*I wan bi president: poems in formal and pidgin English.* (Delta
    Publications, 1988)

Johnson, James Weldon. *God's Trombones: Seven Negro Sermons in Verse.*
    (Viking, 1927).

_____ "Preface: On the Negro's Creative Genius" in *The Book of American Negro
    Poetry.* (Harcourt Brace, 1922, 1931) 9-48. "Preface" to the Revised Edition.
    3-8

Kellman, Anthony. "Projective Verse as a Mode of Socio-Linguistic Protest," *Ariel*
    21, 2 (April 1990) 45-57.

Ndolo, Ike S. "The Case for Promoting the Nigerian Pidgin Language," *Jrl Mod Af
    Studies*, 27,4 (Dec 89), 679-84

Okpewho, Isidore. "The nature of African Oral Poetry" in *The Heritage of African
    Poetry: An Anthology of oral and written poetry* (Longman, 1985) 3-34

Philip, Marlene Nourbese. *She Tries Her Tongue: her silence softly breaks.*
    (Ragweed Press, 1989)

Rohlehr, Gordon. "Introduction: 'The Shape of that Hurt'" in *Voiceprint: an anthology of oral and related poetry from the Caribbean.* (Longman, 1989)

Schipper, Mineke. "Oral Literature and Written Orality" in *Beyond the Boundaries: African LIterature and Literary Theory* (Allison & Busby, 1989)

Smitherman, Geneva. *Black Language and Culture: Sounds of Soul.* Harper Studies in Language and Literature. (Harper & Row, 1975)

Todd, Loreto "*E Pluribus Unum*? The Language for a National Literature in a Multilingual Community," *Ariel,* 15-4 (Oct 84) 69-82.

_____ *Modern Englishes: Pidgins and Creoles.* (Basil Blackwell, 1984)

Survival Strategies and the New Life of Orality in Nigerian and Ghanaian Poetry: *Osundare's* Waiting Laughters *and Anyidoho's* Earth Child

by Ezenwa-Ohaeto
Universität Mainz

Contemporary Nigerian and Ghanaian poetry derives much strength and vitality from Africa's oral tradition. Thus it is possible for a Nigerian or Ghanaian poet to appropriate those oral traditions and subject them, through an individual creative forge, into varied and interesting poetic forms. However, this poetic strategy was given an impetus by a somewhat unfortunate development on the continent. The economic recession in Nigeria and Ghana created a great impact on the publishing industry, which made it impossible for many of the poets to be read by many people. Robert Fraser insists that "the hiatus thus caused was severe, and in the meantime, while the indigenous publishing sector gathered strength, there was a growing tendency for African poets to reassess their priorities." He also makes the insightful remark that "the positive result of these developments was that they thrust the oral tansmission of verse, hitherto regarded chiefly as a standby, into the limelight, and hence procured a much needed rethinking of the way in which highbrow art could learn from the oral tradition. In many cases the consequence was a redisccovery of the immediacy of orality as a means of communications" (314).

This period of economic recession coincided with the now famous statement made by three Nigerian critics Chinweizu, Onwuchekwa Jemie, and Ihechukwu Madubuike—concerning modern African poetry. The three critics had argued particularly that the older Nigerian poets write with "old-fashioned, craggy, unmusical language; obscure and inaccessible diction; a plethora of imported imagery; a divorce from African oral poetic tradition, tempered only by lifeless attempts at revivalism" (165). Although Wole Soyinka, one of the poets criticized, has labeled them "neo-Tarzanists" who are asking for "the poetics of death, and mummification not of life, renewal and continuity" (68), Roger Berger argues that "nearly all critics of African texts, whether or not they agree with Chinweizu, have read (or are in some way familiar with) Chinweizu's criticism. For this reason, the criticism of African Literature can never be the same as it was before the appearance of Chinweizu's book" (148).

It could be argued that the view that Chinweizu and his colleagues propounded coincided with the independent views of the emerging poets, and there is no doubt that they are cultivating those recommended creative strategies. In an interview with Frank Birbalsingh, Niyi Osundare from Nigeria states that the poems of his elders, like "Soyinka, Okigbo, J.P Clark, [and] Kofi Awoonor," were "extremely difficult, particularly those by Soyinka and Okigbo. Our enthusiasm soon fizzled out. When I started writing, this negative influence was in my mind and I felt it was the duty of the new generation of Nigerian poets to bring poetry back to the people. Since everything about our culture is lyrical and musical, how come, when we put this in written form, we alienate the people who created the material in the first instance" (Birbalsingh 9). This notion is amplified by Kofi Anyidoho from Ghana who confesses pointedly that for him, "the primary source of influence and interest...has been the Ewe oral tradition" and that he "had a fairly extensive exposure over all" his life as "a child to various forms of Ewe oral poetry" (qtd. in Wilkinson 8). Thus many modern Nigerian and Ghanaian poets exploit and explore their oral traditions, thereby invigorating and rejuvenating their poetry.

This study uses the poems of the Nigerian poet Niyi Osundare in *Waiting Laughters* and the poems of the Ghanaian poet Kofi Anyidoho in *Earthchild* to discuss the features and characteristics of the new life of oral cadences in modern Nigerian and Ghanaian poetry. The selection of the two poets is informed by several reasons. They are both prize-winning poets, for Osundare has won the Association of Nigerian Authors Poetry Prize, the Commonwealth Poetry Prize, and the Noma Award, while Anyidoho has won the Poet of the Year Award in Ghana, the Valco Prize, and the BBC Arts and Africa Poetry Award. Furthermore, the two poets are critics of African poetry who are also aware of the resources of their oral traditions and their uses in adding new life to modern African poetry.

The twin issue of *waiting* and *laughter* as the major aspects in the collection *Waiting Laughters* provide a thematic focus on hope in the midst of despair as the poet utilizes various devices informed by his oral traditions. This collection, significantly subtitled "a long song in many voices," immediately calls to mind many of those elements associated with music that are usually exploited by the oral performer. The collection is in four sections, and the first section immediately sets the scene through the

SURVIVAL STRATEGIES

123

poet's pervasive use of images. These images are structured in parallels and they engineer responses that are related to the poet's satiric purposes. The poetic scene is set thus:

> I pluck these words from the lips of the wind;
> *Ripe like a* pendulous pledge
> I pluck these murmurs
> From the laughter of the wind
> The shrub's tangled tale
> Plaited tree tops
> And palms which drop their nuts. (2)

This statement of purpose is clearly related not only to the poetic objective to pursue a dedicated creative enterprise in either asking for accounts of "pledges" or insisting on appropriate redemption of those pledges but also to the conscious use of local imagery like "plaited tree tops" and "palms which drop their nuts." These images foreshadow the subsequent condemnation of the injustices associated with inequitable distribution of resources related to the "dropped palm nuts." It is, however, interesting that the poet refers to a "tangled tale," which could be a metaphor for the impediments to the equitable distribution of wealth in the economy of "dropped palmnuts." Futhermore, this image emphasizes the issue of hope because "palms which drop their nuts" symbolize abundant wealth and the remedy to the "tangled tale," which the poet implies is the possibility for the "shrub" to benefit from the tall palmtree; in other words, the deprived people in the society could benefit from the privileged group.

The social concern is illustrated further in the same poem when the poet uses the element of cumulative repetition which blends technique with subject matter. Thus the poet like an oral poet-performer intones:

> And laughing heals so fugitive
> In the dust of fleeing truths
> > Truth of the valley
> > Truth of the mountain
> > Truth of the boulder
> > Truth of the river. (3)

The poet continues in this kind of association of opposites by further linking the truth of the flame with the truth of the ash, the sun with the moon, the liar with the lair, the castle with the caste, and the desert with the rain. All these objects or behavior or status possess their own truths, but the poet implies that those truths cannot subvert the inviolable truth of life, which is the primary focus of *Waiting Laughters*. In depicting these truthts with objects that are in opposition but placed in apposition, the poet clearly seeks to establish the omnipresence of truth, especially in a society that is prone to manipulations of truth. He insists that the truth, for instance, could be in the valley as well as on the mountain and in the flame as well as in the ash, but it still remains the truth.

As the poem progresses through other voices, since the poet conceives his work as a long poem in many voices, the poet's orality becomes part of the poetic movement. His cumulative repetition, which is heavily dependent on Yoruba oral poetics, becomes clear, for part of that poetics includes the creative use of imagery associated with the environment; an apt deployment of refrains and chants; the exploitation of proverbial structures, aphorisms, and even idiomatic expressions, and the deliberate repetition of phrases in order to emphasize or evaluate observations. Thus the poet makes use of repetition:

> Teach us the patience of the sand
> which rocks the cradle of the river,
> Teach us the patience of the branch
> which counts the seasons in dappled cropping,
> Teach us the patience of the rain
> which eats the rock in toothless silence. (7)

The cumulative repetition of what should be taught the persona is portrayed to generate success, which is the expected purpose of patience. The images of rain that "eats rocks" and "the branch that counts the seasons" stress the optimism of the poet that the trope of *laughter* in the title indicates. In addition, the manner in which these images are deployed and the repitition of the phrase "Teach us the patience" produce the semblance of a poet-cantor addressing an audience and clearly involving them in the incantation with the use of the pronoun "us." Thus the envisaged dividend of the education implied in the incantation is the act of obtaining strength like the sand, the branch, and rain for decisive action. In addition, the fact that the poet insists that there is the need to learn wisdom from some of these inanimate objects shows that there is also the need to reexamine the environment and derive from it the kind of knowlege that will enable the people develop and progress.

Repetitions of phrases, whole lines, and even stanzas are regular features of Osundare's poetry. He also uses certain proverbs with regularity. There is a proverb that appears twice in *Waiting Laughters*. The poem "The Feet I See Are Waiting for Shoes," where the poet criticizes the injustice of social deprivation of stomachs "waiting for coming harvests," water pots waiting in famished homesteads, and the eyes "waiting for rallying visions," ends with the following proverb:

> Time it may take
> The stammerer will one day call his
> Fa—Fa—fa—ther—ther's na—na—na—me! (74)

The written orality in that last line, which is aimed at reproducing oral speech, lends credence to Osundare's conscious exploitation of orality. Nevertheless, this same proverb also appears in the poem "Waiting like the Crusty verb of a borrowed tongue," where the poet interrogates the issue of historical experience, the limitations of borrowed languages, and the appropriate utilization of talent for general benefits through an apt medium, as he questions:

> History's stammerer
> When will your memory master
> the vowels of your father's name?
> Time ambles in diverse paces— (41)

Just as the poet states that time "ambles in diverse paces," so his use of proverbial lore is subjected to diverse paces. In this second use of the proverb it is no longer starkly embedded because its intrinsic idea has been worked into the texture of the poem. It is no longer the issue of a child desiring to pronounce the father's name but a fundamental issue where one who is "history's stammerer" or history's destroyer must memorize "the vowels of the father's name," and create positive history in the interest of the society. In effect, Osundare's use of Yoruba proverbial lore has undergone changes as he refines and weaves the associated ideas into the poem rather than leaving them bare as we find in his early collections of poetry. This use of proverbs is much more interestingly presented through a chain of proverbs in the poem "Waiting like Yam for the Knife," which questions the weakness of the oppressed in subduing the oppressor in whatever form. The persona justifies the dedication of the poet to the social use of poetry when he praises himself:

> My tongue has not stumbled
> I have not told a bulbous tale
> In the presence of *asopa*,
> I have not shouted "Nine!"
> In the backyard of the one with a missing finger (70)

These instances of what the persona has not done are part of the Yoruba proverbial lore which states, for instance, that one does not talk about bulbous objects in the presence of an *asopa*, who is a man with swollen scrotum. Nevertheless, these instances of injunctions inserted through the proverbs are used ironically and satirically because the persona has mentioned all the instances of abnormalities in the society through indirect references as well as ridiculing the perpetrators of those abnormalities. This is in the tradition of Yoruba oral poetics, which makes great use of insinuations, and the orality of Osundare's poetic craft derives its energy from such exploitations.

Furthermore, the aphoristic flavor of the poet's Yoruba tradition emerges clearly in the poems. In three short aphoristic poems that exemplify this tradition, the poet expands certain ideas derived from his oral traditions into wider contexts by generating intellectual responses. In "A Baby Antelope," he writes: "a baby antelope/once asked her pensive mother: / Tell me, Mother / How does one count the teeth of a laughing lion?" (72); the second poem reads: "Waiting like the eternal wisdom of /Mosafejo / who gave one daughter / in marriage to six suitors" (75); while a third poem that is clearly political says: "Waiting / like a hyena / for the anniversary of its pounce; / Waiting / like an African despot/for the seventieth year of his rule" (55). The ideas in these poems are locally derived, but Osundare widens their semantic implications, thereby making it possible for the interpretations to refer to other societies. The reference to *Mosafejo* which means "I-am averse-to-litigations," who creates personal difficulties for himself while making contrary onomastic claims, is used to satirize those people who originate destructive activities while claiming innocence. The onomastics in Osundare's poetry is highly illuminating because, in the culture of his people, names possess distinct semantics and they can be exploited in Yoruba rhetoric. The satiric humor in the baby antelope desiring to count the teeth of a laughing lion cautions aphoristically against foolish behavior, while the aphorism of the African despot waiting for the "seventieth year of his rule" distinctly criticizes dictatorship. The association of the hyena "waiting for its pounce"with this despot calls to mind the possibility that the hyena, a carnivorous animal, is related to the despot as a destroyer of human lives.

These aphorisms are sometimes illustrated through songs in some of the poems. The fact that Osundare calls this poem a long song in many voices indicates that he is consciously subjecting the songs to his own poetic ends. Quite early in the collection the poet makes his desire to manipulate the songs clear when he states: "my song is space / beyond wails, beyond walls / beyond insular hieroglyphs / which crave the crest / of printed waves" (25). The songs going "beyond wails" portrays the inevitability of joy and hope because the persona's insistence on the songs' going "beyond walls" indicates an unwillingness to be restricted by mundane impediments. The suggestion in this poem reflects the subtle ways that words can be made to insinuate ideas in the Yoruba oral tradition. Thus, the songs of the poet derive their vitality from Yoruba song traditions. In the poem "Waiting like the Bastille, For the Screaming Stones," which is critical of rulers who misuse power, the poet deploys one of those songs:

Òrògòdodo Òrògòdo
A King who dances with a dizzy swing

Òrògòdo straight he goes. (22)
The poet explains that in Ikere (his hometown) mythology, Òrògòdo is a
remote place of banishment for dishonorable rulers. This song reflects on
the fact that power is transient, for the persona says further that "the crown
is only a cap," the king made of bone and flesh; "the castle is a house of
mortar and stone," while "the chair is wood which becomes a throne." This
particular song establishes the thematic focus of the poem on the hope
implied in the idea of *laughter waiting* to emerge, although there are some
other instances where the song may not possess a didactic bearing on the
poem but could serve as a chorus song, such as the one which says, "the
water is going / Going, going, going / The water is going" (67).

The orality in Osundare's poetry illustrates what J.O.J Nwachukwu-
Agbada identifies when he says that "proverbs, tongue-twisters, riddles,
communal traditions, even folktales in snippety forms are built into poetic
lines, certainly with the intention of Africanizing poetic mediation" (85).
In two poems we find instances of Osundare's poetic mediation with
snippets of folktales. In the short poem "Says the Hyena to a clan of
lambs," the tale concerning a hyena that tells a group of lambs
complaining about his eating habits that they should select a spokesman
who will "come freely to my den / With your woes and sundry views" (62)
becomes a metaphor for the oppressors and the oppressed in most societies.
In the second poem, "Okerebu Kerebu," which means "wonder of
wonders," the folktale dialogue between a hungry snake and a wise toad
indicates that only courageous acts can defeat implacable foes. The snake
who threatens that it will swallow the toad regardless of what it turns into
discovers that when the toad turns into a rock and the snake swallows it,
the stomach fails to function. The parabolic nature of this tale indicates
also that exploiters are restrained only by suitable actions. This is why the
poet ends the poem with the phrase that "our tale is a bride" waiting for
"grooming ears" (64), which means that the tale requires relevant
interpretations. Thus a relevant interpretation justifies the idea of the poet
that the *laughter* (of hope) is just *waiting* to emerge even in the midst of
despair.

There are also poetic devices that reinforce this vision that the
interpretations of creative works must be relevant, and this is done through
cultural associations derived from value-loaded words. The employment of
Yoruba words like "Ibosi o!"—which is a loud cry for help—in the midst
of a poem not only emphasizes the orality of the poetic structure, but it is
also woven into the poetic purpose of hope indicated in the reference to the
act of waiting "for the green fingers of laughing showers" (93). In addition,
the profuse similes that codify the images also reveal through their
associated meanings the undeniable hope of the poet-persona because "the

season calls for the lyric of other laughters" that are like "a boil, time tempered / about to burst" (97). Osundare clearly shows that the craft of his poetry is reinforced by the orality of this Yoruba tradition. This is not surprising, and a previous study has established that his technique "enables the poet adopt abundant materials such as witty aphorisms and phrases from the Yoruba oral traditions" to create "highly political and social" poetry (Ezenwa-Ohaeto, "Dimensions" 161). Other critics have confirmed, after an examination of his early poetry, that his "use of Yoruba words and mythical allusions suggests that many of his pieces have close ties to oral poetry" (Arnold 3); that like "other African poets with an Africa-centered consciousness Osundare finds himself going back to images of nature" (Ngara 184); and also that he makes creative exploitation of "a proverb or a maxim," "Yoruba satirical songs," and "traditional images" (Bamikunle 54-55). These critical observations are devoted to Osundare's earlier collections, *A Nib in the Pond*, *Village Voice*, *Songs of the Marketplace* and *The Eye of the Earth*. But the critical discussion of *Waiting Laughters* here confirms those observations and indicates further development.

However, the orality in Osundare's poetry is not isolated, because in the poetry of Kofi Anyidoho there is the same conscious use of his Ewe traditions. Thus the Ewe dirge tradition is an intrinsic element of the poems. Anyidoho informs us in an interview: "[S]ome of my poems are very closely modeled on Ewe traditional poetry, particularly on the dirge tradition. Partly because my mother and the immediate people around me were very much involved in the dirge tradition and I used to listen to their songs, so that quite a bit of that comes through my poetry" (qtd. in Wilkinson 9). Nevertheless, the dirge impulse proceeds beyond the fact of death, for it projects into what could be described as a synthesization of sadness and hope in terms of projecting beyond current sorrow into the future. The issues of *sadness* and *hope* in Anyidoho's collection of poems entitled *Earthchild* remind us of the themes of *Waiting* and *Laughters* in Osundare's *Waiting Laughters*. But Anyidoho subsumes his own laughter within the ambiance of sorrow, thus making the hope connotative rather than declamatory.

The opening poem, "Fertility Game," is a lament in the true Ewe dirge tradition as the persona insists with a refrain, "Come back home Agbenoxevi Come back home." The implication is that "Agbenoxevi" will return, and in the third stanza the hope in that expectation becomes symbolic when the poet writes:

And your voice shall rise deep across the years
through rainbow gates to the beginnings of things
It will come floating through seasons of glory
thundering through deserts and painfields where

our people died the deaths of droughts and of wars
Where they died and lived again
Where they die   and wake up with
seeds of life sprouting from their graves (1)

The voice of Agbenoxevi is expected to "rise deep across the years" and
even "thunder through deserts and painfields." It is that reference to "pain
fields" which highlights the trope of sadness, for it could be said to be a
"field" where there was tremendous suffering or an image of the terrible
tribulations of the people. However, the ideas that those "who died" would
"live again" or that those who die "wake up with seeds of life sprouting
from their graves" portray the poet's concept in the utilization of the Ewe
dirge tradition to comment on present reality and generate hope. Anyidoho
also strives to incorporate the varied mores and norms of the oral traditions
in the bid to reflect both the orality and the thematic purposes in the poem.
In the later segments of the poem, the persona indicates that "Each
midnight moonlight night I walk naked / to the crossroads," and this
reference recalls a traditional ritual of propitiation or even expiation that is
expected to attract rewards. But more important, this poem illustrates what
has been identified as the achievement of lyricism through "the
organization of verse in such a way that it has an incantatory and mournful
effect" (Ngara 173). This incantatory effect reveals the use of a persona
from both the traditional angles of character and subject matter to create
arresting poetry.

The sorrow prominent in Anyidoho's poetry is not an end in itself, for
in the poem "Honeycomb for Beechildren," the persona stresses that for
"every dirge Adidi sang / I now must weave a song of new birth-cords" and
reaffirms later in that same poem that "long before the reign of
thunderclouds / we were rainbow's favoured child" (6). This optimistic
note and the theme of hope in the exploitation of the dirge tradition may
not be clear to the reader who merely glances at the titles of some of the
poems. Anyidoho, for instance, gives some poems such titles as "A Dirge
for Christmas," "A Dirge for our Birth," and "A Dirge of Joy," thus
illustrating the possibilities in the utilization of paradox and irony in the
exploration of the Ewe dirge tradition. Christmas, births, and joy are
normally socially associated with happiness and merriment but in their
association with the "dirge" in those poems Anyidoho is not only calling
attention to the unreliable nature of contemporary reality but also to the
fact that pleasure and pain, or sadness and hope, sometimes possess
indistinct boundaries. The underlying elements of poetic objectives in these
instances of paradox are thus portrayed through such statements as: "so let
alone our Poets / To mourn Christmas with chants of Easter songs" (62, "A
Dirge for Christmas") and "Now we ask our mothers to confirm / the

things our grandmothers say. / We beg our children to tell us who we were" (63, "A Dirge for our Birth"). The statements therefore generate the view that "these dirges kill our little Joys" (64, "A Dirge of Joy"), which confirms their ironic implications but not at the expense of hope. Anyidoho is clearly distinct in his use of this dirge tradition because he proceeds beyond the normal association of the dirge, which was explained by the celebrated Ghanaian poet Kofi Awoonor in his *The Breast of the Earth* in the following manner: "[T]he Ewe dirge establishes a relationship with the dead in order to emphasize the loneliness of that death, its desolation, and the accompanying sense of loneliness" (202). In the poems, Anyidoho does not focus on particular deaths, but he uses the tone, the tradition of exhortation, and even philosophical concepts to comment on reality. The dimension he adds is the apt use of those features of the dirge form "to evoke contemporary images of fear, pain, hope and joy" (Ezenwa-Ohaeto, "The Poetry of Anyidoho" 22).

In addition, the nature of these dirges reveals a poetic dimension that is significant. Eustace Palmer notes that Anyidoho's "favourite themes are the brutality of regimes, social disintegration, the betrayal of the revolution, the destruction of optimism, the conflict between tradition and Chrisitanity, the clash of contrasting life styles, social deprivation, persecution of innocence and injustice in general" and he also adds that "he can be personal too" (79). It is the use of this personal voice in a manner that widens its horizons which makes Anyidoho's poetry interesting. Thus the dirges could be interpreted to refer not only to Ghana but to humanity in general, although the basic inspirational incidents originated in Ghana. Kofi Awoonor confirms in his essay "Three Young Ghanaian Poets" that Anyidoho's "clear understanding of Ewe dirge has widened his own primary appreciation of the substance of the lyrical form of lament as both a personal and a public statement" (163). Thus in the poem "The News From Home," the poet affirms hope when he states:

> I have not come this far
>> only to sit by the roadside
>> and break into tears
> I could have wept at home
>> without a journey of several thorns (25)

The hope projected here by the dirge is related to the stubborn will for survival even in the midst of social devastations. Later in the same poem, the poet insists: "And I am tired / tired of all these noises of / condolence from those who / love to look upon the anger of the hungry / nod their head and stroll / back home." This attitude accounts for the view at the end of the poem that "those who sent their funeral clothes / to the washerman / awaiting the mortuary men to come" will "wait for the next and next /

season only to see how well earth children grow fruit and even flower /
from rottenness of early morning dreams" (26), which is a reiteration of
the hope of survival in spite of sadness. The socio-political issues are
clearly the substance of these dirges, and in this instance when the poet
writes of the ability of "earth children" to "grow fruit and even flower," his
reference could be extended communally to other societies, other groups,
and other peoples who portray signs of survival in their cultures despite
enormous disasters.

The significance of this communal voice in the poems, which Jawa
Apronti regards as "the poetry of the speaking voice" (41), is the blend of
vision and poetic craft. In the poem "American Fevers," the poet writes
that a "Star-General is urinating peace on Capitol Hill" (20), which
ironically links the positive state of peace with the obnoxious act of
urinating carelessly. In effect the poet is saying that the General is
encouraging not peace but violence. Later in the same poem he writes of "a
broken fence across the backyard of the skies" where a "brood of new
godlings / broke away in the heat of God's nightmares" and " become the
skyrangers who spread rumors / of coming droughts and thunder waves"
(29). The irony portrayed in this dirge is that those in possession of divine
qualities like the "gods" have become destructive elements; this is a
reference to the devastation by most leaders in contemporary societies like
Ghana. On a smaller scale, in terms of subject matter, the poem "Song of a
Twin Brother" dirges on the fact that, "many many moons ago," the
persona had a "twin brother / we shared the same mat / But parted in our
Dreams" (56). The sense of loss here which constitutes part of the dirge
tradition is used to reflect on interpersonal relationships but through
another dimension. The poem entitled "To Ralph Crowder" ends thus:

> We suffer here so much
> But they say your case is worse
> And you've fought with all your blood
> Always fighting on the bleeding side
> And you cannot go on like this...
>   Come Crother Come
>   But I tell you all is not well at *Home*. (112)

The reference in this poem to Ralph Crowder, who is an African
American, deftly links the Ghanaian experience with the Harlem
experience in America. In effect, Anyidoho is exploring not only the fate of
the African but the fate of the race. He suceeds in creating such links
through the fibers of mutual sadness and the repetition of phrases like "all
is not well at home" woven into the poem in a bid to channel the
perspectives on the legacy of suffering towards its general elimination.

The oral poetic strategy in the poetry of Anyidoho also emerges through the deployment of cumulative repetitions and refrains. These refrains are particularly effective in the thematic reinforcements and in the emphasis on the poems' lyrical dimensions. In addition, they also portray the performance strategies intrinsic in the creative works. In the poem "Memory's Call," the poet examines the issue of maladministration by referring to "stolen gold" and the subsequent desire of dedicated leaders like Neto and Biko who "took away our funeral songs / to house of storms sending back / the rhythmic throb of infant hopes" (12) as efforts made in order to enable the people to recover their sense of progress. This hope also counters the feeling of distress encapsulated in the refrain "I hear the harvest songs of Moonchildren / But where are all the planters gone?" (11). The refrains in these poems are clearly consciously fashioned, for in the poem "For Kristofa," the refrain "Expect me my dear Mother expect me / But only when you shall see me coming..." (16) reflects the tragic loss of Kristofa, whose death creates a sense of hopelessness for the members of the family. Interestingly, the other refrains emphasize hope—especially the one in the title poem "Earthchild," where after each description of a disaster the poet stresses:

And still we stand so tall among the cannonades
we smell of mists and of powdered memories (39-42)

It is therefore to be expected, since the people "stand so tall among the cannonades," that in the end they will overcome their tribulations. Thus at the end of the poem the poet reaffirms:

And those who took away our Voice
Are now surprised
They couldn't take away our Song. (42)

It is equally significant that the refrains are fashioned to reflect a communal sensibility that Robert Fraser identifies as the plural sensibility and explains as the "communal experience...which pertains to the well-being of each." In the effect "the poet *is* his people, and they are he, which paradoxically in no way reduces his individuality" (336). Thus the poetic voice becomes the communal voice that echoes the communal ethos and public aspirations, reinforcing the view that the sadness will be erased as well as indicating the hope for a better future.

Another interesting dimension in the poetic strategy of Anyidoho's poetry is his ability to institute varied voices, exhibiting varied characteristics of people of different social status. In the poem "Mr. Poacherman," he uses the voice of a character who is clearly an African American and whose thoughts show the social problems of his cultural environment. The persona in the poem is perplexed by the infidelity of his wife and his address to the poacher is fashioned by the poet to illustrate the tribulations of a man who is the victim of those who "likes to poach for love" and "shoots arrows into virgin territories," thereby scaring "some brother's joys away." The poem ends on a sad note:

> I grabs at things ain't there no more
> I sometimes catches only cobwebs in my dream
> poacherman poacherman please mr. poacherman
> she don't live here no more
> so don't you come here no no more. (22)

The social status of this persona makes his experience particularly sad but his use as a poetic character illustrates the manipulative capability of Kofi Anyidoho. Thus his retrieval of an American experience here confirms the observation by Kofi Agovi that Anyidoho "succeeds in retrieving" the "common store house of values" in order to transform them into "realms of contemporary relevance for *all* Ghanaians" (171). All the same, this utilization of different poetic voices reaches a climax in the long poem "In the High Court of Cosmic Justice," which uses the historical events in Ghana of the sixties and seventies as the focus for an anatomy of contemporary reality. In this poem which is a trial scene of a past Ghanaian leader, several witnesses appear and in their varied voices and varied perspectives they present a scene showing the devastations that occur in society when hasty decisions are taken to discredit past leaders. Several witnesses-personae who appear in the poem are versed in their oral traditions, and both the men and women witnesses in their contrastitive presentation modes reflect Anyidoho's conscious orality in making the words of the characters suit their social status. The sixth witness is most interesting as he introduces himself by saying: "My name is Musa / I am ten years old / I go to Walewale Primary School / when my mother and my father born me / I didn't know how much the world would give to me..." (87), while the seventh witness insists: "Salaam aleikum / Me / I be Malam / And Malam no fit tell lie / Som bigi bigi men—You sabi dem name— / Dey for back / Dey put Malam for flont..." (88). These varied poetic speeches reflecting mother-tongue interferences are used to portray linguistically the social background and status of the characters, and they indicate orally the young and the old, the poor and the wealthy, with either simple or complex minds, and they add to Anyidoho's infusion of new life into African poetry, thereby illustrating the view that his poetry clearly "comes across as a variegated somewhat labryinthine poetry" (Kubayanda 75). Moreover, the artistic use of words from the cultural environment of the poet not only enriches his poetic forms but also echoes the embedded cultural ethos. In the poem "Agbegada," the expression "Miede za Miegbo," which translates as "we went by Night and we came by Night," highlights the tragic implications in a community where the people are driven to bury "a brother alive" because he committed the abomination of "digging a grave into which / he would decoy his Grandfather" (60). In the poem entitled "Okyeame" (118-19), a Ghanaian title indicating that it should be about someone who has become a spokesman and could speak, or be spoken to, on behalf of the group as a recognized channel of communication, the persona in the poem has like "the snake allowed his head into a trap / And / Now must use his tail in self-defence" (119). The significant idea for which Anyidoho uses that culturally loaded word "Okyeame" is the sad disappointment that those who are expected to put their talents in the service of the people could betray that trust. Thus the poetry of Kofi Anyidoho in *Earthchild* clearly complements the poetry of Osundare in *Waiting Laughters* in the exploration and exploitation of the oral traditions of their respective socities and in emphasis on sadness and hope.

In their use of proverbial lore, snippets of folktales, aphorisms, refrains, apt choices of personae, cumulative repetitions, culturally loaded phrases, songs, images, exclamatory words associated with verbal rhetoric, and the dirge tradition, Osundare and Anyidoho have contributed to the distinct tradition of oral cadences in African poetry. They highlight clearly what Tanure Ojaide, another Nigerian poet and critic, acknowledges as "the current shift in poetic materials and themes" (20). This shift also corresponds to the injunction that it is necessary to make "an imaginative deployment of symbols and techniques in a way that resonates the changing expectations and life styles of the society" (Okpewho 24). The poetry of Osundare and Anyidoho effectively portray an enrichment of modern African poetry in terms of craft, and the poets establish that a conscious assimilation of oral traditions could act as both creative inspiration and creative strategy in order to invigorate modern African poetry.

ACKNOWLEDMENT:

The author is grateful to the Alexander von Humboldt Foundation, Germany, and the Institute for Ethnology and African Studies, University of Mainz, Germany, for facilities.

WORKS CITED

Agovi, Kofi. Review of *A Harvest of Our Dreams* and *Earthchild*. *Présence Africaine* 142.2 (19XX): 166-72.

Anyidoho, Kofi. *Earthchild with Brain Surgery*. Accra: Woeli Pub. Services, 1985.

Apronti, Jawa. "Ghanaian Poetry in the 1970s." *New West African Literature*. Ed. Kolawole Ogungbesan. London: Heinemann, 1979. 31-44.

Arnold, Stephen H. "The Praxis of Niyi Osundare, Popular Scholar-Poet." *World Literature Written in English* 29.1 (1989): 1-7.

Awoonor, Kofi. *The Breast of the Earth: A Survey of the History, Culture and Literature of Africa South of the Sahara*. New York: Doubleday Anchor Press, 1975.

_____. "Three Young Ghanaian Poets: Odamtten; Anyidoho and Agyemang." *Ghanaian Literatures*. Ed. Richard Priebe. Westport, CT: Greenwood, 1988. 151-67.

Bamikunle, Aderemi. "Niyi Osundare's Poetry and the Yoruba Oral Artistic Tradition." *Orature in African Literature Today* 18 (1882): 49-61.

Berger, Roger. "Contemporary Anglophone Literary Theory: The Return of Fanon." *Research in African Literatures* 21.2 (1990): 141-51.

Birbalsingh, Frank. "Interview with Niyi Osundare."*Présence Africaine* 147 (1988): 95-104.

Chinwiezu, Onwuchekwa Jemie, and Ihechukwu Madubuike. *Toward the Decolonization for African Literature*. Vol. 1. Enugu: Fourth Dimension, 1980.

Enzenwa-Ohaeto. "The poetry of Kofi Anyidoho." *Daily Times* 10 Jan. 1990: 22.

_____ "Dimensions of Language in New Nigerian Poetry." *The Question of Language in African Literature Today* 17 (1991): 155-64.

Fraser, Robert. *West African Poetry: A Critical History*. Cambridge: Cambridge UP, 1986.

Kubayanda, Bekunuru. "Dream, Betrayal and Revolution: Independent Ghana in the Poetry of Kofi Anyidoho." *Legon Journal of Humanities* 3 (1987): 62-78.

Ngara, Emmanuel. *Form and Ideology in African Poetry*. London: James Currey, 1990.

Nwachukwu-Agbada, J. O. J. "The Eighties and the Return to Oral Cadences in Nigerian Poetry." *African Literatures in the Eighties*. Special issue of *Matatu* 10 (1993): 85-105.

Ojaide, Tanure. "The Changing Voice of History: Contemporary African Poetry." *Genève-Afrique* 27.1 (1989): 107-22.

Okpewho, Isidore. "African Poetry: The Modern Writer and the Oral Tradition." *Oral and Written Poetry in African Literature Today* 16 (1988): 3-25.

Osundare, Niyi. *Waiting Laughters*. Lagos: Malthouse, 1990.

Palmer, Eustace. "West African Literature in the 1980s." *African Literatures in the Eighties*. Special issue of *Matatu* 10 (1993): 61-84.

Soyinka, Wole. "Aesthetic Illusions: Prescriptions for the Suicide of Poetry." *The Third Press Review* 1.1 (1975): 30-31, 65-68.

Wilkinson, Jane. "Interview with Kofi Anyidoho." *Talking with African Writers*. London: James Currey, 1992. 7-16.

Ngugi wa Thiong'o's
DECOLONISING NARRATIVE:
The Allegorical Imperative

by Oliver Lovesey
University of Mainz

Allegory is of particular importance in postcolonial narrative (Ashcroft 28) to counter the falsifications of colonial history, imaginatively reconstruct a fragmented community, and envision a more hopeful future. As Slemon writes, "allegorical writing is associated with 'a belief in the possibility of transformation'" (164). He goes on to detail how the postcolonial project has reappropriated "allegory to a politics of resistance" (163). Critics such as Sharma (169) and Cook and Okenimkpe (130) have traced elements of Christian allegory, and other critics such as Sicherman (347-70) and Dramé (9, 30-31) have examined the centrality of historical rewriting in Ngugi's work; however, in Ngugi's last two novels, the allegorical impetus refigures individual, collective, and national history, but also moves beyond this horizon and envisions a future allowing mental decolonization and social justice. Informed by Mau Mau aesthetics and a Fanonian cognizance of the effects of mental colonisation, *Devil on the Cross* and *Matigari* incorporate various allegorical strains including historical or national allegory, Biblical typology and Bunyanesque allegory, and a type of gendered allegory, but not, I would suggest, postmodern allegory. Contingent upon the pretext of colonial and neocolonial history, Ngugi's counter-discursive fiction draws on a wide range of discourses from oral folk narrative to magic realism and cinematic technique in order to produce a transformational allegory which projects into the future. As a result, these works are a good example of the search for new life in African litertures, for, as Appiah writes, "Despite the overwhelming reality of economic decline; despite unimaginable poverty; despite wars, malnutrition, disease, and political instability, African cultural productivity grows apace..." (157).

The impetus towards allegory in these last two narratives is varied. It is historically grounded in Ngugi's detention; as a colonial prison was the school for national leaders—Robben Island today is called Mandela University—so the neocolonial prison has been a school for national

writers. As explained in *Detained: A Writer's Prison Diary*, in the crucible
of the neocolonial prison, Ngugi came to regard his involvement in the
Kamiriithu Community Education and Culture Centre's communal theatre
production as a continuation of the cultural program of Dedan Kimathi.
Ngugi realized, "I am part of a living history of struggle" (124). His
detention—though he was never charged—probably resulted from the
government's anxiety at the group's success, and is symbolic of the
neocolonial desire to, in Ngugi's words, "[d]etain a whole community"
(80). Like the 17th-century Puritan revolutionary John Bunyan—whose
work Ngugi refers to in *Decolonizing the Mind* (69, 70)—who evolved the
allegorical poetics of *The Pilgrim's Progress* in his autobiography *Grace
Abounding* composed in prison, Ngugi evolved the political aesthetics of
the toilet-paper novel *Devil on the Cross* in *Detained*. His diary's "main
theme was the process of writing a novel under prison conditions" (Ngugi,
Decolonising 63). Through writing this diary, Ngugi seemed to realize
more clearly than ever the symbolic potential of representative individual
experience.

Furthermore, Ngugi's impetus towards allegory derived from what
might be termed his transformational Mau Mau aesthetics, detailed in
Writers in Politics (1981). The Kenyan Land and Freedom Army, he
writes,

> created a popular oral literature embodying anti-exploitation values. They took
> Christian songs; they took even the Bible and gave these meanings and values
> in harmony with the aspirations of their struggle....The Mau Mau
> revolutionaries took up the same song and tune and turned it into a song of
> actual political, visible material freedom and struggle for land. The battle was
> no longer in heaven but here on earth, in Kenya. (27)

Ngugi's transformation of what he perceived to be the tool of the oppressor
into a weapon to fight oppression, then, has revolutionary Kenyan
precedents. These novels also use many phrases and figures from Mau Mau
songs, such as the relationship of the individual to the national house
(Maina 28, 45). Ngugi felt his implied African audience, composed of
peasants and workers, many of whom had direct experience in Mau Mau,
but now weighed down by subalternity, could be empowered by witnessing
such a transformation. The very narrative structures of *Devil on the Cross*
and *Matigari*, in their transformative use of the Bible and other texts,
embody the theme of political renewal and change, and thematize their
own production. By using Gikuyu as his vehicle—and here I am dealing
with the English translation of the Gikuyu originals—Ngugi embedded his
commitment to cultural politics in his narrative medium. Finally, Ngugi's
allegorical impetus was a response to his implied readers' horizons of

expectation. As he explains in *Decolonising the Mind*, he mingled the "biblical element—the parable" (78) with "forms of oral narrative" (77)— man-eating ogres derived from Kenyan popular folk tales and the "human shaped rocks" of Idakho in western Kenya (8l)—in order to reach his audience: "People would be familiar with these features and I hoped that these would help root the novel within a known tradition" (78). Ngugi has also justified the seemingly exaggerated fantasy of *Devil on the Cross* and *Matigari* by reference to Kenyan realities. A case in point is the police attempt to round up the fictional Matigari, rumoured to be roaming the country seeking truth and justice. Realizing their mistake, the police banned the book, which joined its author in exile.

As Sicherman has demonstrated, all of Ngugi's works revision Kenyan history, and Dramé regards Ngugi's first three novels, his "Mau Mau trilogy" (93), as "transformation myths that mirror historical realities" (114) in an "initiatory journey" from alienation to transition and social reintegration (95). Ngugi's last two narratives may be regarded as "national allegories." While being essentialist in its claims at universality and somewhat simplistic in its use of the binary "first" and "third" world construction, aspects of Jameson's aesthetics of non-western literature are valuable. He argues that in

> Third-world texts, even those which are seemingly private and invested with a properly libidinal dynamic—necessarily project a political dimension in the form of national allegory: the story of the private individual destiny is always an allegory of the embattled situation of the public third-world culture and society. (69) (Jameson's emphasis)

Jameson suggests, for example, that it is in part the very different implied audience for such texts and their different "ratio of the political to the personal" which renders them "resistant to our conventional western habits of reading" (69). Writing in 1986, Jameson notes the fascination of first-world theory and cultural practice for "the allegorical spirit" which he defines as "profoundly discontinuous, a matter of breaks and heterogeneities, of the multiple polysemia of the dream..." (73). In *Devil on the Cross* and *Matigari*, however, the allegory is not dehistoricized and postmodern but insists on the reader's interpretation of the coherent, public, political range of reference. Moreover, while Jameson locates the "crisis of representation" at the site of narrative closure in works produced in neocolonial situations, *Devil on the Cross's* and *Matigari's* open closures clearly empower the reader to follow Wariinga into the future, to name Matigari as a collective hero, and to accompany Muriuki to the tree, symbolic of Gikuyu myths of origin which prophesy the coming of a black messiah (Dramé 34-35).

Devil on the Cross and *Matigari* incorporate Biblical narrative into their very structures. Like the freedom fighters' revolutionary adaptation of Christian songs and stories, these narratives use prophetic but demythologized Biblical narrative partly for its transformative potential, because of a peasant/worker audience's familiarity with this narrative tradition. Biblical narrative is also employed as a type of radical anecdote to mass mental colonization and moral degradation, as if a violation of taboos associated with the Bible may engender power over it. However, as *Devil on the Cross's* narrator says, reiterated in *I Will Marry When I Want* (62) and *Nmamba Nene's Pistol* (23), "the voice of the people is the voice of God" (8). In *Devil on the Cross*, the eucharist is a cannibal feast, and in *Matigari*, Luke's account of the disciples' encounter with the risen Christ on the road to Emmaus refigures the return of the mythical Mau Mau fighter General Mathenge. Matigari is recognized as Christ-like when he breaks bread in prison. He warns that "Jesus will find you asleep ... when he returns" (153). Here, the recurrent theme of homecoming in Ngugi's work assumes broader mythical significance. Tropologically, Biblical events relate to the fate of the individual soul; in *Matigari*, freedom from prison and habitation of the literal house, which Settler Williams and John Boy appropriated, are tropes for reclamation of land rights, and national liberation. Analogically, Matigari's attempt to reclaim his house refers not to Christian eschatology, but to the establishment of social justice and the political kingdom not in heaven but on earth, in a new Kenya, in the future.

Aside from these works' strident apocalyptic tone and moral seriousness, and their employment of the journey as a structural device, they share with *The Pilgrim's Progress* the employment of allegorical characters. Like Bunyan's, Ngugi's rhetoric of character exploits caricature, but Ngugi's inspiration may be Fanon rather than Bunyan. Fanon wrote that the revolutionary intellectual writer's work must use "a harsh style, full of images" to express "a hand-to-hand struggle and it reveals the need that man has to liberate himself from a part of his being which already contained the seeds of decay. Whether the fight is painful, quick, or inevitable, muscular action must substitute itself for concepts (220). For Fanon, the national bourgeoisie is not a "replica" of the colonial or imperialist bourgeoisie, but merely a "caricature" of it (175). *Devil on the Cross's* capitalists happily acknowledge colonialism, regarding themselves as conduits for multinational corporations' exploitation of the masses. Like *The Pilgrim's Progress, Matigari* ends at the river, but crossing it leads not to the Celestial City but to the gates of the restored city of new Kenya, and a reassertion of the rights and dignity of the community.

At the end of Part 2 of *The Pilgrim's Progress*, Christiana is welcomed at the Gate by trumpeters, but Matigari finally hears "the distant sound of the siren" before the voices of the patriots close the novel (175), anticipating a future victory. Unlike Christiana and Christian, Matigari's arrival is deferred. The kingdom of heaven on earth, Matigari intimates, will only be established by collective action. Like Bunyan, Ngugi wants readers to envision parallels between the City of Destruction and present social realities. Engaging with Ngugi's narratives, readers must not merely play "with the outside of my dream, " but "[t]urn up my metaphors" (Bunyan 219), and, inspired by a kind of vicarious identification with the hero of the allegory, who in Matigari represents the people's social aspiration, take action to establish the Celestial City on earth.

Ngugi's last two narratives, and especially *Devil on the Cross*, in which Wariinga embodies the potential for renewal and struggle, may also be read as gendered allegories. Both works demonstrate women's role in the story of colonial and neocolonial struggle. In *Devil on the Cross*, called in *Detained* "the Wariinga novel" (166), feminism is equated with revolution, which in turn is allegorized in Wariinga's acceptance of agency. In no way do her actions imply the creation of a feminotipia; rather, her portrayal seems to postulate a transformed sexual politics in a truly democratic society. Exploitation of women here is a trope for the country's political oppression. The image for neocolonial exploitation is incestuous, demonic intercourse between national and international capitalism, and this image is reflected in the apocryphal telling of the story of Wariinga's pregnancy. However, as Florence Stratton explains, in such a representation of the analogy "between the condition of women and that of the state" (144), "it would seem that it is the metaphorical potential of that [female] situation" (167), and not the female's position itself which attracts the writer's gaze. Female abjection remains a metaphor.

These various allegorical strains—the historical or national, Biblical, Bunyanesque, and feminist—and Ngugi's drawing on a carnivalesque fusion of discourses demonstrate the hybridization of Ngugi's narrative project. While obviously grounded in history, Ngugi's last two novels have affinities with the postmodern project inasmuch as they point critically to the loss of coherent reference points in the dominant discourses in Kenya and resist institutionalized master-narratives of the truth. As Appiah points out, both posts, the postcolonial and the postmodern, challenge "earlier legitimating narratives" (1 55). Further they decenter the monolithic power of the authorial narrator. In *Devil on the Cross*, for example, the narrator gives voice to the will of the people who plead with him to tell his tale. Ngugi has celebrated the collective production of his plays and the collective reception of these novels. However, while they are "postrealist"

(Appiah 150), Ngugi's last narratives may be distinguished from the postmodern project, unless one defines postmodernism primarily as a temporal concept, a stage in late capitalist aesthetic production, for, as Spivak has recently written, "In postcolonality, every metropolitan definition is dislodged" (217). Neither of Ngugi's last two narratives is a postmodern allegory. Neither, for example, thematizes the impossibility of meaning, or conceptualizes an ontology of surfaces. These two narratives avoid postmodernism's immersion in the present, what Jameson calls "the loss ... of the sense of the future" (qtd. in Stephanson 52). Their medium is discursive and referential, not merely self-reflexive. The future orientation of *Devil on the Cross* and *Matigari* is indicated not only by their open closures, but by the active engagement they demand from their implied readers.

As Madsen writes, "allegory issues an ideological imperative to the reader" (24). The reader of allegory, she continues, "is deeply implicated ... and it is the awareness of complicity that the narrative translates into significant action" (24). Slemon notes in this context that the reader of allegory has been regarded as "the central character in the allegorical text" (1 60). The metafictional dramatization of the writing and reading situation in *Devil on the Cross*, for example, thematizes the novel's own reception. In *Devil on the Cross* and *Matigari*, the "translation" into "significant action" runs from the barrel of the pen to the barrel of the gun. *Devil on the Cross* ends with Wariinga holding a warm gun striding away from the murdered industrialist; *Matigari* ends with Muriuki digging up the AK 47, and even the children's story *Njamba Nene's Pistol* concludes with the child hero's pistol shining "in the morning sun, on the dawn of a new life" (33). The implied readers of the allegory not only sympathetically engage with the character, but must complete the closure of the novels' social text.

A further indication of the hopeful future orientation of Ngugi's last narratives resides in their focus on the role of children. A similar concern for the destiny of the next generation is also a constant refrain in Mau Mau patriotic songs. *Devil on the Cross* seems to be written for children, the national orphans. The narrator asks: "A child without parents to counsel him—what is to prevent him from mistaking foreign shit for a delicious national dish?" (59). *Matigari* begins with the horror of the returned freedom fighter, who has fought "for the sake of his children" (15) seeking his home and family, when he witnesses children surviving in the ruins of the emblematic Mercedes Benz in a "cemetery" of multinational giants (15) and scavenging the waste of late capitalist over-consumption. This social fragmentation is abandoned when Matigari leads Muriuki from the wasteland: "We will go home together so that you can see that it was not for nothing that I spent all these years struggling against Settler Williams..." (20). The novel ends with the singing of the "patriots of all the different nationalities of the land" singing of victory (175), a moment which is as close as Ngugi has yet ventured in writing a utopian allegory, detailing the realization of his hopes.

Matigari's themes are simplified in the children's story Njamba Nene's Pistol. Set in the 1950s, during the emergency, the story represents political oppression from a child's perspective. The hero, Njamba Nene, is a materially poor, but patriotic and resourceful boy. He will not be one of those boys whom the white settler, Pious Hangbelly Brainwash, in Njamba Nene and the Flying Bus, wishes to genetically engineer. Brainwash's ambition is to manufacture "a small group of Africans who had mouths, legs, arms, hearts, everything like those of white people" (6); similarly, in Devil on the Cross, Nditika wa Nguunji wishes to manufacture spare body parts to enable the rich to "purchase immortality" (180). Like the boy in The Trial of Dedan Kimathi, Njamba Nene is asked to carry a loaf of bread, containing a pistol, to the freedom fighters in the forest. When he is arrested, he uncovers the pistol and trains it on the British authorities, enabling the fighters' escape. As in Matigari, he and his new comrades don soldier's uniforms and sail through the British roadblocks. At the story's end, the boy is rewarded with the pistol for his bravery with the anticipation that his life will be changing. As Ngugi writes, "If people get faith and courage, if people get a clear idea of what they want, yes if they heed the call of their people and nation, they can go through a great change" (9).

Ngugi's allegories of transformation envision community survival. The imperative for incorporating various allegorical strains was the desire to reach an implied audience of Kenyan workers/peasants, and to anticipate—despite the degradation of present social relations proceeding from manufactured poverty and psychological dispossession—a more hopeful future. Ngugi's allegory ultimately projects a future which is cataclysmic and apocalyptic, but also utopian and revolutionary. At the end of Devil on the Cross, Wariinga embraces this future, and at Matigari's closure the collective hero becomes an empowering communal myth. Matigari, in particular, is an extended appeal for its implied audience to accept the hero's challenge and complete his story in the real world. The use of allegory in these novels facilitates a projection into a tumultuous but ultimately triumphant future.

NOTE

This paper, presented at the ALA "After Accra" conference at Rutgers University in April 1994, is part of a larger project on Ngugi's allegory. See "'The Sound of the Horn of Justice' in Ngugi wa Thiong'o's Narrative." *Let My People Go: Postcolonial Literature and the Biblical Call for Justice*. Ed. Susan VanZanten Gallagher. Mississippi UP (forthcoming); "The Post-Colonial 'Crisis of Representation' and Ngugi wa Thiong'o's Religious Allegory." *Religion and Literature in Post/Neocolonial Cultures*. Ed. Jamie S. Scott. Rodopi (forthcoming); "Ngugi wa Thiong'o's *Devil on the Cross* and *Matigari*: Writing the Female Subject." *World Literature Written in English* (forthcoming).

WORKS CITED

Appiah, Kwame Anthony. *In My Father's House: Africa in the Philosophy of Culture*. New York: Oxford UP, 1992.

Ashcroft, Bill, Gareth Griffiths and Helen Tiffin. *The Empire Writes Back: Theory and Practice in Post-Colonial Literatures*. London: Routlege, 1989.

Bunyan, John. *The Pilgrim's Progress*. Ed. Roger Sharrock. Harmondsworth, Middlesex: Penguin, 1965.

Cook, David and Michael Okenimkpe. *Ngugi wa Thiong'o: An Exploration of His Writings*. London: Heinemann, 1983.

Dramé, Kandioura. *The Novel As Transformation Myth: A Study of the Novels of Mongo Beti and Ngugi wa Thiong'o*. Syracuse, NY: Foreign and Comparative Studies/African Series 43, 1990.

Fanon, Frantz. *The Wretched of the Earth*. Trans. Constance Farrington. New York: Grove, 1963.

Jameson, Fredric. "Third-World Literature in the Era of Multinational Capitalism." *Social Text* 15 (1986): 65-88.

Madsen, Deborah L. *The Postmodernist Allegories of Thomas Pynchon*. New York: St. Martin's, 1991.

Maina wa Kinyatti, ed. *Thunder from the Mountains: Mau Mau Patriotic Songs*. Trenton, New Jersey: Africa World Press, 1990.

Ngugi wa Thiong'o. *Decolonising the Mind: The Politics of Language in African Literature*. London: James Currey, 1986.

_____. *Detained: A Writer's Prison Diary* . London: Heinemann, 1981.

_____. *Devil on the Cross*. Trans. by the author. London: Heinemann, 1982.

_____. *Matigari*. Trans. Wangui wa Goro. Oxford: Heinemann, 1987.

_____. *Moving the Centre: The Struggle for Cultural Freedoms*. London: James Currey, 1993.

_____. *Njamba Nene and the Flying Bus*. Trans. Wangui wa Goro. Nairobi: Heinemann Kenya, 1986.

_____. *Njamba Nene's Pistol*. Trans. Wangui wa Goro. Nairobi: Heinemann Kenya, 1986.

_____. *Writers in Politics*. London: Heinemann, 1981.

Ngugi wa Thiong'o and Ngugi wa Mirii. *I Will Marry When I Want*. Trans. by the authors. Oxford: Heinemann, 1982.

Sharma, Govind Narain. "Ngugi's Christian Vision: Theme and Pattern in *A Grain of Wheat*." *African Literature Today* 10. Ed. Eldred Durosimi Jones. London: Heinemann, 1979:167-76.

Sicherman, Carol M. "Ngugi wa Thiong'o and the Writing of Kenyan History." *Research in African Literatures* 20 (1989): 347-70.

Slemon, Stephen. "Post-Colonial Allegory and the Transformation of History" *Journal of Commonwealth Literature* 32.1 (1988): 157-68.

Spivak, Gayatri Chakravorty. *Outside in the Teaching Machine*. New York: Routledge, 1993.

Stephanson, Anders. "Regarding Postmodernism—A conversation with Fredric Jameson." *Social Text* 17 (1987): 29-54.

Stratton, Florence. "The Shallow Grave: Archetypes of Female Experience in African Fiction." *Research in African Literatures* 19 (1988): 143-69.

The Ecstatic Framework:
Language, Music and Dance in Selected Soyinka Plays

by Souley Y. Ousman
University of Ghana, Legon

One cannot ultimately talk of the sources of Soyinka's drama without mentioning its basic projections: language, music and dance. For there is an area of the traditional Yoruba psyche where the metaphysical and mytho-religious, the natural and supernatural meet, and there create a new being and a new awareness; an area of ecstatic upheaval where the most significant and profound feelings and emotional responses take shape, where the scattered fragments of reality combine with mythopoeic images as a grand matrix in traditional Yoruba memory to produce a synthesis of ordered experience. As Soyinka writes in *Art, Dialogue and Outrage*:

> It is unmusical to separate Yoruba musical form from myth and poetry. The nature of Yoruba music is intensively the nature of its language and poetry, highly charged, symbolic, mythembryonic. (Soyinka 1981: 25).

So it is impossible within the framework of this paper to separate language, music and dance from the cosmic world of Soyinka's drama. That is to say, the three themes cannot be separated from all that make up the traditional scene and the general mode of life of the Yoruba community. For the communal nature of their language and music gives them a near-conversational flavor. Moreover, Yoruba dance has a mimic quality and consequently borders on a dramatic performance; thus language, music and dance achieve a complete image of theatre.

Soyinka thus fuses the reality of Yoruba linguistic, musical and dance conception to produce a unified ecstasy. It is in the marriage of the three levels and their active integration as a method of knowing and feeling that the traditional imagination arrives at its precise definition of reality and state of ecstasy. For it is in the context of worship or sacrifice that possession takes place. In this context, it is integrated with music and dance. The Yoruba believe that the state of ecstasy or possession is induced by means of special music closely correlated with specific forms of bodily movement. It is also believed that the gods and ancestral spirits are sensitive to this music. Opportunities are, therefore, sought to call on them while dancing is going on, in the hope that they possess the dancers as they are emotionally prepared to receive them. Thus, the effect of language, music and dance opens a door of knowledge into the deep folds of human consciousness and communion with the wider mysterious Yoruba universe. This process of making contact with the universal essence insinuates and filters through all the coarseness of externality to reach the appreciative soul.

Soyinka in our plays of study shows the immense importance of language, music and dance in the community life of traditional Yoruba people, and how they express predominantly collective emotions. Soyinka has therefore taken the trouble to identify his characters in terms of this general attachment to the musical atmosphere of the traditional society. In citing Yoruba sacred linguistic and musical observances Soyinka even goes so far as to suggest a theory when he says Yoruba tragic music functions

> From archetypal essences whose language derives not from the plane of physical reality or ancestral memory (the ancestor is no more than agent or medium) but from the numinous territory of transition into which the artist obtains fleeting glimpses of ritual sacrifices and a patient submission of rational awareness to that moment when his fingers and voice relate to the symbolic language of the cosmos. (Jefferson 1973: 130)

This raises the question of the nature of language, music and dance in Soyinka's plays, and the relationship of Soyinka's drama to his audience and readers. A consideration of this sort of traditional conception shows why the collective imagination of Yoruba cosmology occupies a central place in Soyinka's drama, but the centrally important fact about the ecstatic framework of Soyinka drama is its sweeping dramatic vitality; thus by staging and watching Soyinka's plays, the performers and audience are made more acquainted with traditional Yoruba religion and thought systems, especially non-Yoruba performers and audiences. That is why following his production of *Death and the King's Horseman* with black and white American performers at the Goodman Theatre in Chicago, Soyinka says:

> Many of them were tone deaf which they could not believe. They were used to singing all the 'yeah, yeah, yeah' and they had earphones clamped to their ears. When I played them the tapes which I had brought from home of some of the songs and said, '"You have to learn this now" they weren't into what they thought. I felt they really had to break down their bones, get them to learn new auditory habits, hear new sounds they never knew existed. That meant that even though they spoke 'English' they had to learn to read it in a rhythm that

is not British R. P. That is a rhythm I needed for what the language of English is saying in my own language. (Gibbs 1987: 91)

Language as Soyinka's Vehicle for Ecstasy

Soyinka does not write English as it is written by the native speaker of the language. He often writes what the English language is saying in his native Yoruba language. It is through this that his cosmic message could be delivered without much distortion. It is fairly well agreed that as other parts of the English-speaking world have their own brands of English, determined by their mother tongues, so also are the English-speaking Yoruba entitled to their own cosmic brand.

Soyinka adapts the English language to his own needs in an intelligent manner. Any foreigner reading his play may find that it contains expressions with which he is not familiar, but they are not difficult enough to obstruct his comprehension. His characters speak in a natural tone and say the things that are expected of people in their traditional society, in the way they normally would. In its form, this language perfectly reflects the people's religious and thought systems.

Soyinka's basic tool as a dramatist is language. The way he portrays his characters' actions on stage, their inner feelings and thoughts, his ordering of incidents and events to convey traditional Yoruba cosmology, these are all conveyed by his manipulation of language. His reliance on the Yoruba spoken language roots his plays within Yoruba traditional ethos, especially as the language is often reinforced by physical gestures, facial, vocal inflections and other arts of the performer. This clearly marks the plays with a unique linguistic technique. That is why Bernth Linfors says in his paper 'Wole Soyinka and the Horses of Speech':

> Soyinka, as a dramatist, must pull all his words into the mouths of his characters; he can never speak in his own voice or in the guise of an omniscient chronicler. (Ibid.)

The location of Soyinka's plays within a fundamentally Yoruba ethos, in which traditional values are still integral to the functioning culture that exists side by side with a growing modern tradition, means that the English language used may be modified by the language of the traditional Yoruba society. As Kofi Asare Opoku says:

> The importance of our language for our development cannot be over-emphasized and I can say without doubt that our 'underdevelopment' or lack of self-confidence as a nation, is due largely to our use of a foreign language. If we are to become a self-reliant, self-assertive nation respected by other

nations, we have to actively promote our own languages and lingua franca which is African. (Opoku 1992: 25)

This explains why Soyinka attempts to recapture traditional Yoruba speech through translation from the vernacular into English. J. P. Clark, in an influential essay titled "The Legacy of Caliban," has advanced the thesis that authentic works could be created by the artist capable of utilizing a "reliance upon the inner resources of language. These are images, figures of meaning and speech, which expert handling can achieve for his art (through) a kind of blood transfusion, reviving the English language by the living adaptable properties of some African language." (Clark 1970: 37)

Thus Soyinka's use of fossilized expressions is important, as they reveal beliefs and concepts of the universe and of life that are collectively shared and transmitted by the Yoruba language. In this regard, fixed expressions form the main basis of the permanent linguistic tradition. These expressions form a criterion of linguistic authenticity in our plays of study.

Transformation is a functional view of cosmology and its main vehicle is language. Thus the ecstatic or emotional significance of the relationship of language to our selected Soyinka plays must be appreciated from various levels: language of the word, language of the music, language of the drum and language of the dance. In a sense Soyinka resorts to a device which gives it an ecstatic effect. And since his cosmic principles incorporate various levels of existence, his use of the English language provides an appropriate framework for his cosmology. As he himself asserts:

> When we borrow an alien language to sculpt or paint in, we must begin by co-opting the entire properties of that language as correspondences to properties in our matrix of thought and expression. We must stress such a language, stretch it, impact and compact it, fragment and resemble it, with no apology, as required to bear the burden of experiencing and experiences, be they formulated or not in the conceptual idioms of the language. (Soyinka 1975: 67)

While it is agreed that language is basically used to convey information, it can also be argued that at the level of an ecstatic communication, especially one involving a cosmic context, language does more than just inform; it provokes emotions and attitudes, it invokes the spirits and affects sensibility. In the ecstatic framework of Soyinka's drama, language is an all-embracing denominator. At once 'mythopoeic' and effecting the 'masonic union of sign and melody,' it is largely a device beyond linguistic communication and apprehension. It is the ecstatic element of transformation.

The Uses of Proverbs and Everyday Sayings

The cosmic significance of proverbs in Soyinka's drama is brought out by their close connection with other forms of traditional Yoruba linguistic decorum. Proverbs in general are condensed or short witty statements which express collective ideas, beliefs and feelings, sentiments or wisdom of a people in verbal terms. The Yoruba have a saying that, " proverbs are the horses of speech, if communication is lost, we use proverbs to find it" (Leslau 1962: 5). Soyinka uses the proverbs and sayings from his everyday culture to convey weighty mythological and religious messages to his audience and readers. As Fadipe A. Nathiel says:

> It is in proverbs that the profound expression of wisdom by many sages have been stored over a long period of time. Such expression usually summarize cosmic events in the purest Yoruba idiom and they are, at once, precise and didactic. In modern times when the language is becoming more and more adulterated by indiscriminate borrowing from foreign languages, particularly English, proverbs have remained ... for maintaining the purity of their language, for maintaining a sense of continuity and rootedness in the Yoruba cultural tradition, and for defining one's position in the cosmos. (Nathiel 1970: 17)

Kongi's Harvest perhaps offers one of the best examples of Soyinka's use of language as an element of his cosmology. In his grasp, proverbs yield easily to formal manipulation and convey insight into character and give pattern to ecstatic action. That is to say Soyinka's use of proverbs and adages in this play carries his audience into the heart of Yoruba cosmology.

The character of Oba Danlola can only be explained fully by analysis of power and personality motifs embodied in proverbs. For the old order is represented by Oba Danlola and his followers whose choice of language sharply marks them off from Kongi's breed. That is to say that Danlola's language has a concreteness of metaphor and imagery which recalls traditional beliefs and practices. Let us by way of analysis consider Danlola's remark when Kongi's superintendent stops his drummers:

> DANLOLA: Good friend, you merely stopped my drums. But they were silenced on the day that Kongi cast aside my prop of wisdom, the day he drove the old Aweri from their seat. What is a king without a chain of elders? What will Kongi be without Sarumi, what name was it again? (Soyinka 1973: 65)

Oba Danlola is a king and a pillar of the traditional Yoruba society. Each of his appearances is a masterpiece of linguistic property. Most important is the presence of an enormous store of philosophy that is inherent in his speech. It is this feature which carries the mind away to the spheres unseen. It is also this feature which makes the listener reflect, and it is also this feature which touches the innermost realms of ecstasy. Thus the language of Oba Danlola reveals that which was used long ago, as the most proverbial expressions date far back. That is why, in response to Kongi and his followers, he bombards them with traditional Yoruba proverbs and everyday sayings. Let us take another example in which he reminds his followers of the danger looming over the society:

> DANLOLA: But he says I must. Let me prostrate myself to him [Again the gesture. He and his retainers get involved in a mock struggle]. ...
>
> Curse? Who spoke of curses? To prostrate to a loyal servant of Kongi—is that a curse? All is well. The guard has waived his rights and privileges. The father now prostrates himself in gratitude. (65-66)

Danlola's speech illustrates traditional Yoruba linguistic decorum. These proverbs and everyday sayings are an ironic coda to the play; they both prepare the way to the end, and apply directly to the audience. For a purely dramatic purpose, these proverbs become a defining point of the play's action and so serve in heightening emotional response to the action. That is why Kongi's superintendent finds these sayings so threatening he has to apologize profusely:

> SUPERINTENDENT: Only a foolish child lets a father prostrate to him. I didn't ask to become a leper or a lunatic. I have no wish to live on sour berries.... I waived nothing. I had nothing to waive, nothing to excuse. I deny rights and beg you not to cast subtle damnation on my head...[Forestall him by throwing himself down]. I call you all to witness. Kabiyesi, I am only the fowl dropping that stuck to your slippers when you strolled in the backyard. The child is nothing, it is only the story of his forebears that the world sees and tolerate in him. (66)

The Use of Poetic Language and Praise Singing

Soyinka reinforces normal English language and syntactical forms with traditional, derived images and idioms. He appropriates rhythmic patterns of traditional speech and builds them into normal linguistic patterns of English to produce a powerful ecstasy. As Anozie says:

> Soyinka in his poetry makes ... an attempt to erect a bridge between the poet's competence in his native Yoruba language, via his performance in the literary language of English, and the native speaker's intuition of English, that is, generative grammar. (Gibbs and Lindfors 1993: 195)

What Soyinka does is to build his language around traditional linguistic characteristics and to fuse them, by applying the verbal habits of traditional Yoruba people into a mythopoeic medium. His characters speak in a language which most Yoruba will recognize and rouse strong religious fervor through verbal invocations which has ecstatic impact on both the characters and audiences.

It is noteworthy that the first voice heard in *Death and the King's Horseman* is that of the Praise-Singer. Yoruba poems of whatever type are performed by people who have acquired an unusually sweet voice. The Praise-Singer's appearance sets the tone of the play:

> Praise-Singer: Are you sure there will be one like me on the other side?
>
> Elesin: Olohun-iyo!
>
> Praise-Singer: Far be it to belittle the dwellers of that place but, a man is either born to his art or isn't. And I don't know for certain that you'll meet my father, so who is going to sing these deeds in accents that will pierce the deafness of the ancient ones. I have prepared my going, just tell me, Olohun-iyo. I need you on this journey and I shall be behind you.
>
> Elesin: You are like a jealous wife. Stay close to me but only on this side. My fame, my honor are legacies to the living, stay behind and let the world sip its honey from your lips. (Soyinka 1976: 9-10)

The praise-singer's ability to manipulate in a pleasing manner the tone and rhythm of the language is an essential attribute of the Yoruba oral poet. This makes it possible for one to get the proper feeling of Yoruba poetry in its actual performance. Thus the dominant cadence in the play is unmistakably Yoruba, not of Yoruba everyday speech, but of Yoruba poetry. In its measured utterances, the play belongs in the same tradition as *ijala* (the poetry of the hunters) and *rara* (the poetry of the praise-singers) all wrapped up in the total echoes of the Yoruba language. An example of this is Elesin-Oba's anecdotes on the "Not-I-Bird." These are reminiscent of those in *ijala* poems of the hunters:

> Elesin: I, when that "Not-I-Bird" perched upon my roof, bade him seek his nest again. Safe, without care or fear, I unrolled my welcome mat for him to see. Not-I flew happily away, you'll hear his voice no more in this lifetime— you all know what I am. (14)

Even Elesin's response to his praise-singer and the market women are prophetic statements on the larger burden of his life. According to the Praise-Singer, his riddles are more than the nut in the kernel in hot embers that dares a man's fingers to draw it out. That is why Elesin is capable of singing his own elegy:

> My faithful friends, let our feet touch together this last time, lead me into the other market with spurts that cover my skin with down yet make my limbs strike earth like a thoroughbred. Dear mothers let me dance into the passage even as I have beneath your roofs. (41)

Elesin's poetic language contains an idiom and tone which accord with the ecstatic requirement of a particular genre as determined by tradition. So Soyinka's choice of words is deliberate, to hammer in at every opportunity the point that what the audience is witnessing is not just the inevitable death of Elesin-Oba, but a rite of passage deep-rooted in Yoruba tradition. This also explains why the proverbs, the everyday sayings and the poetic language are no longer the physical expression of merriment, but largely a dance into the passage.

Music and the Dance of Possession

In the ecstatic framework of Soyinka's drama, music does more than just provide entertainment; it provokes emotions and attitudes, it invokes the spirits and affects sensibilities. For 'the Yoruba are a singing people. In their singing, which comprises songs, lyrics, ballads, minstrelsy, they tell stories of their past, and their hopes and fears of the future.' (Idowu 1962: 10). So, one can see why music is one of the key realities of the Yoruba people.

Soyinka as a playwright does not only draw his ideas from the religious and ritual activities of his people, but musical and dance perceptions are also part of the humanity of the Yoruba people, and Soyinka finds in them material for his immense desire to paint for ecstatic response. That is why he says 'our forms of the theatre are quite different from literary drama. We use spontaneous dialogue, folk music, simple stories and related dances to explain what we mean' (Nkosi 1962:10).

This explains why the Praise-Singer in *Death and the King's Horseman* is fully identified with music. Soyinka naturally associates traditional music with specific scenes of the play to portray Yoruba cosmology. Soyinka thus shows the immense importance of the Praise-Singer in the community life of his traditional society. For the Praise-Singer is closely informed by a sense of historical truth of the Yoruba people:

> PRAISE-SINGER: (Elesin in this motion appears to feel for a direction of sound subtly, but he only sinks deeper into trance dance). Elesin Alafin, I no

longer sense your flesh. The drums are changing now but you are far ahead of the world. It is not yet noon in heaven, let those who claim it is begin their own journey home. So why must you rush like impatient brides, why do you race to desert your Olohun-Iyo? (Elesin is now sunk fully deep in his trance, there is no longer sign of any awareness of his surroundings). (44)

Cosmic values are expressed through the music. For every musical type sung in community life has a tradition behind it, a tradition which governs its mode of performance, its repertoire, its choice of musical instrument as well as the tradition that governs the context in which it should be sung. Those familiar with these aspects of musical improvisations may recognize them in dramatic performance and may therefore be disturbed if there are serious departures, For there seems to be cosmic value in the renewal of experience:

> PRAISE-SINGER: Does the deep voice of gbedu cover you then like ... the passage of royal elephant? Those drums that brook no rivals have they blocked the passage to your ears that my voice passes into wind, a mere leaf floating in the night? Is your flesh lightened? Elesin, is the lump of earth I slid between your slipper to keep you longer slowly sifting side now stuming skin with ours in Osugbo?

> Are these sounds there I cannot hear, do footsteps surround you which poured the earth like gbedu roll like thunder round the dome of the world? Is the darkness gathering in your head Elesin? (38)

The praise-singer provides an accompaniment to action and serves as an integrative force (a means of holding the society together).

A remarkable phenomenon of Soyinka's drama is the poetry played on the drum. The expression of words through the drum rests on the fact that the Yoruba language is highly tonal; that the meanings of words are distinguished not only by formal semantic element but also by their tones. It is the tonal patterns of words that transmit the message in drum poetry. The drum builds its effect in this play by arousing visions of grandeur and power which though rising within the individual imagination are soon objectified as collective images of Yoruba history. As Olunde explains to Jane:

> Olunde: Listen .... You can't hear anything against the music.

> Jane: What is it?

> Olunde: The drums, can you hear the change? Listen (the drums come over, still distant. There is a change of rhythm; it rises to a crescendo and then, suddenly it is cut off. After a silence, a new beat begins and resonant). There. It's all over.

Jane: You mean he's....

Olunde: Yes, Mrs. Pilking, my father is dead. His will-power has always been enormous; I know he is dead. (55)

Like *Death and the King's Horseman*, the musical interest of *Kongi's Harvest*, especially the spontaneity and expression of the gbedu rhythm in song and dance, is an aspect of the traditional Yoruba idyllic nature:

> [to the beat of gbedu' drum steps into slow royal dance].
>
> *Ema gun'yan ba kere O*
> *Ema gun'yan oba kere*
> *Kaun elepini ko se e gbe mo*
> *Eweyo noin ni ni fi yo' nu*
> *e ma gun'yan oba kere*
> 'Don't pound the king's yam
> In a small mortar
> Small as the spice is
> It cannot be swallowed whole
> A shilling's vegetable must appease
> A half-penny spice. (62)

This explains why the dramatic use of dance finds its highest ecstatic expression in Soyinka's play. As Judith Hanna (1973) explains 'dance is composed of purposefully, intentionally, rhythmically, and culturally patterned sequences of non-verbal body movements and gesture which are no ordinary motor activities, the motion having inherent value.' It is also a psychological behavior, in the sense of being an emotional experience which affects the quality of an adjustment to an individual's self-existence and group life. That is why William Fagg says,

> There is strong reason to believe that in tribal society all dancing, whether sacred or profane, is held to increase the life force of the participants, that a person in stylized movement is 'ipso facto' generating force. (Fagg 19..:122-23)

This may explain why Soyinka uses the Yoruba dance to teach and reinforce cultural patterns. Thus the movement of characters on the stage in *Kongi's Harvest* is determined by the music:

> Danlola, totally swelled, steps down from his throne and falls in step with Sarumi. The two obas cavort round the chamber in sedate, regal steps and the bugles blast a steady refrain. Danlola's wives emerge and join in; the atmosphere is full of ecstasy of the dance. (111)

The dance by Danlola contributes to the attainment of societal goals. As an accompaniment to religious obligations, the dance stimulates the individual's involvement, and generally makes the objection less of a chore. That is why James Frazer says, 'in Onitsha the king is required to dance before his people at the annual yam feast to retain his position of honor' (Frazer 1929). There is therefore a royal quality in the dance of Oba Danlola and his retinue. The words of Oyin Ogunba (1984: 18) seem to pay further tribute to the might and majesty of the king's dance:

> The king's dance is the dance of the community by its divine leader, a re-enactment of the whole living tradition of the people. It is thus a life-giving ritual which has to be done in epic (form) to demonstrate the higher aspiration of the community.

It is clear from our analysis and discussion in this paper that Soyinka sets language, music and dance within the social and cultural environment of the Yoruba people. Language, music and dance, as we have seen, are formulated from human experience and reflections, and are handed down from the past by ancestors who are believed to have qualities of wisdom, authority and responsibility. It is these qualities that lead the characters and audiences into a state of deep reflection and also of ecstasy.

REFERENCES CITED

Clark, J.P. "Aspects of Nigerian Drama." *The Example of Shakespeare,* Longman, London, 1970, p. 37.

Fagg, William. *Nigerian Images,* ... 122-23.

Frazer, Sir James. *The Golden Bough: A Study of Magic and Religion,* The Book League of America, New York, 1929.

Gibbs, James. "Soyinka in Zimbabwe," *The Literary Half-Yearly,* Vol. xviii, No. 2 July 1987, p. 91.

Gibbs, James and Bernth Lindfors, *Research on Wole Soyinka.* New Jersey, Africa World Press, 1993.

Hanna, Judith. "Towards a Cross-Cultural Conceptualization of Dance and Some Correlated Consideration." *International Congress of Anthropological and Ethnological Sciences.* August 1973.

Idowu, Bolaji F. *Olodumare, God in Yoruba Belief,* Longman, London, 1962.

Jefferson, D.W. *The Morality of Art,* Cambridge University Press, London, 1973, p.130.

Leslau, Charlotte and Wolf. *African Proverbs,* Mount Vernon, 1962, p. 5.

Nathiel, Fadipe A. *The Sociology of the Yoruba,* Ibadan University Press, 1970

Nkosi, Lewis. *Home and Exile,* Longman, London, 1962.

Ogunba, Oyin. *African Literature Today,* No. 4, (1984).

Opoku, Kofi Asare. "The Traditional Foundations of Development." *Uhuru*, Vol . 4 No. 7, 1992.

Soyinka, Wole. *Art, Dialogue and Outrage,* New Horn Press, Ibadan, 1981.

_____. *Death and the King's Horseman,* Eyre Metheum Ltd., London, 1976.

_____. "Aesthetic Illusions: Prescription for the Suicide of Poetry," *Third Press Review*, Vol 1, No. September/October, 1975.

_____. *Kongi's Harvest,* Oxford University Press, London, 1973.

INA CESAIRE:
Telling Theatricalized Tales

by Judith G. Miller
University of Wisconsin—Madison

I propose here to analyze three of Ina Césaire's theatre pieces in terms of their interconnectedness with the Caribbean oral tradition, in particular the orality of tale-telling.[1] To get at this interconnectedness, I will use the notion of "intertextuality," understanding that the "text" of "inter *text* ual" is *the performance text* (which can be defined here as the cathexis of the theatricality [or theatrical potential] of the linguistic text and its realization in performance). This use of "intertextuality" does not exclude thematics or poetics, but, rather, apprehends both in light of how staging (or telling) gives physical shape and rhythm to thought and to what might be termed "word-music." While I will, then, touch on thematics and poetics, I will do so by embedding them in a more detailed discussion of three aspects of Césaire's theatre: the spatio-temporal dimension and related stage action of her plays, her characterization, and her plays' rhythmic structure and subsequent emotional impact. I hope to show how these three aspects mirror similar aspects of oral tales. I'd like to conclude, however, by suggesting the particular innovations of the theatricalized tales Ina Césaire tells, for in them she both twists the traditional emphasis on

---

[1] Because the text seems to be lost, Césaire's 1990 play *La Saison Close*, [Closed Season], an adaptation of *Cell 478*, Sevgun Soysol's recounting of imprisonment in a Turkish jail, will not be examined. I will, however, analyze Césaire's 1986 play, *Mémoires d'Isles : l'Histoire de Maman N et Maman F,* translated by Christiane Makward and myself as *Island Memories: The Story of Mama N and Mama F*, in *Plays by French and Francophone Women: A Critical Anthology* (University of Michigan Press, 1995) ; also *L'Enfant des Passages ou La Geste de Ti-Jean* (1988), which for the purposes of this presentation will be called *The Child of Passages or the Epic of Ti-Jean*; and, finally, *Rosanie Soleil* (1992), published by Ubu Repertory Publications in my translation as *Fire's Daughters* (*Plays by Women*, 1993).

male characters prevalent in the tales and creates an expanded mythic origin for Martinican people.[2]

I consider it useful to begin by briefly summarizing each play, fully cognizant of the ways in which a résumé of this nature, by foregrounding the "story," disfigures Césaire's theatre, making her plays appear less idiosyncratic and more linear than they actually are. And further on codicils, in my analysis I assume a public fully receptive to the world of Césaire's plays. In speaking for that public, I recognize I'm making a speculative and empathic leap.

Césaire's first play, dating from 1986, *Mémoires d'Isle: L'Histoire de Maman N et Maman F*, translated as *Island Memories: The Story of Mama N and Mama F*, draws upon the reminiscences of several elderly Martinican women.[3] Césaire places the recollected memories in the mouths of characters Aure and Hermancia, half-sisters who seem, nonetheless, to have lived oceans apart. Aure, a mulatto from the protected southern part of the island, is educated, refined, even if somewhat stuffy. Hermancia, feistier, a woman of the people from the wild northern side, sings and taps her cane as she celebrates more tangibly the matriarchy which formed their personnalities. By play's end, both characters show themselves to be incredibly strong-willed, passionately connected to their physical surroundings, and deeply bonded to each other. In an evening's conversation on the veranda, they recreate the contemporary history of Martinique through recalling their own daily reality.

Césaire's second play, *l'Enfant des Passages ou la Geste de Ti-Jean*, which I shall call in English *The Child of Passages or The Tale of Ti-Jean*, dates from 1988. It is more ostensibly metaphorical than *Island Memories* and imagined as a play of constant physical movement, taking the wily adolescent Ti-Jean and his wimpering brother Yin-yin through a series of frightening experiences to the pinacle of questionable success. Along the way, Ti-Jean encounters a sorcerer, an enraged tiger mother, and a fishy

---

[2] My readings of the performance text of Ina Césaire's plays are based on performances I have seen or directed: *Island Memories*, Ubu Repertory Theatre, N.Y., 1991; *Fire's Daughters*, Ubu Repertory Theatre, N.Y., 1993; *L'Enfant des passages*, University of Wisconsin-Madison, 1992). I do, nevertheless, hold to the notion that within the written text the performance text is a virtual stage "reality." My analysis of Ina Césaire's theatricalized tale-telling should, then, be able to stand on its own even without reference to an actual production.

[3] *Island Memories* is based on interviews with female relatives of Ina Césaire and with foremothers of the two Antillean actresses, Mariann Mathéus and Myrrah Donzenac, who helped develop the play in rehearsal.

tonton-macoute. He commits inexplicable acts of violence: burning down his house, cannibalizing his Turtle-Savior, and killing a baby-tiger; and he confronts strange new worlds: ones that are upside-down, or shaped from his own fantasies, or infinitely dark. At play's end, this hero who is, in fact, an *anti*-hero, destroys the seven-headed monster which has victimized an entire kingdom. Ti-Jean thus restores the light and lays claim to a great reward. His victory, nevertheless, looms hollow. He may have won half a kingdom and the hand of the beautiful Princess, but the latter cannot think her way out of a barrel. It appears that achieving wealth and status by doing business with "the King" has serious drawbacks.

Césaire's third play, the 1992 *Rosanie Soleil*, translated as *Fire's Daughters*, returns to the intimacy of an island home and women's conversation. The anthropomorphized figures from *The Child of Passages* do not people this apparently domestic drama. However, the play's deep-set meaning lies precisely in the figurative implications of the female characters' quest. The time is 1870, the Third Republic has been declared in France, but justice and economic prosperity are still out of reach of the former slave population of Martinique. Four characters: Mama Sun and twin daughters Rosa and Anna and their neighbor Sister Smoke, exchange through ellipses, proverbs, and understatement, news and feelings about the revolt brewing among the people of their commune. Mama Sun tries to protect her daughters from getting involved in the struggle; but she has already introduced into their home a mysterious revolutionary leader. His very presence engages them in the current conflict and, as he has come from Haiti, also links them symbolically to the country in which Caribbean republicanism got its start. At play's end, all four women prepare to join their compatriots on the battlefront in demanding from French authorities full recognition of Martinican rights.

The preceding synopses of Césaire's plays always arrive, as becomes apparent, at the play's end. Suggesting that each play has a definite and conclusive ending, however, or, in other terms, that Césaire's plays are plot-driven, misprizes their impact as well as their intent. The spectators are not primarily seduced into wondering what will happen next. Neither do they worry about the fate of the main characters. Instead, Césaire's plays, like oral tales, compel the spectators' adhesion through the process of transporting them to a different space. Like tales, Césaire's plays evoke and make palpable a simultaneous sacred and subversive space, one enlivened and reinforced by song and dance.

Island Memories, for example, is prefaced by a *vidé* dance scene in which the actresses who play Aure and Hermancia perform first the "Devil-Women" of Carnival. The devil-women break up their raucous dancing with riddles in the creole language, signaling both their African heritage and a uniquely and authentically Caribbean cultural *métissage*. Their performance establishes immediately the radicalizing folly which Carnival materializes, a topsy-turviness which permits the exorcism of social and political oppression and which evacuates specific time and space frames. The actresses further reinforce a sense of atemporality by changing before the audience's eyes into old ladies about to tell their story. This metamorphosis into old ladies brings to life the veranda where Aure and Hermancia sit, rock, and remember, a threshold space neither in nor out, but encompassing at once what is in, what is out, and what is in-between. From this unclassifiable space, not unlike that of the long liminal nights of funeral wakes when creole storytellers perform, Aure and Hermancia weave their tales.

The mere evocation of the name "Ti-Jean" calls forth the space of tale-telling; for he is the ubiquitous hero of Caribbean folk tales.[4] In Césaire's Ti-Jean play, however, no storyteller character introduces this liminal dimension. Rather, characters spring to fully fleshed-out life as soon as the curtain opens. The obvious phantasmagoria of the spatial changes and interactions during Ti-Jean's voyage nonetheless create an out-of-space, out-of-time feel. Moreover, the presentational acting style required to propel the text makes palpable the spatial changes which occur within each character's psyche. Actors move in and out of their roles as "Eagle," "Zamba," "Dame Keleman," "Ma'am Tiger," and so on, marking clearly the transition from one performance mode to another. They perform the dance of the trees, the song of the Inverted Man; *mazurka piqués, lérozes,* and other syncopated or fast-stepping tunes. Using the storyteller's slippery technique, they glide from telling to showing, from musical commentary to scene. Their movement establishes a time which is no time (because many times) and a space which is no space (because many spaces). To reinforce this multi-dimensionality, in the concluding banquet scene Césaire brings all the characters together from the four different domains Ti-Jean has traversed. Their celebration of Ti-Jean's exploits integrates, as if in a dream or hallucination, the mental worlds of the play.

Of the three plays examined, *Fire's Daughters* would seem to have the closest interface with Martinican "history," if we understand history in its traditional conceptualization as a narrative constructed through the use of archives and legal documents. Indeed, the need to write the play impressed itself upon Césaire when she was researching the Southern

---

[4] Once again my readings of the performance text of Ina Césaire's plays are based on performances I have seen or directed.

Insurrection of 1870, a moment in Martinican history omitted from French chronicles.[5] Rendering on stage the actual historical events was not, however, her overarching goal. She felt quite free to change court reports on real-life insurgents, blur the details of the spontaneous uprising (which left some twenty-five plantations burned to the ground), and metaphorically collapse the Southern revolt of Martinique into the earlier Haitian Revolution.

What manifestly inspired Césaire was again the desire to establish a space of liberation, another out-of-time unboundedness. In *Fire's Daughters*, the four women characters explode the shackles of the oppressive colonial power structure through the liberating medium of telling. The enfolding space, once again a veranda, sees them simultaneously cover up and uncover for each other their involvement in each stage of the insurrection. With the same syntaxical quirks as found in creole story-telling, the two "mother-figures," Mama Sun and Sister Smoke, recount past dreams of freedom.

Sister Smoke and Rosa even begin to tell "The Tale of the Unknown Beauty" (another splendidly convoluted Ti-Jean quest) at a particularly tricky moment when government troups are about to search their home.[6] Telling the tale helps camouflage the action of shifting the revolutionary leader taking refuge in their house from one hiding space to another. Telling tales, making tales of their own lives, finding themselves in the tales they tell, adopting the suggestivity of the tale's structure as the fundamental means of communicating with and protecting each other from too brutal a confrontation with the truth—are strategies used by the characters which also complicate, thicken, and enrich the spatiotemporal dimension of the play.

Despite what would seem to be well-defined historical time frame for *Fire's Daughters*, as well as for *Island Memories*, despite the apparent importance of the ending of the *Ti-Jean Tale*, what really matters in all three plays, what gives them their special force, is the creation of a spatio-

---

[5] The Southern Insurrection of 1870 saw over 500 agricultural or other workers jailed, and resulted in fierce repression by the colonial government. In the year following the uprising, there were seven consecutive trials which resulted in the imprisonment of some 100 people (cf. Odile Krakovitch).

[6] "The Tale of the Unknown Beauty," one of the tales collected by Ina Césaire during a long period of ethnographic research on Caribbean orality, is another extremely interwoven Ti-Jean story, in which the boy hero finally ends up with the beautiful Princess after a series of impossible tasks imposed on him by the horrible King.

temporal dimension which is *out* of real time and real space. Césaire's plays, like tales, carry their audience to a liminal place, a place where deep psychological effects may indeed take hold.

Such profound effects are also made possible through strategies of characterization. The patently allegorical nature of characters in oral tales and of characters created by Césaire powerfully binds the audience and performers in a rite of lesson-giving and emotional release.[7] In none of her plays does she focus on an individual character's psychological development or self-revelation. The strength of Césaire's stylized characters lies in their stereotypical nature which, through situation and performance, takes on mythic dimensions which speak directly to the collective consciousness.

In her most salient borrowing from the oral tradition, *The Child of Passages*, the character Ti-Jean and his dozen cohorts possess the same traits and dispositions as their counterparts in a multitude of Ti-Jean tales. "Tiger," for example, is a hard-working but somewhat stupid peasant; "Blowfish," the treacherous henchmen of tyrants; "The King," a representative of the neuresthenic white or mulatto ruling classes. Both Ti-Jean tales and Césaire's play rely on these encoded references to communicate their criticisms or offer a lesson. But any morality derived from such stories escapes the iconic confines of the Christian "good man."[8]

In a world of "eat or be eaten," all of Césaire's characters use cleverness, cunning, and guts to get what they want. They refuse the virtues of humility, poverty and acceptance which would undermine their life force. They strive to overcome great obstacles by giving vent to the rage that inhabits them.[9] The oral tradition's adolescent Ti-Jean might, then, be considered an ur-figure for all of Césaire's creations, the real source for her impulse to write plays. Ti-Jean, orphaned (which can also be interpreted as torn from the community of Mother Africa), represents for Césaire the deep psychic structures of Caribbean peoples. Always hungry, always miserable, always having "to walk and walk and walk and still learn how to walk," Ti-Jean exercises his wits to get the best of "The Good Lord," or "The King," "The Devil," "The Giant," or "The Seven-Headed

---

[7] In tale-telling once the teller calls out, "Cric" (Let's begin!), the audience responds, "Crac" (Yes, let's!). In other words, the "fire" is lit.

[8] In this vein, in *The Child of Passages*, the Sorceror tells Ti-Jean what he already knows: "Kabrit ki pa malin pa gra" ["A stupid goat never gets fat."]

[9] In the case of characters Sister Smoke and Anna, their inability to express this rage has led to madness and muteness, infirmities overcome in the course of *Fire's Daughters* through their revolutionary commitment.

Monster"—whatever figure or figures stand for tyrannical and greedy colonial and neo-colonial control.

In *Island Memories*, Aure and Hermancia together represent the resistance force of Martinique and its people. Their separate experiences and sensibilities (the one accepting her "Frenchness," the other foregrounding her African lineage and responding in creole) can be seen as complementary facets, albeit uneasily linked, of the same Caribbean subject. Césaire twice makes this explicit. In the introductory didascalia, she praises them both for their "indomitability." The second time, at the play's end, she juxtaposes a series of comparisons between each woman and the island's prodigious natural treasures. She finishes by building a complicated equine metaphor which positions both Aure and Hermancia as "lightning willed, untethered, and noble."

The women characters in *Fire's Daughters* also stand for a potent wondrousness in the Martinican spirit: burning and vital. Like *Island Memories'* Aure and Hermancia, *Fire's Daughters'* Mama Sun, Sister Smoke, Rosa, and Anna possess elemental strength. They respectively evoke through behavior, personal idiolect, and what they communicate to others, earth, wind, fire, and water. Like Aure and Hermancia, Rosa and Anna are "inverted mirrors" of each other, creating a suspenseful dialectic. With Mama Sun and Sister Smoke, they constitute the past and the future, preserving memory and stretching towards a new direction in which to change and develop. Paradoxical symbols, participating in several worlds, naive and rusé, these characters are meant to generate hope for a new tomorrow. The purifying fire of Rosa, in particular, clears the way of old traditions and constraints.

In Césaire's plays, riddles, allusions, secrets, that which is hidden, and that which needs to be deciphered pull the audience into a movement of mounting expectation and suspense. Yet, as mentioned earlier, the audience is not so much interested in "what happens next" as engaged in basking in the many layers of possible meanings, an engagement not unlike the one elicted in a tale-telling session. Passages leading to more passages, tales embedded in more tales, dance steps frozen as if to recommence in the next moment, and an abundant use of *mise en abyme* endow Césaire's plays with a densely resonant texture. Whether in *Island Memories*, *The Child of Passages* or *Fire's Daughters,* the liminal quality, the sense of not moving linearly but rather plunging more deeply, destabilizes the sense of progress.

Nevertheless, a psychological voyage is underway; and it is a voyage which counts the audience among the travelers. As should be apparent by now, Césaire's plays, like oral tales, like, indeed, ritual theatre and psychodrama, mean to help exorcise major demons, to reconcile the audience-participants to the energies of living and to their own particular lives. Told tales and Césaire's theatricalized ones participate in the community's efforts to keep itself (or make itself) healthy by providing a symbolic space for release and celebration.

Césaire's theatre, then, is quite unlike the 1970s theatrical experiments in the Caribbean which developed what became known as "le nouveau récit," in which tales were rewritten to express pressing political demands.[10] Her plays, like traditional tales, are not meant to spill over into real-life activism; but, rather, provide an opportunity for creative laughter and spiritual blossoming. In *The Child of Passages,* she even adds the character of the "Inverted Man," a figure from her own private psychological arena, to help foreground the relativity of all truth systems. The Inverted Man washes with sand, stands on his hands, sleeps outside his house, and generally presents Ti-Jean with the possibility of reimagining his entire epistemological field.

While "proclaiming Truth" might make her anxious, Césaire does not hesitate to reorient the reigning mythopoesis of the French Antilles by reinserting history into her plays. Her contribution regrounds legendary Caribbean figures and moments closer to her own "home." In incorporating into her dramatic world the Southern Insurrection of Martinique of 1870, by giving it centrality in *Fire's Daughters* as the fragmented main tale, and according it the status of progenitor in *Island Memories* (Aure's mother having been born in the context of the Insurrection), Césaire awards this historical moment pride of place. She thus establishes the Southern Insurrection as the founding moment for her own mythopoeses of the French Caribbean. In this way, she inflects her father Aimé Césaire's impassioned designation of the Haitian Revolution as originary myth. Her tales ultimately link symbolically (and dialogically) several Caribbean islands, nations, and peoples in an effort to birth the Caribbean out of something other than European voyages of "discovery."

By privileging women characters in her plays, Césaire also rethinks the patriarchal bias of the oral tradition which not only posits men as the legitimate storytellers but also consigns female characters to roles of dreaded witches, dead mothers, or dumb-bell fiancées.[11] Her plays, then,

---

[10] This information and other background on Caribbean theatre comes from an interview in Paris with anthropologist Dominique Rolland, January 1994.

[11] The absence in the tales of adult *male* characters who might accompany Ti-Jean also finds an echo in Césaire's plays. Her plays seem to recognize Caribbean men's difficulty in becoming adult heroes when burdened by the history of

are not merely theatricalized transcriptions of tales. Ina Césaire has produced a new theatrical object for potentially building another, perhaps more complex, collective self-image.

WORKS CONSULTED

Césaire, Ina. "Au temps où le bon dieu était un petit garçon," *Diagonales/Le Français dans le monde*, no. 14., avril 1990. pp.16-17.

Césaire, Ina. *Contes de vie et de mort aux Antilles.* (with Joelle Laurent) (Paris: Editions Nubia, 1989).

Césaire, Ina. *Contes de nuit et de jour aux Antilles.* (Paris: Editions Caribéennes, 1989).

---

enslavement and a mythic structure forever threatening "zombification," or transformation into endless servitude.

In *Island Memories*, only one moment calls for the presence of a male character on stage. This moment, however, represents in mime the archetypal rape scene of a white master overcoming a slave. It is a frightening and discouraging scene, both because of the violence inflicted on the female character and because of the evacuation of any possibility of retaliation.

In *Fire's Daughters*, the male character, meant to represent the founding father, the link with Haiti and with Africa, never apppears on stage. Rather, his presence is transmuted into the sound of an off-stage *ti-bwa* (a horizontal percussion instrument local to the islands), itself connected to an on-stage *Assotor* (the symbolic drum of the voodoo religion). Thus, percussion and musical symbolism, instead of flesh and blood, reproduce "the man."

_____ *L'Enfant des passages ou la Geste de Ti-Jean.* (Paris: Editions Caribéennes, 1988).

_____ *Mémoires d'Isles: l'Histoire de Maman N et Maman F.* (Paris: Editions Caribéenes,1986).

_____ *Rosanie Soleil.* np MS.

Gautier, Arlette. *Les Soeurs de Solitude.* Editions Caribéennes, 1985.

Krakovitch, Odile. "Le Rôle des femmes dans l'Insurrection du Sud de la Martinique en septembre 1870," *Nouvelles Questions Féministes,* no. 9-10 (Printemps 1985), pp. 35-51.

Nicolas, Armand. *l'Insurrection du sud de la Martinique (sept. 1870),* Fort de France, 1971, 47 pp.

Pago, Gilbert, "l'Insurrection du sud de la Martinique," *l'Histoire des Antilles,* 1980, T. IV, chap. III, pp. 221-300.

BLOOD, MEMORY AND VOICE

by Peter Hitchcock
Baruch College, CUNY

The inscription of the voice remains a vexing problem for politics and philosophy, indeed a politics of philosophy, since it offers a conundrum about subjectivity, presence, and ontology. The Derridean critique has attempted to undo the privileging of the spoken through the différance of writing but this too comes with a significant pause, for the hermeneutic reverie attached to the sentence (death sentence or *l'arrêt de mort*) might also seem to elide the violence within speech, the power relations that trace the curve between the word and silence. It is ironic that so much postwar French philosophy has been concerned to untie the Gordian knot of speech in Western discourse when many of the philosophers concerned emerged in the shadow of North African decolonization, a postcolonial critical consciousness based, in part, on the insurgent voice.[1] The topic is a complicated one, but for the sake of this argument the disabling of the Master's Voice should not imply the displacement of voice *tout court*, for this would seem to conspire with those ideologies that insistently confer a panoply of silence on those whose voices would otherwise transform it.

Such lessons are not lost on Abdelkebir Khatibi (from Morocco) and Assia Djebar (from Algeria), two writers whose work artfully *de*-scribes or deconstructs French colonial discourse while not sacrificing the scriptible voice that informs such delinking. The complex range of resistance that their works enunciate cannot be sufficiently engaged in the space provided, but I do want to indicate why writing the voice informs North African philosophies of language. I would argue that gender is the central fact of the latter because i) gender differentiation drives the colonial episteme, the desire for the Other constructs the Other as woman, that which must be possessed and assimilated to the Self of masculine certitude; ii) the Law of the Father pre-exists the colonial adventure—it is inscribed in the social

---

[1] This topic is a huge one but it would be interesting to track how thinkers like Derrida, Cixous, and Lyotard steer the Scylla and Charybdis of writing and voice as a postcolonial *de*-scription. While the privileging of voice within Western metaphysics has been rightfully critiqued the question of voice in, say, Algerian culture offers a different order of "being," one with which such philosophers must surely be familiar.

discourses of the Maghreb, sometimes reduced to patriarchal
interpretations of Islam, but also functioning within a more general code
assumed to sanction gender hierarchy (this includes interpretations of
tribal and class-inflected economies of difference); and iii) gender riddles
the language of difference, not just between the alternative and alternating
registers of colonizer and colonized discourses, but also within the
languages of state which have often produced a celebratory masculinism in
articulating the "imagined community" of Nation, however important the
concept of nation has been in delegitimating colonial subjugation. In this
light, both Djebar and Khatibi address a central problem in the languages
of liberation: how can one enunciate a new sense of being (the postcolonial
subject, for instance) when the very process of delinking is grounded in
ontologies of the Male whose power seems to give to that process its logical
integrity?

Several strategies recommend themselves, including *écriture féminine*
(women writing) and *parler-femme* (speaking [as] woman) which both
suggest a deterritorialization of masculine space in language. Again, both
writers are aware of such theoretical approaches—their cosmopolitanism
includes debates with and within Paris (Khatibi, for instance, has been
making use of deconstruction since the early seventies). Yet the point is
that their writing the voice is a politics *in situ*, discursive schema that
differ not only from the perquisites of the Parisian scene, but also from
each other for the Maghreb itself, as Khatibi in particular attests, is plural
and contradictory. For him the central problematic is an *écriture metissée*,
a form of body bilingualism whose apotheosis is the figure of androgyny.
In *Maghrib Pluriel* the counter critique emerges in the realization of
woman's invisible inscription between God and man in Islam: she is "la
mise en abyme de l'ordre théologique."[2] Androgyny then is a doubling in
language, in sexuality, in culture, in being—an ontological iterability.
Djebar reads this agonistic function in postcolonial subjectivity as
irrevocably engendered (that is, before women can be androgynous they
must be themselves) and therefore articulates a "scriptive discontinuity"[3]

---

[2] See, Abdelkebir Khatibi, *Maghrib Pluriel*. Paris: Éditions Denoel, 1983: 23.
Here the invocation of "woman" is explicitly linked to what Khatibi calls the
process of thinking the other in decolonization. In a later chapter, "La sexualité
selon le Coran," ("Sexuality according to the Koran") Khatibi uses the same notion
to question the veiling of women in some interpretations of Islam. It is this, what
he calls "hallucination," of the visible that signs an aporia in Islamic thought.
Djebar, much more than Khatibi, connects this sense of viewing to voicing.

[3] This operates at several levels, not just in the way Djebar's writing breaks from
Algerian forms of masculinism, but also in the disjunction she figures in the

—a discourse of what has been seen as a prelude for what might become. In the interanimation of these diverse counter-hegemonic voices a heteroglossary begins to emerge, one whose philosophy of language is always already a politics of language in contemporary Maghrebi aesthetics.

The first difference in différance in this regard is the tatoo, the literal inscription of the body, a mark or measure that signs are not decolonized univocally, or indeed, unisexually. Khatibi writes of this in *La mémoire tatouée*, his autobiographical novel of 1971, a book that, like much Maghrebi postcolonialism, makes French a stranger to itself. Of course, this also traces the dilemma of subjectivity in the narrative, for the protagonist struggles through an "inner exile" to articulate a Berber dialect transcribed into Arabic then written in French. This is what Khatibi terms "bi-langue"—a language that is neither one nor another, but is the untranslatable, the intractable, the space between languages, the "entretien en abyme" (*Maghrib* 179), the impossible exchange. James McGuire has suggested that this bilingualism registers an attempt to reconstitute the "riven self"[4] but this would imply a whole that pre-exists the disruptions of linguistic codes, yet the translation at issue is much more a "sujet en procès" (subject in process) whose becoming does not mark an a priori self but a subject that has not been. The tatooed memory in this sense, is a trace (la trace) of being under erasure; paradoxically, it is the indelible design of a life Khatibi has not lived (because it is a fiction), but not an origin to which he aspires (e.g. before the French, before the Turks, before the Arabs, before the Romans, before the Berbers, before....).

The tatoo is obviously a cultural signifier in the literal sense, since many Moroccan tribes have used tatoos for symbolic effect (facial and body tatoos may be applied to women prior to marriage, sometimes to men as well—the practice appears in various parts of the Maghreb). Khatibi's

---

relationship of Western and Algerian women (seen, for instance, in her short story "Women of Algiers in their Apartment"). For more on Djebar's sense of this disjunction see the "Afterword" by Clarisse Zimra (which includes an interview not available in the French edition) in Assia Djebar *Women of Algers in Their Apartment*. Trans. Marjolinjn de Jager. Charlottesville: University Press of Virginia, 1992.

[4] See, James McGuire, "Forked Tongues, Marginal Bodies: Writing as Translation." *Research in African Literatures* 23:1 (1992): 107-116. McGuire's essay provides a cogent analysis of Khatibi's translation theory and the "bi-langue" it inscribes. My point here is to note that the splitting of language that Khatibi's writing signifies does not constitute the "wholeness of the bilingual body" somewhere between French and Arabic, but instead registers a profound irreconcilability in the composition or composure of such a body language.

narrator does not remember this form of tatooing, however; what he does recall is his circumcision: "l'éclosion d'une fleur de sang, tatouée entre les cuisses"[5] ("the blooming of a flower of blood, tatooed between the thighs"). While Lucy Stone McNeece correctly underlines that the narrative in general eschews cause and effect, clearly some events tatoo the narrator's being more than others.[6] The narrator remembers his obsession with the scissors tearing his sex and connects this to writing and the imagination as "a motif of his generation."[7] For him, it is a confirmation of patriarchal law, an initiation rite, but it comes with a profound ambivalence, as if he is made neither man nor woman—a pause underlined by his hands being stained with henna accompanied by the exhortation, "Sois homme, sois femme!" (*Memoire* 28) ["Be a man, be a woman!"]. Khatibi's text continually folds back on itself, parabolically, as it tears at the languages and cultures that inform it, but in this moment at least we are made aware that the flux of identity itself is the indelible mark of violence, even as the centrifugal force of "bi-langue" reinscribes this violence within a more general economy of patriarchy, religion, and colonialism. The parabola is also a parable (in French parabole means both).

The parable of decolonization narrates difference, but I would argue that the gendered doubling, the linguistic fracturing, signs differently through and by subjectives states of "being" woman. Khatibi is sensitive to this differentiation—how else to understand the creative intellection of *Amour bilingue* (*Love in Two Languages*)[8] —even as the "threshold of the untranslatable" is drawn through heterosexual erotics. My point is that the masculine autobiography meets its own abyme in envoicing the trace of

---

[5] Abdelkebir Khatibi, *La mémoire tatouée*. Paris: Éditions Denoel, 1971: 27. All French translations are mine unless otherwise indicated.

[6] See, Lucy Stone McNeece, "Decolonizing the Sign: Language and Identity in Abdelkebir Khatibi's *La Mémoire tatouée.*" *Yale French Studies* 83 (1993): 12-29.

[7] Of course, Khatibi is using this image figuratively but it remains a problem, especially in cultures where genital mutilation is engendered differently. Male circumcision, metaphorical or otherwise, is not the equivalent of clitoridectomy.

[8] See, Abdelkebir Khatibi, *Amour bilingue*. Paris: Fata Morgana, 1983. This novel is available in English as *Love in Two Languages*. Trans. Richard Howard. Minneapolis: University of Minnesota Press, 1990. Although I will not be dealing with this superb book on this occasion the inference here is that Khatibi's "bi-langue" is overdetermined by a politics of sexuality that marks a difference with feminism. In a longer version of this essay I consider how love is written otherwise *between* Khatibi and Djebar.

violence, for patriarchy, religion, and colonialism are not primarily, or nominally, a violence against men. There is another way to read this bloody tatoo.

Djebar's *Femmes d'Alger dans leur appartement* (*Women of Algiers in their Apartment*) begins with a scene of torture, a woman is being electrocuted, scarred for her work in the Algerian war of independence. Both Sarah and Leila carry these scars because they carried fire (in the war there were women who attacked the occupying army with grenades— Djebar calls them the "fire carriers," *porteuses de feu*): the tatos are born of insurrection. For Djebar as for Khatibi, scars and scarring are a touchstone of memory, something that must be voiced. But this is not just a question of artistic creativity but one of access to language, to the arena of the *Le Verbe* (that is why in Djebar's quartet, as Mildred Mortimer has pointed out, French ecriture is opposed by Arabic *kalaam*, the colonizing male is disarticulated by the indigenous peasant woman, *l'ecrit* by *les cris*[9]). In the torture scene male violence is written onto the body of the woman: for Djebar, that inscription cannot or should not be silenced, secluded, or veiled. This is one cadence of the discourse of postcoloniality.

The colonizer has memories too, as Djebar evokes in her extraordinary "Postface" to *Women of Algiers* by reference to the "intoxicated gaze" of Delacroix, whose brief encounter with a harem in Algiers in 1832 produces the famous painting (indeed, Djebar borrows the title for her collection of stories). The final essay, "Forbidden Gaze, Severed Sound," dramatizes why a philosophy of language must also write the cognitive and corporeal space of sight and sound specific to women's being, specific to the complex scriptability of an unraveling discourse of domination. Djebar argues that within Delacroix's "stolen glance" (which is also the viewer's who sees this painting) "Elles demeurent absentes à elles-même, à leur corps, à leur sensualité, à leur bonheur" (*Femmes* 173) ["They—the women—remain absent to themselves, to their body, to their sensuality, to their happiness." (*Women* 137) In a sense, they are looking nowhere because, in a cunning reversal and unlike the spectator who mischievously pores over this phantasm, they do not have the right to look.

---

[9] See, Mildred Mortimer, *Journeys Through the French African Novel*. London: Heinemann, 1990: 147-164. Mortimer argues that Djebar explores the space between two languages by writing the Arabic voice into French. This, of course, is part of Khatibi's project but the difference is in the transposition of women's voices in the decolonization of French and, by implication, the Maghreb. Significantly, Mortimer also analyzes how this reinscription is simultaneously a struggle over women's space. See, in particular, Mildred Mortimer, *Assia Djebar*. Philadelphia: CELFAN Monographs, 1988.

Yet it is not just the voyeurism of the colonial gaze that marshalls this figurative absence: it is also the surveillance by the women's own culture that, a century and a half later, and despite a "progressive" relaxation of social codes, continues to situate or condition an affective absence (which is Djebar's way of accentuating that postcoloniality does not imply postpatriarchy).

Like many other writers of Maghrebi decolonization (a list would include Tahar Ben Jelloun, Abdellatif Laâbi, Rachid Boudjedra, Driss Chraïbi, and to some extent the "Beur" voicing of Leïla Sebbar) for Khatibi and Djebar realism is not the medium of counter critique. As the Moroccan Mohammed Khair-Eddine notes in the first issue of *Souffles*, the aim is "un roman complexe où poesie et delire seraient un"[10] ("a complex novel in which poetry and delirium would be one"). In its form and content, Khatibi's *La Mémoire tatouée* displays all the experimental flair of Kateb Yacine's *Nedjma* (indeed, at one point in Khatibi's novel his narrator pays explicit homage to Kateb's inspiration). The prose is marked by consummate digression, irreverence, alienation, displacement, euphoria, citation, but most of all, a commitment to the deracination of French. Thus, Khatibi remarks "la langue française n'est pas la langue française" (*Maghrib* 188) ["French is not French"] and "Chacun de nous souffrait de sa langue maternelle, un seuil de l'affolement. Et peut-être celle qui prend la place de la mère doit devenir folle." (*Amour* 61) ["Each of us suffered from our Mother tongue. And perhaps the language which takes the place of the mother must become mad"] But, as we have already noted with the violence of inscription, the task of postcolonial *de*-scription is not engendered blindly.

Djebar knows that in highlighting the woman question, merely by having women speak (that is, in recording their oral expressions), she runs a gamut of oppositional critique. First, to oppose the marginalization of women in the new society is seen to detract from the integrity of Algerian nationhood (feminism itself can be attacked as colonial baggage). Second, feminism, while certainly not anathema to Islam, is regarded as an affront to conservative interpretations of the Koran and *hadith* and as a profane symptom of non-Arab modernization (given the violence of 1988 and 1992, and the continued instability of Algerian politics this makes Djebar's interventions all the more remarkable). Third, the use of French, even when it attempts to tongue tie His Master's Voice, can be read as complicitous, a cosmopolitanism that again allows the woman question to

---

[10] Quoted in M'hamed Alaoui Abdalaoui, "The Moroccan Novel in French" trans. Jeffrey S. Ankrom, *Research in African Literatures*, 23:4 (1992): 15.

be cathected to an anti-nationalist agenda (of course, that Djebar has
attacked the policy of "Arabization" because "Official Arabic is an
authoritarian language that is simultaneously a language of men" [*Women*
176] has only fanned those particular flames).[11] Fourth and most crucial,
given my own position vis-a-vis Maghrebi writers, there is a strong
tradition of criticism in Maghrebi postcoloniality (the *Souffles* group for
instance) that is highly suspicious of works that (intentionally or not) feed
the ethnographic desire of the West. As M'hamed Alaoui Abdalaoui has
commented on Moroccan novels in French, "in France (and elsewhere in
the West), [such] novels are still universally read as sociological
documents (the most highly prized being those that deal with the condition
of Muslim women)." (Abdalaoui 31) This is not just a knee-jerk
masculinism but is a position shared among some Maghrebi feminists
(Marnia Lazreg for one has pointed out that narratives focusing on the veil,
seclusion, or clitoridectomy play into the obsessive interests of the Western
colonial unconscious—a fetishism inexorably inclined to ingest images of
the oppressed woman *elsewhere*). The last point is difficult, to say the
least, but one that I have attempted to critique at length in my book,
Dialogics of the Oppressed.[12] Here I will say only that the position of
adjudication (or what Foucault calls the subject of the statement) cannot be
produced by the simple displacement of the woman question into categories
of ethnography, sociology, or indeed neo-colonialism (which seems to unite
the other two). If Djebar's fiction has a material correspondence with

---

[11] For more on the contradictions of Arabization see, John Ruedy, *Modern Algeria*.
Bloomington: Indiana University Press, 1992—especially Chapter Seven. What
Djebar "loathes" is not only the patriarchal norms that gird aspects of the Arabic
language but also the fact that the privileging of Arabic is made at great cost of
Kabyle and other Berber languages. The situation is complicated, however, since
historically the Kabyles themselves were the most inclined to Francophonie under
colonialism and in general held higher social ranks than their indigenous
counterparts. Clearly, Arabization was in part aimed at the privilege that had
accompanied the use of French.

[12] This is a controversial topic that cannot be settled here but it remains difficult for
Maghrebi women themselves to articulate an oppositional politics without
reference to the forms of oppression that structure their lived realities. Lazreg's
main target is, of course, Western feminism and its religion/tradition paradigm
where Arab women are concerned. The argument is a forceful one and is
unresolved (if not unresolvable) within the scholarship on this issue. See, Marnia
Lazreg, "Feminism and Difference: the Perils of Writing as a Woman on Women
in Algeria" *Feminist Studies* 14:1 (Spring 1988): 81-107. See also my *Dialogics
of the Oppressed*. Minneapolis: University of Minnesota Press, 1993—especially
Chapter Two.

specific inequalities within Algerian society it is not out of a desire for Western readers (we should remember that *Women of Algiers in Their Apartment* was first published in Algeria), and even if it is, would this constitute adequate grounds for dismissal from *within* the very texture of that lived inequality? Certainly, Euramerican colonial desire remains problematic and continues to be actively undone but there is too much at stake for Djebar to allow the decentering of that desire to detour or defer women's enunciation—a condition that requires even more than a war of independence, but social transformation more broadly construed.

In the first two novels of her quartet (*L'amour, la fantasia* and *Ombre Sultane* translated as *Fantasia* and *A Sister to Scheherazade*) Djebar suggests that the first priority must be the woman's story (l'histoire femme) which artfully links the scriptible voice to memory and so to history.[13] Both books depend upon a canny oscillation not just in the space between languages, but in that which marks the field of the intersubjective and diachronic eventness. These are the weave of the dialogic, itself a significant mark of Djebar's novelistic discourse, but here the point is that Djebar's biculturalism is Khatibi's bi-langue internally distanciated by the woman's voice. This utterance is the product of an arduous collocation of historical research and a painstaking attention to oral traditions. Thus, even as *Fantasia* proceeds by a clever juxtaposition of the French invasion of 1830 with the events leading to the liberation of 1962 the central *histoire* is writing the voice, a question of women's performativity directly linked to aspects of Djebar's upbringing, her acculturation. At one point the narrator comments on the differences among the veiled women of her community, especially that which refuses the realm of silence: for instance, women shouting between their patios:

> To refuse to veil one's voice and to start "shouting," that was really indecent, real dissidence. For the silence of all the others suddenly lost its charm and revealed itself for what it was: a prison without reprieve.

> Writing in a foreign language, not in either of the tongues of my native country—the Berber of the Dahra mountains or the Arabic of the town where I was born—writing has brought me to the cries of the women silently rebelling in my youth, to my own true origins.

---

[13] Assia Djebar, *L'Amour, la fantasia*. Paris: Jean Lattès, 1985. Translated as *Fantasia: An Algerian Cavalcade*. Trans. Dorothy S. Blair. London: Quartet Books, 1989. Assia Djebar, *Ombre Sultane*. Paris: Jean Lattès, 1987. Translated as *A Sister to Scheherazade*. Trans. Dorothy S. Blair. London: Quartet Books, 1987.

Writing does not silence the voice, but awakens it, above all to resurrect so many vanished sisters. (*Fantasia* 204)

Voice does not confirm presence, at least not in the philosophical sense of ontology, but it does imply a thread, one which ties, sometimes imperceptibly, in a historical chain of dissidence in dissonance. The voice is interventionist not just because it textualizes the testimonials of those who have often been confined to the realm of silence or the unheard (and therefore the *inconnue*) but also because it is an agonistic archive, a restless register of what can be said, and differently. Thus, even when the "chronicles of defeat," the defeat of 1830, are the reminiscences of men in the narrative the presence of women begins to seep through: "Ces lettres parlent, dans le fond, d'une Algerie femme impossible à apprivoiser" (*L'Amour* 69) ["between the lines these letters speak of Algeria as a woman impossible to tame"]. H. Adlai Murdoch has suggested that Djebar feminizes the figure of invaded Algeria but in a sense this is always already inscribed in what Jenny Sharpe calls "an allegory of empire."[14] The point is that, while she does not falsify the records, Djebar scrupulously marks the gender trouble that conditions their very possibility, so that the invasion "reverberates with the sound of an obscene copulation" (*Fantasia* 19), one which attempts to objectify and possess in the same instant.

Like Khatibi, Djebar recognizes that the colonial episteme requires a fantastic overinvestment in the colonized as Other. For her part, she presents this delirium as a *fantasia*; specifically, *la fantasia*, the warlike display of Arab horse riding skills in which the riders charge the audience only to stop just before they overrun it, but also the musical reference (common in Europe from the sixteenth century) in which the form of composition is made subservient to "fancy." Surveying Algiers in 1818, Blaquiere described the fantasia as a "paroxysm of passion" which for me connects the violence of one act to the creative reverie of the other. (During a fantasia in Djebar's novel, Haoua, a young Algerian woman is [accidentally!] kicked to death by a horse ridden by a lover she had rejected. The historical incident from which Djebar draws is recorded by Eugene Fromentin in 1852 during the occupation). Today, the Maghrebi fantasia is not just a measure of tribal masculinism but also a bizarre mirror of orientalist desire (and can include "flying carpets," belly dancers,

---

14
See, H. Adlai Murdoch, "Rewriting Writing: Identity, Exile and Renewal in Assia Djebar's *L'Amour, La fantasia.*" *Yale French Studies* 83 (1993): 71-92. I would read Djebar's textual practice as outlined by Murdoch as a de-scription rather than a rewriting, although the general strategies of displacement pinpointed are surely the sine qua non of postcolonial subjecthood. See, also Jenny Sharpe, *Allegories of Empire.* Minneapolis: University of Minnesota Press, 1993.

snake charmers, and any number of generalizations worthy of the tourists' gaze). The fact remains that Djebar tracks the fantastic projections of desire within and without the discourse of culture she articulates (one could also connect this theme to the letter-writing campaign of the adolescent girls in the first part of the narrative).

Khatibi takes the delirium of the fantasia almost to madness, "Cette folie qui nie en s'affirmant dans un double fondement...." (*Amour* 11) ["This madness which repudiates as it affirms itself in a double foundation"). The discrepant doubling invoked occurs at the level of language, sex, location, and indeed in the difference of writing and speech, and writing and music.[15] The "jouissance de l'intraduisible" (the ecstasy of the untranslatable) that Khatibi describes in *Maghreb pluriel* is the paroxysm of passion that drives his *La Mémoire tatouée, Amour bilingue*, and *Le Livre du sang*. My contention is that while Khatibi deploys this violent passion to destabilize the binary logic that fixes the Moroccan subject in subjection he risks reducing the inequalities of social hierarchization purely to functions of language (interestingly, Abdallah Mdarhri-Alaoui refers to this aspect of *Amour bilingue* as a "textual game"[16]). Clearly, Khatibi is as radical as Djebar in challenging the linguistic assumptions of ethnic absolutism in and outside the Maghreb but the ecstasy of bi-langue does not resolve itself in the condensation of androgyny, just as postcoloniality in itself is the process not the product of dysjunction. The *concept* of androgyny is not at issue (for one thing, its etymology is insistently ambivalent and includes not just notions of a simultaneously female/male subject but also intimations of effeminacy and the representation of the eunuch). One could say much more, for instance, about Khatibi's narrator in *Love in Two Languages* stating "And men? They are the women in me." (117) In addition, androgyny complicates theories of the orientalist gaze.[17] But while Khatibi's *métissage* constitutes

[15] This is a point productively developed by McGuire and is essential to understanding the rhythmic complexity of *Amour bilinque*.

[16] Ibid.

[17] . See, Adballah, Mdarhri-Alaoui, "Abdelkébir Khatibi: Writing a Dynamic Identity." Trans. Patricia Geesey. *Research in African Literatures* 23:2 (1992): 167-176. Again, Khatibi is well aware of the political valence of such gaming even as he risks trivializing the strategies he deploys.

[18] For instance, think of the provocation in this snippet from Sir Walter Besant and James Rice's novel of 1878, *By Celia's Arbour*: "A woman without the mystical veil is no woman, but a creature androgynous." A whole history of colonial masculinism fans out from such distinctions.

a radical philosophy of language that is feminist in inclination, woman in his texts is not quite the Other who is artfully deconstructed. When one writes the psyche perhaps one needs Toril Moi's reminder that women are not oppressed because they are "irredeemably Other" but because they are women. Since that is Djebar's starting point perhaps I can close with a comment on her novel of 1991, *Loin de Médine*.[18]

Like *Fantasia*, this novel uses a close reading of history to speak to Algeria's present, in this case to offer a narrative of Islam's flexibility in the final days of the Prophet's life and the aftermath of his death. Djebar supports her tactical contextualization of this moment through respected sources like Ibn Sa'd and al-Tabari, an essential although still a dangerous move in the current political climate (although Djebar was trained as a classical historian). Djebar attempts to round the characters and their everyday interactions by accentuating what is latent in the classical histories; that is, that the wives of the Prophet and other women in their environs were "women of the Verb" and women of action, and were respected as such even if part of their power derived from patriarchal genealogies (for a non-fictional account of this period the work of Leila Ahmed is highly recommended.[19]) The lesson is consistent with Djebar's other works, her double words or dual words are an exhortation to remember, and in that memory to conjure a subjectivity deferred or confined: "Ah, far from Medina, to rediscover the wind, the exhilaration, the incorruptible youth of rebellion." (*Far* 275) This is not idealism, but an utterance contracted to the specificity of context. In October of 1988 in Algiers Djebar saw "blood flowing in the streets." *Far from Madina* is, thus, her book of blood—not a call to arms but a meticulous reconstruction of the spaces through which the voice is engaged. As the singer of satires, the poetess says to Muhajir before he has her teeth pulled out and her hands severed, "My eloquence, my voice will remain when you are dust."

19 See, Assia Djebar, *Loin de Médine*. Paris: Albin Michel, 1991. Translated as Assia Djebar, *Far from Medina*. Trans. Dorothy Blair. London: Quartet Books, 1993. For an informative discussion of this book and an interview with Assia Djebar see, Clarisse Zimra, "'When the Past Answers the Present.'" *Callaloo* 16:1 (1993): 116-131.

(*Far* 106) While hardly a philosophy of language in the accepted sense, it inspires a dissonant writing that now claims greater urgency.

French and British
COLONIAL LANGUAGE
POLICIES:
A Comparative View of
Their Impact on African Literature

by Fredric Michelman
Gettysburg College

"Ma patrie, c'est la langue que j'écris."
Antoine Rivarol

"In 1915, Edmond Laforest, a prominent member of the Haitian literary movement called La Ronde [...] stood upon a bridge, calmly tied a Larousse dictionary around his neck, then proceeded to leap to his death by drowning."

This astonishing event, as reported by H. L. Gates (66), brings into relief the dilemma of the non-European writer trapped in the language of the colonizer (past or present). In particular, it can be seen as symbolic of the problematic linguistic legacy bequeathed by France to her colonial peoples in sub-Saharan Africa.[1] For Africans colonized by the British,

---

[1] It should be pointed out that, more than any other colonial power, French has also maintained tight political and economic control over its former African colonies. With permanent military forces located in strategic areas on the African continent, it has been able to foil several coups and make or break leaders of "independent" francophone nations over the past three decades. It is only recently, with the

similar burdens exist to be sure, but, as I will argue here, French colonial policies had far more serious consequences for African literatures than did those of Great Britain. As one considers the literary output of Africa south of the Sahara, one is struck by two phenomena: first, the vast bulk of writing in *African* languages is to be found in the former British colonies, and, second, those writing in English have, on the whole, demonstrated a greater degree of adaptability of African speech patterns to the language of the colonizer. How can one account for this paucity of African language literatures and a greater fidelity to the "mother tongue"—i.e., French—in francophone Africa? At the outset, I believe it is essential to examine the unique importance that the French attach to their language and culture. How this vision was translated into certain specific policies in the colonies will then be compared with the attitudes and policies of the British. Finally, the ways in which these differing policies resulted in divergent linguistic legacies will be outlined and briefly illustrated by comparative literary texts. It is important to understand that, insofar as writing in English and French is concerned, what is being discussed here involves relative, not absolute, divergences, and any such demonstration would be misleading if it did not take into account the few francophone writers who do not fit the theoretical mold.

"Tout Français, ou presque, se sent ou se croit grammairien de droit divin" (Almost every Frenchman believes himself to be a grammarian by divine right.).[2] This tongue in cheek remark by the linguist Pierre Alexandre, contains more than a grain of truth. Indeed, he goes on to note that, "La France est, autant que je sache, le seul pays au monde où la plupart des journaux populaires possèdent une chronique grammaticale régulière" (35) (France is, as far as I know, the only country in the world where most popular newspapers have a regular column on grammatical usage). More alarming (and even less comprehensible to native English speakers) is the declaration by Sorbonne professor René Etiemble: "The French language is a treasure. To violate it is a crime. Persons were shot during the war for treason. They should be punished for degrading the language" (quoted in Lockwood). Surely, few native French speakers would subscribe to this extreme position, but the foregoing does reflect the unique preoccupation—some would say, obsession—the French have exhibited with their language for centuries.

---

devaluation of the CFA Franc which is closely tied to the French Franc, that France's economic grip on these countries has begun to weaken somewhat.

[2] All translations my own unless otherwise indicated.

The British, by contrast, have rarely displayed this protectiveness of and almost mystical attachment to their native tongue. In 1539, François I signed an ordinance at Villers-Cotterêts imposing the use of French in all official documents. This historic event not only signaled one of the first French acts of liberation from Latin, but also marked the beginning of a policy suppressing other languages spoken throughout France in the affirmation of centralized power. The 16th century also saw the publication of DuBellay's celebrated *Défense et illustration de la langue française* (1549), a manifesto of the Pléiade group affirming the excellence of French as a literary language. But it was in the 17th century, with the writings of the poet Malherbe and the grammarian Vaugelas and the founding of the Académie Française by Richelieu (an institution that has survived into the 20th century), that the purification and reform of the language began in earnest. The claim of the superiority of French, owing to its crystal clarity and rigor which dates from this period, as well as a vigorous protection of it from outside impurities, continues even to our day, as the above quotation from Etiemble attests. A recent *New York Times* article reported on the French government's proposal of a law to prohibit the use of foreign words from virtually all public government and commercial communications "whenever a 'suitable local equivalent' exists in French" (Simmons A1).

This attempt by the French at legislating language usage is nothing new and is of course a circling of the wagons against the pervasive incursions of English into modern-day French. But it also reflects a long-standing and deep-seated conviction that their language is intimately tied to their identity and grandeur as a nation and as a civilization. In the above-cited *New York Times* article, Prime Minister Edouard Balladur asserts that defending the French tongue is "an act of faith in the future of our country" (Simmons A14), and his Minister of Culture, Jacques Toubon, would later declare in support of the law that, for the French, their language "is their primary capital, the symbol of their dignity, the passageway to integration, the diapason of a universal culture, a common heritage, part of the French dream" (quoted in Riding). Indeed, language is seen as the supreme civilizing force and, given the belief in the superiority of theirs, over the centuries the French have deemed it their sacred mission to bring its benefits to those unfortunate enough not to speak it. If "inferior" languages do exist, however, there are no intrinsically inferior peoples, in keeping with the egalitarian ideals of the French Revolution, only those who are at a lower level of development. Western humanistic values, best embodied in French culture and language, the argument runs, are therefore "universal" and are accessible to all. Thus the 18th century writer Rivarol could assert: "Sure, sociable, reasonable, it is no longer only the French language, it is *the* human language" (quoted in Gordon 203; emphasis in the original); and the 20th century philosopher Etienne Gilson could write: "Notre particularité, c'est notre universalité" ("Our particularity is our universality") (quoted in Betts 27). Many critics have characterized this so-called "universalism" as blatant ethnocentrism (Gordon 8-9), and it is clear that this principle justified for France the "civilizing mission" carried out in Africa and elsewhere in the French Empire.

If the French colonial policy was based on the concept of "identity," that is, the belief that the political and cultural destinies of their subjects would eventually coincide with their own, the attitude of the British was rather one of "differentiation" which envisioned separate development of African peoples "and maintained, therefore, a social and cultural gap between European and African" (Spencer 542).[3] Although both philosophies are based on convictions of cultural superiority, as we will see, they resulted in rather different colonial language policies.

As a general rule, the British encouraged the use of indigenous languages in their colonial schools, in literature and even occasionally in administration. Albert Gérard has shown the important role that Protestant missionaries played in British Africa during the early years to foster direct knowledge of the Scriptures through the transcription and teaching of African languages (177-182). He points out that, unlike the spiritual and institutional centrism of the Catholic Church, Protestantism, with its emphasis on the individual's direct relationship to God, was intensified in Britain by that nation's tradition of individual rights and parliamentary democracy. Such missionary activities had important consequences, not the least of which was the virtual creation of African linguistics by German-speaking Protestant missionaries in the 19th century. In British Africa, with time, the transcription of strictly religious African language texts was expanded to the publication of secular ones. Some African pupils were even encouraged to try their hand at original composition, and the origins of modern *written* African language literatures can be traced to these modest beginnings.[4]

Insofar as educational policies are concerned, the issuance of the Phelps-Stokes Fund reports after World War I, emphasizing the vital importance of the use of native languages in schools, doubtless had an

---

[3] The conventional term describing the British colonial approach is "indirect rule."

[4] Although prior to Western colonization, most Sub-Saharan African languages existed only in oral form, several written indigenous literatures have thrived for hundreds of years in both East and West Africa. See Gérard x-xii.

important impact. They stated emphatically that "no greater injustice can be committed against a people than to deprive them of their own language" (Gérard 183). Shortly after the publication of these reports, the British government issued official guidelines which asserted the "primary importance of the use of African languages in its schools" (Gérard 183). Indeed, it became standard practice throughout the British territories to introduce local languages as the medium of instruction during at least the first two years of primary school. But beyond this, from the 1920's on, serious efforts were made by various governmental, missionary and private organizations to foster creative writing in African languages, including the regular awarding of literary prizes. Over the years, these efforts have borne fruit and important bodies of literature have appeared in Twi, Yoruba, Hausa, Swahili, Zulu, Xhosa, Sotho and other languages spoken in areas once colonized by the British.

The situation in French Africa proved to be quite different. Two major factors were at work here: first, in the earlier days of colonization, education was in the hands of Catholic missionaries who had inherited from the Roman empire a strong tendency toward linguistic and cultural centrism. This inclination, coupled with France's strong propensity for cultural imperialism, led to schooling that was virtually entirely in French and to the resulting devaluation of African languages. Around the turn of the 20th century, missionary influence waned rapidly and the French government assumed responsibility for colonial education. Echoing earlier directives, the decree of 10 May, 1924 clearly stated: "Article 64: Le français est seul en usage dans les écoles. Il est interdit aux maîtres de se servir avec leurs élèves des idiomes du pays" (Moumouni 55) 'French only is to be used in schools. It is forbidden for teachers to speak to pupils in the local languages.' But beyond this prohibition was the intimidating ban imposed on the students themselves by means of the infamous system known as "le symbole": an object (such as a box of matches) was circulated from student to student as each was caught by his classmate speaking his native tongue. At the end of the day, the unlucky holder of the "symbole" was subjected to corporal punishment by the teacher. Moreover, neologisms and ungrammatical French were severely suppressed. (Yves Person has pointed out that "French is the only language in the world where the same word [une faute] signifies a moral offense and a spelling [or grammatical] error" [102].) Alexandre sums up the situation with his usual sardonic verve:

> La politique coloniale française en matière d'éducation et d'administration est facile à définir: c'est celle de François Ier, de Richelieu, de Robespierre et de Jules Ferry. Une seule langue est enseignée dans les écoles, admise dans les

tribunaux, utilisée dans l'administration: le français, tel que défini par les avis de l'Académie et les décrets du ministre de l'Instruction publique. Toutes les autres langues ne sont que folklore, tutu panpan, obscurantisme, biniou et bourrée, et ferments de désintégration de la République. (111-12)

French colonial policy regarding education and administration is easy to define: it is that of François I, Richelieu, Robespierre and Jules Ferry. Only one language is taught in the schools, allowed in the courts, used in the administration: French, as defined by the judgments of the Academy and the decrees of the Minister of Public Education. All other languages are nothing but folklore, gibberish, obscurantism, mumbo-jumbo and seeds of the disintegration of the Republic.

Frantz Fanon, in *Black Skin, White Masks*, analyses the almost pathological response of educated West Indians vis-à-vis the French language: anything less than pure Parisian (such as the use of Creole or a West Indian accent) relegates the speaker to a less human category. In the same vein, Paulin Hountondji, wrote in *Présence Africaine*: "The linguistic behavior of the African, when expressing himself in French, has all the characteristics of a neurosis." He describes this neurotic obsession with the search for linguistic perfection in French as contributing to the intellectual's increasingly impoverished rapport with his native language (13 and 20). As a corollary to the draconian imposition of French in the schools, there was thus a simultaneous devaluation of African "dialects" (a "dialect" presumably being something less than a "language"), justified in part by the spurious theory of superior and inferior languages (see Calvet Chapter 5 and passim). In these circumstances, it is not at all surprising that no encouragement was given by the French government to the transcription and use of African languages in its colonies.

Before proceeding to the consequences of these policies, an observation on French colonial policy is in order. Although the assimilationist principle of making all Africans French cultural clones persisted as an ideal throughout the colonial period, in practice it was only seriously applied in education after World War II. During the first half of the 20th century, this approach was modified by the principle of "adaptation" whereby a very limited number of African children were exposed to a simplified curriculum designed to train a small cadre of loyal, mainly low-level subordinates to assist the colonial administration. A very few were able to obtain more standard university-level degrees and it is from their ranks and from those of the immediate post-World War II university graduating classes that most of the contemporary francophone writers emerged.

One of the most obvious legacies of the two respective colonial systems—the British and the French—is that until recently, as we have noted, writing in African languages was to be found almost exclusively in the former British territories. This applies not only to imaginative literature, but to non-fiction, religious materials and various forms of print journalism as well. By contrast, in the areas once controlled by France, virtually all books, newspapers, and magazines were (and still are) in French.

The French colonial language policy has had other inhibiting consequences as well. Figures dating from the late 1950's indicate that school enrollment ratios, literacy rates and other cultural indices were considerably higher in the former British colonies.[5] For Abdou Moumouni, the explanation of this state of affairs lies "not in any philanthropic tendency of English colonization compared with the French, but rather in the objectively greater possibilities of cultural development which flow from even partial use of African languages in schools" (172). And psycholinguistic studies strongly support the view that a child's cognitive development is enhanced when learning occurs in the mother tongue (Schmied 103). Moreover, the imposition of French at the earliest stages of schooling, accompanied by a curriculum valuing exclusively French civilization, created an unnatural dichotomy in the mind of the child: French becomes the language of literacy, modernity and culture, the mother tongue being relegated to the oral vehicle of a supposedly outdated tradition. (It should be noted parenthetically that, especially since independence, the governments of some former French colonies have encouraged the development of literacy and written literature in indigenous languages. Their activities in this respect are very likely to increase.)

When one turns to the vast and flourishing literatures from Africa written in English and French, the impact of the respective colonial legacies may be somewhat less obvious but it is nonetheless real. In a convincing example of what he calls "extending the frontiers of English so as to accommodate African thought patterns," Chinua Achebe writes:

---

[5] See Moumouni 169-176. Figures for 1984 continued to show significant disparities, especially in primary enrollment ratios and literacy rates:

	Primary Enrollment Ratios	Literacy Rate
Francophone Africa:	46	18
Anglophone Africa:	77	40

(Bray et al., cited in Moroney 1090)

Allow me to quote a small example, from *Arrow of God* which may give some idea of how I approach the use of English. The Chief Priest is telling one of his sons why it is necessary to send him to church:

"I want one of my sons to join these people and be my eyes there. If there is nothing in it you will come back. But if there is something there you will bring home my share. The world is like a Mask, dancing. If you want to see it well you do not stand in one place. My spirit tells me that those who do not befriend the white man today will be saying had we known tomorrow."

Now supposing I had put it another way. Like this for instance:

"I am sending you as my representative among those people—just to be on the safe side in case the new religion develops. One has to move with the times or else one is left behind. I have a hunch that those who fail to come to terms with the white man may well regret their lack of foresight."

The material is the same. But the form of the one is in character and the other is not." (29)

But had not Camara Laye in *L'Enfant noir*, writing in French sixteen years earlier, already provided in a sense, the kind of "out-of-character" example imagined by Achebe? The situation is similar: young Laye's father is encouraging his son to attend school in France:

"Chacun suit son destin, mon petit; les hommes n'y peuvent rien changer. Tes oncles aussi ont étudié. Moi—mais je te l'ai déjà dit: je te l'ai dit, si tu te souviens quand tu es parti pour Conakry—moi, je n'ai pas eu leur chance et moins encore la tienne. . . .Mais maintenant que cette chance est devant toi, je veux que tu la saisisses; tu as su saisir la précédante, saisis celle-ci aussi, saisis-la bien! Il reste dans notre pays tant de choses à faire. . . .Oui, je veux que tu ailles en France; je le veux aujourd'hui autant que toi-même: on aura besoin ici sous peu d'hommes comme toi. . . .Puisses-tu ne pas nous quitter pour trop longtemps!. . ."(247)[6]

"Each one follows his own destiny, my son. Men cannot change what is decreed. Your uncles too have had an education. As for me—but I've already told you; remember what I said when you went away to Conakry— I hadn't the opportunities they had, let alone yours. This opportunity is within your reach. You must seize it. You've already seized one, seize this one too, make sure of it. There are still so many things to be done in our land. . . .Yes, I want you to go to France. I want that now, just as much as you do. Soon we'll be needing men like you here. . . .May you not be gone too long!" (182)

---

[6] While it is true that I have argued elsewhere (see my "From *L'enfant noir* to *The Dark Child*: the Drumbeat of Words Silenced") that certain repetitive passages in *L'enfant noir* might have been influenced by the Malinké oral tradition, the fact remains that, overall, Laye's prose, although compelling, falls well within the bounds of standard French literary usage.

The fathers in both these novels are meant to be speaking their mother tongue, but whereas, by all accounts, Achebe has masterfully captured the flavor of Ibo imagery, the reader is hardly aware that Laye's dialogues are being spoken in his native Malinké. Certainly this scene is touching, given its context, but Laye's language does not impart the sense of authenticity created by Achebe's prose. It has often been noted that especially the first generation francophone novel "remained very close to French models," frequently echoing the manner of a Balzac or a Zola (Dabla 13-15; 50-54). There is little in these works to compare with the experimentation, the "stretching" of the European language as Soyinka has called it, that has occurred in such anglophone authors as Gabriel Okara or Ken Saro-Wiwa, or with the more or less "unconscious" liberties that Amos Tutuola or the "Onitsha Market Literature" authors have taken with the Queen's English. Limitations of space preclude further extensive quotation, but a final comparative example will suffice to make the stylistic point. Both of the following texts describe a sunset, the first being drawn from Cheikh Hamidou Kane's *Ambiguous Adventure* (originally written in French) and the second from *The Voice* by the anglophone writer Gabriel Okara:

> A l'horizon, il semblait que la terre aboutissait à un gouffre. Le soleil était suspendu, dangereusement, au-dessus de ce gouffre. L'argent liquide de sa chaleur s'était resorbé, sans que sa lumière eût rien perdu de son éclat. L'air était seulement teinté de rouge et, sous cet éclairage, la petite ville soudain paraissait appartenir à une planète étrange. (93)

> On the horizon, it seemed as if the earth were poised on the edge of an abyss. Above the abyss the sun was suspended, dangerously. The liquid silver of its heat had been reabsorbed, without any loss of its light's splendor. Only the air was tinted with red, and under this illumination the little town seemed suddenly to belong to a strange planet. (68)

> ***

> "It was the day's ending and Okolo by a window stood. Okolo stood looking at the sun behind the tree tops falling. The river was flowing, reflecting the finishing sun, like a dying away memory. It was like an idol's face, no one knowing what is behind. Okolo at the palm trees looked. They were like women with hair hanging down, dancing possessed. . . .And, on the river, canoes were crawling home with bent backs and tired hands, paddling. A girl with only a cloth tied around her waist and the half-ripe mango breasts, paddled, driving her paddle into the river with a sweet inside. (26)

The passage from *Ambiguous Adventure* is very beautiful but lies strictly within the purest French classical literary tradition. The English of *The Voice* has been molded to reflect the imagery and syntax of the author's native Ijaw. Okara has written the following on his intentions:

> As a writer who believes in the utilization of African ideas, African philosophy and African folk-lore and imagery to the fullest extent possible, I am of the opinion the only way to use them efficiently is to translate them almost literally from the African language native to the writer into whatever European language he is using as his medium of expression. I have endeavored in my words to keep as close as possible to vernacular expressions. For, from a word, a group of words, a sentence and even a name in any African language, one can glean the social life of a people.
>
> [A] writer can use the idioms of his own language in a way that is understandable in English. If he uses their English equivalents, he would not be expressing African ideas and thoughts, but English ones.
>
> Some may regard this way of writing in English as a desecration of the language. This is of course not true. Living languages grow like living things, and English is far from a dead language. ("African Speech" 137)

It seems clear that the language policy, indeed the entire educational enterprise imposed by the French in their colonial territories, inhibited this kind of linguistic adaptation and sent the very distinct message to their students that such deviation would very surely be a "desecration" of the language and spirit of Racine and Descartes, a desecration that could not be tolerated.

It would be grossly misleading, however, to leave the impression that no efforts have been made by francophone writers to break through the constraints of linguistic orthodoxy in order to forge a new language resonating with African speech patterns. The example that first springs to mind is the very successful novel by Ahmadou Kourouma, *Les soleils des indépendances*, and others can certainly be cited. But as Chantal Zabus has demonstrated in her important study, *The African Palimpsest*, francophone authors who have attempted to "indigenize" their texts are not only far fewer in number, but generally neglect a technique she terms "relexification" which uses European vocabulary, "but indigenous structures and rhythms" (the formulation is Loreto Todd's, qtd. in Zabus 101).[7]

Zabus also raises, but does not pursue, an interesting hypothesis: the more successful indigenization on the part of anglophone writers may be due in part to the inherent flexibility of English as opposed to the "intrinsic rigidity of the French language" (see Zabus 23, 122; see also Saro-Wiwa's observation on the same subject, qtd. In Zabus 174). This is an idea that certainly merits further research but is also one requiring expertise in

---

[7] See also Zabus's discussion of pidgin usage and other anglophone/francophone comparisons: 23, 91-93, 122, 157-58, and 170-71.

comparative linguistics and familiarity with the African language(s) in question.

Finally, no discussion of the use of European languages by African writers can ignore the larger language controversy currently raging in African literary circles. Many Africans have called into question the authenticity of any work by an African not composed in an African language. One of the most vocal spokesmen for this point of view is of course the Kenyan writer Ngugi wa Thiong'o who holds that books by such authors as Soyinka, Armah, Sembène or Senghor belong to English or French literature and cannot be called "African." At the very most, one can term them "Afro-European literature." By their very choice of language moreover, these writers cut themselves off from the great mass of the African public who, by and large, do not know enough English or French to read them. "Some are coming round to the inescapable conclusion," Ngugi asserts, "[that] African literature can only be written in African languages" (27). Many Africans writing in English or French do not share this view as can be inferred from the passages quoted earlier from Achebe and Okara. Only time will sort out this immensely complex issue.

Whatever directions written African literatures may take away from the European model in the next few decades—whether involving increased use of African languages, greater indigenization of European language texts, or, as is likely, a combination of the two—it seems clear that writers from countries once colonized by the British have a distinct head start on their French-speaking counterparts.

In the long term however, the situation in francophone Africa is not beyond hope. As neocolonial influences gradually wane, it is highly probable that most African writers will create in the idioms actually spoken by their people. In some cases this will be in the more tenacious of the existing African languages; in others, creolized versions of French will establish themselves as legitimate literary languages. This should close the unnatural gap that now exists between many African authors and their rightful audience.

WORKS CITED

Achebe, Chinua. "English and the African Writer." *Transition* 4.18 (1965): 27-30.

Alexandre, Pierre. *Langues et langage en Afrique Noire*. Paris: Payot, 1967.

Betts, Raymond F. *Assimilation and Association in French Colonial Theory 1890-1914*. New York: Columbia UP, 1961.

Bray, Mark, Peter B. Clarke, and David Stephens. *Education and Society in Africa*. London: Edward Arnold, 1986.

Calvet, Louis-Jean. *Linguistique et colonialisme*. Paris: Petite Bibliothèque Payot, 1979.

Dabla, Séwanou. *Nouvelles écritures africanes*. Paris: L'Harmattan, 1986.

Le français hors de France: Dakar 1973 (5e Biennale de la langue française). Dakar: NEA, 1975.

Gates, Henry Louis, Jr. *Loose Canons*. New York: Oxford UP, 1992.

Gérard, Albert S. *African Language Literatures*. Harlow, Essex: Longman, 1981.

Gordon, David C. *The French Language and National Identity 1930-1975*. The Hague: Mouton, 1978.

Hountondji, Paulin. "Charabia et mauvaise conscience." *Présence Africaine* 61 (1967): 11-31.

Kane, Cheikh Hamidou. *L'aventure ambigüe*. Paris: Julliard, 1961. Trans. By Katherine Woods as *Ambiguous Adventure*. New York: Collier-Macmillan, 1969.

Kourouma, Ahmadou. *Les soleils des indépendances*. Paris: Seuil, 1970.

Laye, Camara. *L'Enfant noir*. Paris: Plon, 1953. Trans. as *The Dark Child*. New York: Farrar, Strauss and Giroux, 1969.

Lockwood, Allison. "Legislating Language: Will It Work?" *The Wall Street Journal*, 13 Mar. 1973: 22.

Michelman, Fredric. "From *L'enfant noir* to *The Dark Child*: The Drumbeat of Words Silenced." *Toward Defining the African Aesthetic*. Ed. Lemuel A. Johnson. Washington, DC: Three Continents, 1982. 105-11.

Moroney, Sean, ed. *Africa, Volume 2*. New York and Oxford: Facts on File, 1989.

Moumouni, Abdou. *L'Education en Afrique* (2nd ed.). Paris: Maspero, 1967.

Ngugi wa Thiong'o. *Decolonizing the Mind*. London: James Currey, 1986.

Okara, Gabriel. "African Speech. . . . English Words." *Transition* 3.10 (1963), 15-16.

———. *The Voice*. New York: Africana, 1969.

Person, Yves. "Impérialisme linguistique et colonialisme." *Les Temps Modernes* 324-326 (1973): 90-118.

Riding, Alan. "Mr. 'All-Good' of France, Battling English, Meets Defeat." *The New York Times*, 7 Aug. 1994: 6.

Rivarol, Antoine. *Discours sur l'universalité de la langue française*. 1784.

Schmied, Josef J. *English in Africa: An Introduction*. London: Longman, 1991.

Simmons, Marlise. "Bar English? French Bicker on Barricades." *The New York Times*, March 15, 1994: A1 and A14.

Spencer, John. "Colonial Language Policies and their Legacies." *Current Trends in Linguistics, Vol. 7, Linguistics in Sub-Saharan Africa.* Ed. Thomas A. Sebeok. The Hague: Mouton, 1971, 537-547.

Zabus, Chantal. *The African Palimpsest: Indigenization of Language in the West African Europhone Novel.* Amsterdam: Rodopi, 1991.

The Current State of Writing and Publishing in National Languages, LITERATURES IN MALI TODAY: The Case of Bamanankan

by Bob Newton
University of Wisconsin, Madison

To begin this presentation on "The Current State of Writing and Publishing of National Languages Literatures in Mali Today: The Case of Bamanankan" (known as Bambara to many, the most widespread language in Mali), I would like to point out the contradiction in the title of the conference, "Beyond Survival: African Literature and the Search for New Life," as it applies to Mali. The oral tradition continues to flourish in Mali today as it enters into new forms with the expansion of independent and affiliated radio stations, the explosion of the cassette industry, and the dramatic spread of television and videos. Yet the efforts put forward to establish literacy and literatures in the national languages since independence have yet to prove themselves as sustainable. What has become apparent in the course of post independence efforts to promote national languages literacy and literature is that survival is not possible without the ability and the will to envision that state which lies beyond mere survival. What needs to be developed is an environment in which national languages literatures not only survive but blossom and bear fruit, constantly interpreting and transforming the cultural heritages from which they have grown. They need to continue to inform and to express the lives and the relations of the people in the communities of their readers and writers. In particular, I would like to emphasize the need for the creation of national languages literatures in order to make possible the programs of functional literacy that are so needed and sought after in Mali today. Although most current projects follow the conventional wisdom in presuming the need to focus on the obvious prerequisite of literacy first, literacy and literature must develop together if either is to be successful.

After putting forward some of the arguments for the need to create national languages literatures and describing some of the current conditions and difficulties they face, I will look at the personal and working experiences of two writers currently expressing themselves in the Bamana language, Ismaila Samba Traore and Berehima Wulale, to illustrate these points. In examining their writings, the forces that compelled them to write, and the struggles to get these publications to their readers, we can see that the development of literacy and of national languages literatures are not independent concerns in the case of Mali. What is needed for both to be successful is the creation of a general environment conducive to the use of written languages and the development of a viable publishing industry for national languages. It also becomes apparent that the need for individual initiative and courageous commitment needs to be accompanied by coordination and collaboration in the use of limited resources.

The first argument for the necessary development of national languages literature is the need for reading materials which engage the new readers of the various literacy projects in Mali. Secondly, in order for any of the literacy campaigns to succeed, they must take place within an environment conducive to the achievement and maintenance of these skills. Such an environment must include the incentive of practical applications of national languages literacy. What is needed to establish these practical incentives is the general popularization and expansion of national languages into all domains. Although certain initiatives have been taken on the part of the media television, radio, and especially the growing number of national languages newspapers, the government has shown more sensitivity than comprehensive planning or concrete action in regard to expanding their use in government or education. For example, all ministers and top level administrators are required to become literate in a national language of their choice but all national identity cards are written only in French and the government and its ministries have yet to develop and implement a final plan in regard to the expanded use of national languages in the formal school system, even after studies and evaluations of almost fifteen years of national languages experimental schools.

The Direction Nationale de l'Alphabetisation et de la Linguistique Applique, or DNAFLA, as well as producing journals in national languages, has been the principal publisher of texts designed for general literacy programs and for those of specific development projects. But linguists are not necessarily creative writers. Teachers, students, and development workers alike have complained of the dryness of these texts; they fail to engage the readers through their own cultural expressions and genres, or the social contexts and activities of their everyday lives. And they lack the narrative excitement that is found in the oral genres which are still the main form of verbal expression and entertainment in Mali today.

The creation of vigorous national languages literatures is a necessary complement, not a threat to continued interest in oral genres or French language literatures. In regard to the former, the art of *jeliya*, the use of speech and music by the occupational caste of *jeliw* who engage in the public performance of epic histories, family genealogies, personal praise, as well as for purposes of general advice, negotiation, and public speaking, has gone through a major transformation in response to new technologies and changing economic and social relations. The advent of recording studios and state run radio stations has been followed in the last decade by the introduction of television, audio and video cassettes, and most recently, a proliferation of affiliated and independent radio stations. These developments have provided new means of contact, new fame, and new economic opportunities for many *jeliw* but have altered the nature of *jeliya* in the process.

Many of the longer narratives of the epic traditions have now made their way onto cassette, but it is the *jelimusow* and some of their male counterparts who have saturated the Malian cassette market and the airwaves, largely reducing the practice of *jeliya* to the performance of praise songs. The bonds that linked members of this occupational caste to a particular host family have been loosened and, as a result, many of the critical features of *jeliya* have been lost: notably the recounting of family, community, and regional histories; the imparting of advice regarding personal conduct and social relations; and in general providing the continuity of the cultural heritage as contained in the once popular longer narratives.

To fill this gap, new masters and guardians of the word must take up the challenge to provide narrative forms using cultural expression for social education. They must address themselves to the differing levels of literacy and education, social location, and activities and interests found in the various communities throughout the country. As well as reaching the newly literate of the countryside, these writers must engage recent migrants to the cities and urban intellectuals. Whereas they cannot be all things to all people, these writers must take up the task of expanding the use of national languages writings into new domains capable of expressing new ideas and issues, and at the same time express them in a form which reflects the styles and genres of established and popular practice. Many of the intellectuals who have dedicated themselves to writing in national languages were educated in French. For them it is the first language of literacy and certain intellectual domains. Initially they began thinking and writing many of their compositions in French first and then translated into a national language, and only through the development of new habits have they been able to achieve a fuller written expression in their first spoken language. Clearly, translating into Bamana thoughts and expressions orignally conceived in French is not sufficient. Nor should readers of Bamanankan be restricted to transcriptions of oral performances. Written and spoken languages should complement, not compete with one another.

In regard to French language literatures, the resistance to the development of national languages literatures and other media productions found in the policies of the institutions of Francophonie presumes an inevitable competition, cultural and economic, within a limited market. The evidence, however, is to the contrary. Studies conducted on learning within bilingual or multilingual contexts in general, and evaluations of Mali's experimental schools in national languages, have cited the efficacy of the convergent method in which students are first taught in the first language. In teaching literacy first in the language of the cultural and social context in which the students are living and learning, it is then possible to transfer the developed lingistic understanding to that of another language. Learning in the two languages is carried on simultaneously rather than one replacing the other. The result of evaluations of students in Mali have demonstrated that those who are educated in their own languages first, through use of the convergent method, outperform those who have conducted their studies in French, even on the French language portion of the exams. Given that the figures on literacy (and French proficiency) in Mali are still well below 20%, among the lowest in the world, the emphasis on French competency first is clearly a mistake in a country where it is the first language of virtually no one and where Bamana is the first language of 40% of the population and spoken by 80% overall.

As this pertains to the development of a viable publishing industry in Mali, in any language, the first obvious constraint is the lack of a readership. Literacy skills need to be developed first but the incentive and desire to read must follow. Incentive is related to the expansion of national languages use into new domains and activities. Desire is created and satisfied through the writing, production, and availability of interesting written materials. In order to develop the structures needed to foster an incipient publishing and distribution, there must be the coordination and collaboration of interested parties in the use and expansion of limited resources and professional skills.

A small number of publishing houses have developed in the wake of the demise of the previously state-run publishing industry which lacked in responsiveness to its limited market and failed to develop effective distribution networks or professionally trained workers. Most bookstores and libraries in Mali have many shelves but few books. The first challenge is to publish high-quality, affordable materials that are of interest to a developing readership.

In 1986, the Jamana cultural cooperative became the first independently owned and operated publishing house and distribution company. Its dedication to the development of national languages was and is tied to a continuation of the push toward independence, democracy, and decolonization. In general, the question of distribution has taken a back seat to its many other activities including the immense effort to establish the viability of a self-sufficient publishing and printing house independent of collaboration with foreign companies and agencies. It enjoyed reasonable success, but currently has suffered frequent attacks and significant damage from anti-government opposition forces due to the prior involvement of the current president of the republic in its development.

Sahelienne Edition, on the other hand, has begun by procuring significant funding from several sources, especially through non-governmental organizations and the donors that fund them. It has concentrated on developing the distribution network that is critical for success, mostly through personal contacts with adjustments to ensure professionalism and efficacy. In realizing this goal of correcting the imbalance regarding the availability of writing in national languages vis-a-vis those in French, it has relied heavily on input from international organizations interested in literacy and education. As well as publishing the monthly Bamana language newspaper, *Saheli*, it has several publishing projects in national languages and holds week-long seminars to encourage and train developing national language writers.

The approach taken by Jamana is in keeping with the quest for a truly independent publishing house. Sahelienne Edition, however, takes advantage of the overwhelming presence of non-governmental development organizations in Mali today and uses their money and support to set up the structures for the publishing and distribution of national languages materials. In their view, it is first necessary to supply the potential reading public with affordable books and newspapers in order both to inform them and to establish reading habits, leaving the question of establishing a financially independent publishing industry for later.

Ismaila Samba Traore

Ismaila Samba Traore began his literary career in French, like those of the novelists of the generation before his, many of whom had dedicated themselves to the Negritude project of legitimating and recognizing the value of their own cultural heritage. But the concerns of Traore and his generation were neither the colonial presence nor the validation of their own cultural heritage but rather the correction of the cultural imbalance left in the wake of colonialism, conditions which carryover into the present. His novel, *Les Ruchers de la Capitale*, which made use of several Bamana words to reflect cultural specificity in his descriptions of the conditions of the disenfranchised of the capital city and their struggles with the new power elite, was published by l'Harmattan and released in December 1982. Shortly after that he was elected to the position of secretary general of the Malian Writers' Union, a post which he held from 1984-88.

In January of 1985, Traore held the regular meeting of the writers' union to which he invited the members of Benbakandungew, a group of intellectuals dedicated to the creation and promotion of the Bamana language and its literature. This was one of the first meetings which brought together the Francophone writers being read and recognized and published in Paris and the Bamanaphones who were engaged in the struggle to extend the use of national languages and gain recognition not only as a matter of cultural validation, but as a national necessity. Despite the confrontational nature of the encounter, contact had been made between the two groups. In the same year, Traore launched the review *Kalimu* (or "pen" in Bamana) for the Union of Malian Writers and reserved 2-3 pages for poems and other writing in Bamanankan for the members of Benbakandungew.

Throughout his professional life in research and educational projects with various governmental and academic institutions, Traore has maintained his affections for the Bamana language, its cultural heritage, and social history. In 1992, after having written several texts drawn from oral performances as well as socio-economic histories, he published *Hine Nana*, a social and political anthroplology of the sahelian region of Kala Kuruma using a combination of French narrative summation and the text of his informants own words in Bamana. This project exemplifies the intersection of forces currently involved in the production of national language writing. The newly formed Sahelienne Edition, to which Traore now devotes all of his time and where he also publishes its Bamana language monthly journal, *Saheli*, was in charge of publishing and distribution. Financing was made possible through the Royal Dutch Embassy. Editing was carried out by Moussa Sidibe of the Insitutut Pédagogique National, or IPN, and John Hutchison of Boston University who has worked extensively on national language publications in Mali in conjunction with DNAFLA, IPN, USAID, and several specifically funded projects. Printing was done on the presses of LINO. The preface, which stresses the importance of expanding the use of national languages, was written by Issa Ndiaye, a professor of philosophy, who was the minister of

Culture and Scientific Research at the time, and a member of Benbakandungew.

Traore's stress on the need for political will and courageous personal commitment comes from a grounded understanding of the structural and political forces that national language promotion faces. The inherited structure of the educational system and the long tenure of French language use for government, administration, and commerce represent the habitual practices that must be transformed. The persistent economic and political pressure from the institutions promoting Francophonie to produce and disseminate French language cultural productions and to foster ties to a greater French language network of countries, is a more active deterrent. To meet this challenge, Traore is determined to reverse the conditions that currently present French as the language of first choice for most educated writers.

Berehima Wulale

In the writings of Wulale we can detect the multiple influences of his family and community life, his education and training, his professional teaching career, and those factors that compelled him to intiate his Bamana language writings and made possible their publication. As a *jeli* born into and living within a family of *jeliw* active throughout the region just to the east of Segu, he was raised within an environment strong in the use of the spoken word. The practice of *jeliya*, the use of language and music for the performance of epics, genealogies, family histories and praises as well as for negotiation, mediation, and public speaking for the families and communities to which the *jeli* are attached, was learned from his father and grandfathers. From his mother he learned innumerable stories and songs. Proverbs and the recounting of relations and events in people's lives were frequently employed for purposes of argument and illustration.

His success in the educational training provided in French both under the colonial regime and in the early years of independence brought other influences and opportunities. In pursuing his teaching career, he maintained and strengthened his relations within various towns and villages to the east of Segu. And he continued to employ the skills and forms of speech learned from his family for teaching and for the critical community negotiations necessary to establish and maintain local schools.

In the early 80s Wulale began his work with the experimental schools in national languages. From 1982-1985, the Third Educational Project was carried out with funds from the World Bank. The number of experimental schools and the national languages employed increased significantly. As the experimental school project expanded, its deficiencies became apparent. Lacking an overall plan for development, supervision, and evaluation, it also lacked appropriate curricula, methodologies, human resources, and educational materials. Like many others designated as agents for the national languages instruction by the Direction Régionale de l'Education de Base, he was given a 15-day training course, a dictionary, and a guide to transcription and assigned the task of translating the next week's lesson into his national language, Bamanankan.

In 1986 and 1987, he attended training sessions in Belgium which stressed the convergent methodology, a means by which students learn in their own language first and then, with the addition of a second language, continue their study of the two languages simultaneoulsy, using the skills gained in learning their first language to support the second. This method also emphasizes the students' active participation in the learning process, including an appreciation of the cultural and social environments in which they live. After three years of study, this method of teaching was introduced into two experimental schools in Segu in October of 1987.

While working on this project, Wulale found that the materials that had been provided him by DNAFLA were not suited to this teaching method. He began to write his own texts for lessons. He then assembled 62 of these texts and showed them to the director of experimental teaching in Segu who then forwarded copies to DNAFLA, IPN and DNEF (Direction Nationale de l'Enseignement Fondamentale). His texts, which featured stories, life histories, literature, and the events and activities from daily life, caught the attention of Moussa Diaby at DNAFLA. Wulale was subsequently offered positions at DNAFLA and later at IPN, both of which he turned down in favor of remaining in Segu to carry on his teaching and writing in Bamana.

In 1990, he completed a retrospective of Bamana cultural and social life in the region of Segu which he sent to DNAFLA and was subsequently lost. Totally discouraged, he was encouraged to rewrite it by Abou Diarra of IPN to whom he submitted it in 1991. John Hutchison, a linguist at Boston University who has had a long history of involvement with Malian national languages, was present at the time carrying out projects associated with IPN, DNAFLA, and USAID. He not only followed through on the publication of this book, *An ka ko file doonin*, but encouraged Wulale to write other books for his publishing project with USAID.

Conclusion

If it is possible to break away from the domination of foreign-based French language publishing houses which address themselves to only the European and Francophone reading public which supports them, this will make possible not only the publication of works in several languages but also encourage writers from the many regional and social locations of Mali to express themselves in styles and genres linked to the oral traditions and verbal expressions within their own communities. DNAFLA continues to conduct seminars for writers who live outside of the urban centers and apart from the influence of major educational institutions to learn the styles and structures of various genres reflecting blends of written and oral narrative forms. Some literacy campaigns have incorporated projects in which the participants engage in the writing of their own life experiences and daily languages in their own first language. This democratization of written expression will encourage the expansion of communication and self-expression by satisfying the demands and tastes of many communities.

If national language literatures are to become viable, they need to fashion themselves in the image of existing social experience and to develop in the cultural context provided by the extensive and persistent oral tradition. Much of the initial writing published in national languages consisted of transcriptions, often with accompanying translations, of performances of the raconteurs of epics and stories. As Francophone writers move into national languages and as the narrators of oral genres begin to apply themselves to the written word, new genres, styles, and voices will find original ways to meet the conjuncture of a long-standing oral tradition and the circumstances and conditions of people's lives today. Other writers, like Wulale and Traore, must develop their own genres, styles, and literary devices to provide the continuity between spoken and written cultural forms and between the activities of reading and writing and those of daily life in order to bring the same meaningful vitality to the emerging national language literature as is expressed in Mali's impressive oral tradition.

SECTION D:

New Life II:

Resistance Strategies/ Performing Resistance

Fanon And Beyond:
The "Nervous Condition" of the Colonized Woman

by Renee Schatteman
University of Massachusetts

The epigraph to the novel *Nervous Conditions* recalls a line from Jean-Paul Sartre's introduction to Frantz Fanon's *The Wretched of the Earth*: "The condition of the native is a nervous condition introduced by the settler among civilized people with their consent" (20). All of the characters in Tsitsi Dangarembga's work demonstrate the mental anxiety that Sartre describes. But, interestingly, the Fanonian ideas that seem most applicable to *Nervous Conditions* are not those contained in the writing that Sartre introduces but rather are found in Fanon's earlier work, *Black Skin White Masks*.

These two works by Fanon, written nine years apart, have significantly different emphases. In the first, Fanon carefully analyzes the psychological instabilities of his patients in the Antilles, offering his explanation for the social factors that engender psychoses. In this 1952 writing, Fanon seems content to limit himself to a psychoanalytical interpretation of the effects of colonialism—what he refers to as "a complete lysis of this morbid body" (9)—without offering any prescriptive conclusion other than the hope that exposure of the colonial complex might lead to its destruction.

In *The Wretched of the Earth*, however, Fanon is speaking from his involvement in the Algerian war for liberation. He writes with a greater certainty of how to cure the mental illnesses of domination, for in the intermittent years Fanon has moved from pure psychiatry into a politics based on psychological findings. No longer is analysis a sufficient defense against colonialism; as Derek Wright notes in "Fanon and Africa: A Retrospect," "Personal liberation is now to be found in the context of political revolution" (681).

Dangarembga opts to place her narrative in a pre-independence Rhodesia before the armed struggle against the government has entered the consciousness of the common people, a time more related to the ideas expressed in *Black Skin White Masks*. Fanon's battle cry of *The Wretched of the Earth* does not resound in *Nervous Conditions.* Rather, Dangarembga ends her narrative on an ambiguous note, with her main characters still struggling to overcome their neuroses on an individual and not a national level. *Nervous Conditions,* then, works as a fictional representation of the theories of Fanon's earlier work, demonstrating both the psychological manifestations of the colonial structure and the responses of the colonized psyche.

Fanon's overall contention in *Black Skin White Masks* is that every colonized person has been afflicted with an "arsenal of complexes" (23), for a system based on the illogic of racial supremacy must necessarily play upon the nerves of the entire society. "It is not just this Antillean or that Antillean who embodies the neurotic formation," Fanon writes, " but all Antilleans" (151). In his essay "Remembering Fanon: Self, Psyche and the Colonial Condition," Homi Bhabha emphasizes that for Fanon all forms of social and psychic alienation are not linked to the soul of the individual but rather are always explained as "alien presences, occlusions of historical progress, the ultimate misrecognition of Man" (136).

This insistence that every abnormality is situational rather than individual may appear hyperbolic. But Fanon, no doubt, would argue that his absolutes are called for since the dynamics of systemic racism unavoidably lead the colonized subject into predictable patterns of behaviour.

Fanon details these patterns by first outlining the psychological underpinnings that go into the establishment and maintenance of a colonial power. He describes the colonists' two-pronged approach of first abolishing the native's sense of self and then replacing it with a white-defined notion of blackness. The first step—the death and burial of the local inhabitant's customs and metaphysics—fosters the internalization of inferiority, and that feeling is furthered in the second step when the colonized person is conditioned to accept the archetype of the black as a being that is inhuman, aggressive or exceedingly sexual.

Fanon goes on to explicate the two contrasting responses of the colonial subject who is faced with a self that is defined as being ahistorical and immoral—defensive anger or eager imitation. The first response resides in the rage provoked by the colonists' unquestioned sense of superiority. Fanon writes, "Black men want to prove to white men, at all costs, the richness of their thought, the equal value of their intellect," (9) and in effect to disprove the assumptions made about blackness. The other reaction to oppression involves accepting the artifact of blackness and thereby learning to "distrust what is black in me" (136) and to attempt a whitewashing of all aspects of the self. As Homi Bhabha notes, "The compulsory identification with a persecutory 'They' is always an evacuation and emptying of the 'I'" (142).

Both of these responses equally destabilize the victim of colonialism since both inevitably lead to failure. The defensive reaction is problematic since it still depends on white approval which can never be given within an exploitative framework. The imitation of white ways also proves fruitless since the colonial subject cannot escape the blackness of the skin and is "forever in combat with his own image" (137). Ultimately the white mask that Fanon refers to in his title is but a mask. Colonialism seduces the victim with the glories of whiteness but then betrays with the unalterable reality of skin color. Fanon laments, "I am overdetermined from without" (82).

The frustration produced by these ineffectual reactions to colonialism is further exacerbated by the coexistence of both of these opposing impulses inside the one person, causing an internal scission. Homi Bhabha suggests that "the very place of identity, caught in the tension of demand and desire is a space of splitting. The fantasy of the native is to occupy the master's place while keeping his place in the slave's avenging anger. 'Black skin, white masks' is not ... a neat division; it is a doubling, dissembling image of being in two places at once" (138).

How then, according to Fanon, can the colonized person mend the divisions of the self and be "dealienated" back into the indigenous context? Fanon calls for a new construct which will be able to obliterate the fabricated myth of blackness in order to achieve "nothing short of the liberation of the man of color from himself" (8). But he resists giving specifics on how this myth-shredding should be done in this earlier writing. He closes instead on a less practical and a somewhat idealistic note, appealing to the white power structure to enter into responsible and healthy dynamics with the colonized. Fanon concludes this work by saying, "I, the man of colour, want only this: . . . That the enslavement of man by man cease for ever. . . . That it be possible for me to discover and to love man, wherever he may be" (165). Homi Bhabha suggests this unexpected outflowing of optimism is Fanon's method of countering the overall bleak analysis of colonial relations of the rest of the work. "Such a deep hunger for humanism, despite Fanon's insight into the dark side of Man, must be an overcompensation for the closed consciousness ... to which he attributes the depersonalization of colonial man" (143).

While Tsitsi Dangarembga does not conclude her novel with such a hopeful appeal, she does set out to illustrate the psychological manipulation that has taken place in her society under Rhodesian rule. White characters are relatively absent from the action of *Nervous*

Conditions, but the consequences of white domination are very apparent in the interactions of black characters.

The theme of neurosis in the novel is felt in a general sense by the strained atmospheres that characterize both of the settings, the homestead and the mission. Maiguru complains of being unnerved by "the inmates of her house" (113); Babamakuru demands that his household remain silent because his nerves are so tense; and, of course, Nyasha suffers from bulemia, the most severe and life-threatening mental disorder presented in the novel.

As Fanon theorized, the numerous anxieties in this novel are clearly brought on by the sociopolitical climate of the country and not by personal idiosyncracies. In fact, all the possible responses outlined in *Black Skin White Masks* are found here. The angry defense of blackness is most clearly illustrated in Nyasha's rage as she tears up her history book and screams, "I won't grovel, I won't die" (200). The desperate imitation of whiteness is most evident in the character of Nhamo who desires to cast off his father's name as soon as he leaves for the mission. And, finally, the splitting of a self to accommodate both these reactions is seen especially in the character of Tambu. At one point in the novel Tambu suggests that her tension is simply due to the adjusting she must make as her life changes. But her instability clearly is caused by more disturbing factors. Her personal story actually chronicles the entire process that a colonized person goes through in response to European domination as it is outlined in Fanon's *Black Skin White Masks* theories.

To begin with, Tambu's precolonial past is symbolically negated by colonial forces that intrude upon her childhood. She is barred from the "deeper, cooler, more interesting pools" (3) of her river when the government's Council Houses, and the accompanying businesses, gradually make their presence known in her village. In addition, though she still has no direct contact with whites, she begins to be affected by the reports of the world outside of her childhood sphere that come to her through the stories of her grandmother and the boasts of her brother. She is quickly attracted to the thought of white-run education which leads her to question the value of her childhood identity in comparison to what is being held up as the ideal. Her parents are no longer the authorities they once were to her; their world becomes invalid and foolish when compared to the white-structured world of her aunt and uncle.

Even before she has left the homestead, then, Tambu has begun the mental journey that Fanon speaks of. She has set herself on a path to imitate the white ideal by transforming herself into someone free from the restrictions of rural poverty. She anticipates her new identity when saying,

"At Babamakuru's I expected to find another self, a clean, well-groomed, genteel self who could not have been bred, could not have survived, on the homestead" (58). Once she is at the mission environment, Tambu's desire for whiteness becomes full-blown. She strives to capture the beauty of the white missionaries' children by "approximating my idea of a young woman of the world" (93), one who is well-versed in the European classics from Enid Blyton to the Bronte sisters.

In conjunction with this elevation of whiteness, Tambu further debases any reminders of her past life. When she visits the homestead, she begins to imitate the ways of her brother, whom she criticized so harshly when he was alive. The complaints he had made about work on the farm are echoed in her disgust with the sanitation of the toilets. And his tendency to remain away whenever possible is seen also in her delight over Babamakuru's generous agreement "to allow me to stay on at the mission until we all went home for Christmas" (108).

In a way, she outdoes the selfishness of her dislikable brother for her determination to fulfill her destiny of education causes her to be insensitive to her mother's greater needs. There are two moments when her mother threatens to call Tambu back to help on the homestead, once when she is deciding whether to leave her husband and once when she falls into a non-functional lethargy. Tambu simply cannot consider assisting her mother at either moment. What is paramount in her mind is the desire to get as far from her past life as possible. Ngugi wa Thiong'o, like Fanon, would explain this by saying that the cultural bomb which annihilated these people's identities ..."makes them see their past as one wasteland of non-achievement and it makes them want to distance themselves from that wasteland" (*Decolonizing the Mind* 3).

Dangarembga complicates this narrative of a girl who strives to imitate the white world by having Tambu experience the other response to colonialism that Fanon explains—that of defensive anger—in a very dramatic way. The stimulus that pushes Tambu toward this reaction is found in the character of Nyasha, in many ways Tambu's alter ego.

Nyasha is an interesting character in that she so clearly occupies "the space of splitting" that Bhabha refers to. She is an extreme embodiment of the white-masked black with her desire for slimness, her definite British accent and her western concepts of feminism. On the other hand, she defends her blackness by preferring a black mission school to the nun's institution, by calling for the traditional cleansing ceremony as opposed to the Christian wedding service for Tambu's parents, and by being the only character to show an interest in the politics of colonialism. Nyasha painfully recognizes the schism in herself when she states, "I'm not one of them but I'm not one of you" (201).

Her consciousness of her own internal division cannot but have an impact on Tambu, although Tambu stubbornly resists the influence. Both at the homestead and the mission Tambu is plagued by "complex, dangerous thoughts that I was stirring up" (39), but she repeatedly pushes them aside, preferring to pursue without question an unexamined life committed to educational advancements.

But Nyasha's continual questioning of all of the structures of their society, in particular those advocated by Babamakuru, weakens Tambu's resistance to her own personal turmoil. Sally McWilliams notes in her article "Tsitsi Dangarembga's *Nervous Conditions*: At the Crossroads of Feminism and Post-Colonialism," that Nyasha problematizes Tambu's adherence to the white model of success and thereby "ruins Tambu's linear plans for her education and for a clear-cut, wholly unambiguous sense of identity" (105). Tambu changes in the course of the novel from disapproving of Nyasha's lack of decorum to applauding her cousin's ability to "pluck out the heart of a problem and present it to me in ways that made sense "(151). Under Nyasha's tutelage, Tambu begins to reexamine the identity she has been seeking for herself away from her family's homestead.

Nyasha's promptings do help to prepare Tambu for the crisis moment that she faces when her uncle pushes the white archetype of blackness to a point that she can no longer justify. When he insists that her mother be married in a Christian tradition, Tambu cannot suppress anymore the thoughts which now "linger and chip away at my defenses" (150). Although she cannot even conceive of opposing Babamakuru's value system, she also cannot incorporate his suggestion that her family life resided in the realm of sinfulness. Tambu can't accommodate the myth of blackness when she too is drawn into the evil circle.

And so, Tambu's psychological response to this dilemma is to engage in the division of the mind that Nyasha has modeled. By physically leaving her body on the morning of her crisis, Tambu is able to allow for the internal splitting that must occur for her to have the ability to say, "I'm sorry, Baba, but I do not want to go to the wedding" (166).

Thus, Tambu has come to experience all that Fanon predicted for the psyche of the colonized person. She finishes her story speaking of her new consciousness of the doubleness of her existence, but she still occupies that same ambiguous space. McWilliams notes that, "She vacillates between the two positions, never able to secure an absolute position on one or the other side of the divide" (109).) That the older Tambu who is narrating the story calls her acceptance into the white school an escape—as opposed to an entrapment—indicates that she is still pursuing the white ideal of education and advancement. That she is driven to record the lives of the women who inhabited her past speaks of her defense of her blackness. That she embodies both reactions to colonialism suggests that the nervousness which characterized her earlier life will continue to be with her much as it appears to be abounding in the life of the fragile Nyasha.

Nervous Conditions, then, does serve to bring Fanon's suppositions to life. But Dangarembga's novel also explores other psychological realities that Fanon leaves unexamined—most specifically the role of gender in the colonial context. His theories are recognized today to be gender-biased in both his examples and in his emphasis on the loss of manhood. Bhabha explains that "the problem stems from Fanon's desire to site the question of sexual difference within the problematic of cultural difference—to give them a shared origin—which is suggestive but often simplifies the question of sexuality" (148).

Dangarembga, writing from a later time period and a female perspective, extricates the issue of sexual identity from that of colonial identity and proposes that the colonizer/colonized dynamics are reverberated in the relations between men and women who share the status of the oppressed.

Firstly, the harsh treatment that the women in the novel receive at the hands of the husbands or fathers who dominate their lives suggests that the existence of the colonized woman is invalidated by the men of color in much the same way that the selfhood of all colonized people is annihilated by the Europeans. Tambu argues that "the needs and sensibilities of the women in my family were not considered a priority, or even legitimate" (12). Other female characters are equally ignored: Maiguru earns money for her family but then has no voice in determining how it is spent; Tambu's mother must live with a husband who has an affair with her own sister and who is then only concerned about offending Babamakuru; Nyasha is ordered about by a tyrannical father who continually questions her moral decency.

The notion of the archetype of male blackness analyzed by Fanon and included in *Nervous Conditions* finds its parallel in the archetype of womanhood that constrains many of the women in the novel. Tambu is encouraged to curb her unnatural inclinations (33) that cause her to behave more aggressively than what appropriately suits the male notions of the female gender. The frustration that she and all the other women experience because of the assumptions that form this archetype echoes the defensive anger felt in the colonized subject over the misconceptions surrounding the myth of blackness. Maiguru and Tambu's mother both give numerous hints of the repressed rage they harbor over their assigned roles though they attempt to hide these feelings under attitudes of excessive submissiveness in the case of the first or indifference in the case of the latter. Tambu herself says, "What I didn't like was the way all conflicts came back to the question of femaleness. Femaleness as opposed and inferior to males" (116).

But while colonialism and patriarchy are seen here to use similar means to oppress, Dangarembga does not appear to be paralleling the way the colonized subjects and the female subjects respond to the strictures placed upon them. For all of the women in this novel, the nervousness that characterizes their relationships with the men in their lives reaches a crisis point which results in actions that grant momentary relief. Maiguru, exasperated from the strain of being caught between her husband and her daughter, walks out on Babamakuru for the first time in her life when he insists on punishing Tambu unfairly. She returns soon enough but with a changed attitude, no longer willing to coo over her husband or to suppress her own opinions.

Tambu's mother experiences a trauma over the news that her second child is going to be taken far away to the nuns' schools. Her extreme reaction proves to do her good, for it brings Lucia, who nurtures her and provides her a temporary rest from the burden of motherhood.

Nyasha secretly does violence against her own body to articulate her protests against her father without inspiring the type of fighting that marked their earlier relationship. McWilliams notes that Nyasha "uses her body to threaten her life and through this threat to try to shake her father's authoritarian hold, all the while never having to bring into the open the problems between them" (110). Once her disease reaches a critical stage, it also enables her to receive extended care in the city, away from the daily tension of life in her father's home.

And, finally, the out-of-the-body experience that Tambu experiences during her confrontation teaches her a new mode of interacting with her uncle, one which enables her to demand the space she needs to occupy when dealing with her mother's marriage. "This act of internal distancing from her body makes it impossible for anyone to control her because they aren't aware that her spirit has fled her physical form. When Tambu realizes she can react to Baba's categorical demand to get up without being implicated and controlled by his words, then she slips back into her body. Against his code of acceptable female behavior, she speaks to her uncle, refusing to capitulate to his desires" (McWilliams).

Sue Thomas suggests in her article "Killing the Hysteric in the Colonized's House" that the various types of hysteria displayed by the women when their internal conflicts become extreme actually constitute minor acts of resistance, not forceful enough to remove them entirely from their tense environs but significant enough to provide them with a healing space that can better prepare them to handle the ambiguities of their positions within the society.

The partial liberation that all of the women gain in *Nervous Conditions* implies that female enslavement can be more readily overcome than the oppression imposed by colonial structures. Sue Thomas suggests that men like Babamakuru may be less able to participate in acts of hysterical resistance since they are so much more invested in their oppression than are the women. Baba's subservience to the colonial school system grants him a masculine authority over his immediate and extended family that he would be denied if he did not hold such a complicitous position in this colonial society.

By the time Frantz Fanon writes *The Wretched of the Earth* he is convinced that it is only through violence that the colonized person can be freed of his inferiority complex and can restore his self respect. Fanon also celebrates the creative and positive qualities of violence. Dangarembga's text perhaps offers a revision of Fanon by suggesting that the subject of a colonial world, like the woman of a patriarchal structure, can take creative steps between victimization and armed rebellion to relieve the strain of a life inherently marked by deprivation and uncertainty.

WORKS CITED

Bhabha, Homi K. "Remembering Fanon: Self, Psyche, and the Colonial Condition." in *Remaking History*. Eds. Barbara Kruger and Phil Mariani. Seattle, Washington: Bay Press, 1989: 131-148.

Dangarembga, Tsitsi. *Nervous Conditions*. Seattle, Washington: The Seal Press, 1988.

Dangarembga, Tsitsi. "This Time, Next Year..." *The Women's Review of Books*. Vol. VIII, Nos. 10-11 (July 1991): 43-44.

Fanon, Frantz. *Black Skin White Masks*. London: Grove Press, Inc., 1967.

Fanon, Frantz. *The Wretched of the Earth*. New York: Grove Press, Inc., 1963.

McWilliams, Sally. "Tsitsi Dangarembga's *Nervous Conditions*: At the Crossroads of Feminism and Post-colonialism." *World Literature Written in English*. 31, 1 (1991): 103-112.

Thomas, Sue. "Killing the Hysteric in the Colonized's House: Tsitsi Dangarembga's *Nervous Conditions*." *The Journal of Commonwealth Literature*. 27, 1 (1992): 26-36.

Ngugi wa Thiong'o. *Decolonizing the Mind: The Politics of Language in African Literature*. Portsmouth, New Hampshire: Heinemann, 1986.

Wright, Derek. "Fanon and Africa: A Retrospect." *The Journal of Modern African Studies*. 24, 4 (1986): 679-689.

Techniques of Survival: *Artful Dodges in Nigerian Urban Fiction*

by William Sharpe
Barnard College

For many of those who look "Beyond Survival," the dream of making it in the big city has loomed ever larger as the century has progressed. Throughout the 20th century there has been a worldwide population shift toward urban centers, and Africa is no exception. For example, in the next twenty years Lagos—which in 1970 had an estimated population of 1 million—is expected to grow from its current population of around 9 million to over 21 million. This massive transition from agrarian to urban society has profound implications for all aspects of African identity: economic, political, cultural, social. In keeping with actual trends, the protagonists of Nigerian urban fiction usually have a rural past that continues to shape their responses to the contemporary city.

What are the techniques needed to "make it" in the big city? With its fluid social order, its vast array of occupations, its dangerously shifting sands of political and economic power, the urban environment forces formerly rural people to reconsider their social roles and personal identities. This process may be liberating, in that the city offers newcomers a chance to start new lives by creating new selves: amidst urban anonymity one can embark on a quest to refashion the self by taking on new roles, a quest that may seem pointless in a rural setting where everyone already knows everyone else. But the dramatic and stimulating transition from rural to urban life can also insidiously undermine the newcomer's sense of self; it is a disorienting and potentially disastrous process. In an effort to adapt and survive, some urbanites yield, willingly or not, to the theatrical possibilities that the city's anonymity encourages. They turn to such "artful dodges" as role-playing, storytelling, even outright deception, and they risk losing sight of who they really are. This paper focuses on role-playing in three very different classics of urban Nigerian literature: Cyprian Ekwensi's *Lokotown and Other Stories* (1966), Buchi Emecheta's *The Joys of Motherhood* (1979), and Chinua Achebe's *Anthills of the Savannah* (1988).

The protagonist of Ekwensi's story "Glittering City" is an urban
chameleon who will pretend to anything as long as it brings him some
advantage, whether social, financial, or sexual. Fussy Joe is a ladies' man,
musician, fast-talker, and seducer who uses his charm and good looks to
make things happen. In a typical night he tricks a young girl from the
country into coming home with him, saying she will be arrested for
loitering if she continues to wait for her mother at the train station; by
dawn, he is spinning a new yarn to another woman:

> He told her he was secretary to a leading firm in an enterprising corporation,
> that he had gone to England as a delegate . . . and had only just returned. They
> exchanged lies, each one knowing that the other one was putting up a good
> show and not worrying to check the facts. (119)

"Exchanging lies" is how people in the city get to know one another,
Ekwensi suggests; "putting up a good show" is what matters most. When
the new girlfriend worries that his wife will appear, Joe calms her fears,
while thinking to himself: "there were at least three girls who answered to
the description of his 'wife.' And the fun was that each of them believed
that she was *the* wife" (119).

There are, however, some roles that Joe is unwilling to play. The
woman closest to him is Lilli, and they have a son, but when she tells him
to "accept his responsibilities as a father and a man" (21) he resists. "She
was honest and dutiful to him, and he was deceitful, tricky, and untrue to
her" (120). Joe's refusal to accept a well-defined social role is signaled by
his lack of a fixed address, for although he has a flat in Lagos where he
entertains his pick-ups, he also lives with Lilli in the suburbs: "Many
people ... thought he lived outside the city. It was the address he gave when
he wanted to be naughty and knock the heads of Lilli and another girl"
(123).

But eventually all his stories begin to backfire, as the city does not
seem big enough for his fantasies:

> Fussy Joe played a variety of parts. One had to play so many parts. To some
> people he said he was a journalist ... to others he was a legal practitioner ... to
> others he was a band leader, or a film star. It was difficult to remember what
> he was expected to be at any particular time. (124)

The people he meets in various guises begin to meet each other, and
violent confrontations erupt, particularly as Lilli slugs it out with her
rivals. Amid several close calls, Joe remeets Essi, the country girl he
picked up on her first night in Lagos, and finds out he has ruined her
marital prospects. Then he gets in trouble with his boss's wife, and the
band leader deals him a public humiliation as all his tricks unravel:

The band-boys were laughing at him. They knew him for what he was, The Brainer, the glib inventor of lies, the city boy who was a victim of his own virility and codelessness. (136)

Sweating with fear and shame, he feels his flashy clothes turn soggy; "gone were all the studied movements ... the poses struck for effect. Only the man Joe was left: and he was no man at all." (136)

Although Ekwensi clearly delights in the fabrications of his hero, he also emphasizes that such role-playing can be dangerous. While it might be useful as a survival strategy, the trading of lies ultimately leads to a loss of personal and community identity. In quick succession Joe's contacts are arrested, his women rebel, and the band leader repossesses Joe's trumpet, the instrument of his sexual success. Divine retribution is in store: "unseen forces were moving beneath the traffic lights of Lagos City. Joe did not know it at the time, but the wheels of fortune were rolling .... Plans for his destruction were already in progress." (143)

Condemned for his devil-may-care life, Joe is killed while fleeing the police. But as he dies near the railway station where he began his seduction of Essi, he repents and tells Lilli he loves her. Ekwensi thus represents life in Lagos as a world of mirrors and facades, but through the mirror of his own fiction he paradoxically reassures his readers that truth will ultimately prevail.

Yet Ekwensi the moralizer cannot quite restrain the impulses of Ekwensi the story-teller. For, at the very moment Joe dies, Essi is on the platform preparing to return to her village—where she is apparently going to tell her own lies. Essi had already lied to Joe when he ran into her a second time: she pretended that she was not out looking for a pick-up. Now, when she hears about Joe's death, she weaves a comforting fable about her seducer for the benefit of the other train passengers: "Such a good boy ... he was so kind to me— ... so handsome, and such good manners" (152). The city, it seems, compels one to fabricate, to make one's own life as satisfying and idealized as the city itself is reputed to be.

In the short time Essi has spent in the city, she is already becoming like Joe, which suggests that in Ekwensi's Lagos, smooth talking and shape-shifting is not exclusively male behavior. In the title story, "Lokotown," it is a woman, Konni, who has been deceiving honest railroad workers. She is an extreme version of Ekwensi's most famous character, the wily prostitute Jagua Nana. Konni signs the names of her various lovers on the bills she runs up, and spends her nights at bars attracting and ruining still more men. These deceits are made possible by her skill at covering up the signs that her body is aging, for "her beauty had now become a fading illusion" (6). "Deprive her of her creams and paints and she would frighten a wizard" (18). Konni has four children and a husband in her past, but she uses the anonymity of the city to conceal this: "when they separated she was a complete wreck and Lagos was a good place in which to hide her identity" (6). She hangs out at crossroads looking for men with money: the trick was to "be inviting and look easy to seduce. She had practised it a thousand times" (7). When she is with her friend Anna, they stand around and pretend to talk animatedly: "their conversation became a kind of stage performance" (11).

All of this artifice works its magic: Konni drives three men to desperation. One tries to murder the other, but both are saved from self-destruction by the third, Nwuke. When Nwuke's infant son is killed in a scuffle between Konni and his wife, all three men turn their wrath on Konni. Konni crumbles, and like Fussy Joe, her smooth wiles fail in adversity:

> She had suddenly become very old. Deep lines ran around her neck, and her hands were wrinkled. Hair undone, eyes wild, an unlit cigarette in her hands, a torn dressing gown against her body. None of her thousand admirers would have looked at her twice now. (33)

In Ekwensi's stories, fancy clothes are the trappings of deception, and they are stripped away to make a moral point. Earlier, her cloth-seller had told Konni that "clothes make a woman" (9), and now, without her clothes or her make-up, Konni is defenseless.

In the end, Konni realizes she does not belong in the city: "Lokotown was..... not a town for spongers and parasites who only brought..... heart-breaks to honest, well-meaning wives" (40-41). After Konni commits suicide, the men who once pursued her gather at a bar to ponder her death. One man is momentarily overcome with grief, but now feels ready to marry his faithful unsophisticated fiancee at last; her natural rural goodness triumphs over artificially stimulated lust. But as in "Glittering City," the torch of urban drama seems to be passed on to another character at the end: "Nwuke appeared to be enjoying himself, or was he merely play-acting?" (42).

Ekwensi takes a moral tone in the "Lokotown" stories—falsehoods, fabrications, and the fast lives they temporarily sustain are always contrasted with solid homelife and the rural, domestic virtues of good women and steady men. For centuries, people have gone to the city to escape the weight of tradition, to fashion new selves free of the expectations of family and community. But if the city offers the freedom to make oneself anew, it also carries with it the pitfalls that Ekwensi depicts: prostitution for women, corruption and crime for men. Though the lively surfaces of his stories indicate that he is himself enchanted with the creative talents and physical attractiveness of his villains, Ekwensi conveys the message that urban actors cannot succeed for long; fidelity to the truth is the best policy. In both stories, lying characters are threatened with arrest as "unlicensed guides." Ekwensi seems to be saying that the city is too complex and dangerous for readers to traverse without the aid of a "licensed guide" such as himself, the writer who can unmask the authentic and vulnerable identity beneath the sham.

Ekwensi's fascination with self-destructive storytelling is perhaps a reaction to a fluid urban society where so many unconventional ways of behaving are suddenly available, and where the loss of traditional roles leaves people groping for new ones. But Buchi Emecheta's ironically titled novel *The Joys of Motherhood* shows what can happen when a woman tries to fulfill her traditional role in an urban world that undermines all her efforts. The novel opens with the main character, Nnu Ego, in despair— her baby has just died, and she wants to kill herself if she can't be a mother. Though she has left her native village and moved to Lagos to marry, she seeks her selfhood only through motherhood, a role that the city renders increasingly difficult.

Always blaming herself, Nnu Ego believes that she lost her baby because "she'd been trying to be traditional in a modern urban setting ... this time she was going to play it according to the new rules" (81). So when more babies arrive, she gives up her aspirations to earn a living. In her village, "women made a contribution, but in urban Lagos, men had to be the sole providers; this new setting robbed the woman of her useful role" (81). For Nnu Ego, "the pride of motherhood" is worth the loss of market income. But it is ironic that her scope of action is now more constricted: the "new rules" insure that women in Lagos have fewer roles available to them than before. They can only be wives and mothers, not breadwinners, and must depend on what their husbands are willing to hand them.

Nnu Ego's life is not so much one of deception, like that of Fussy Joe or Konni, as it is of self-deception: she innocently hopes to do her duty and "be satisfied" (81). But eventually the truth of her situation comes home to her: "It occurred to Nnu Ego that she was a prisoner, imprisoned by her love for her children, imprisoned in her role as senior wife" (137). She is shocked and chagrined when Adaku, her husband's second wife, leaves the struggling family in order to become a successful prostitute. "Many people put the blame on Lagos itself" (170), but the city has only suggested a course of action that Adaku chooses of her own free will. And in fact this oldest of urban professions enables Adaku to become a happier, more fulfilled person. She plows her profits into well-paying investments and educates her daughters, while Nnu Ego's daughters must sacrifice their chances to her ungrateful sons. When a new junior wife appears, Nnu Ego resigns herself to her fate: honored by strangers for her children's accomplishments, she is gradually abandoned by her selfish family. Emecheta's Lagos, with its emotionally numbing struggles for survival and advancement, is the opposite of Ekwensi's passionate, brawling, mercurial city. But playing by the rules turns out to be no more rewarding than breaking them: the protagonists of both authors come to grief.

Chinua Achebe's *Anthills of the Savannah* suggests a possible way out of this urban impasse. The novel rejects superficial role-playing, endorsing instead a self-conscious evolution of personality that acknowledges the multiplicity of elements constructing any single identity. The book's narrative style mirrors this process—the apparently fragmented accounts of several first-person narrators eventually combine to form a unified story of a city in crisis. Although Achebe avoids the earnest moralizing of Ekwensi and the relentless ironies of Emecheta, there are parallels. As in Ekwensi, the male characters take on new identities as occasion demands, with fatal results. Only the women survive, yet, as in Emecheta, they suffer for their refusal to be other than what they are. But in the end the possibility of a new identity appears, one that merges traditional culture with urban education and adaptability.

The biggest role-player in *Anthills* is the country's president: His Excellency, or Sam, as his friends call him. The discrepancy between august title and pedestrian name hints at Sam's inner conflicts. As a young man he imitated the English gentlemen he met at Sandhurst; now he models himself on the aging dictators he meets at the OAU. Spying the dramatic possibilities in the role of an African head of state, he alters his wardrobe and polishes his act. His friend Ikem reflects that a "sense of theatre" defines the president: "He is basically an actor and half of the things we are inclined to hold against him are no more than scenes from his repertory to which he may have no sense of moral commitment whatsoever" (45). But absolute power and play-acting are a lethal combination; soon no one can tell whether Sam has any "moral commitment" left at all.

Ikem tries to save both Sam and the country with his sense of humor and bold truth-telling: "worshipping a dictator is such a pain in the ass," he observes wryly (41). He wants to keep the leader from taking himself too seriously. But Sam has forgotten how to laugh at himself, indeed has forgotten who he really is. Surrounded by sycophants and seduced by his own theatrics, Sam loses himself and loses sight of the needs of his troubled country. From Lokotown low-lifes to British-educated elite, role-playing proves self-destructive.

At the novel's turning point, the government arrests a village storyteller, prompting Ikem to make an outraged speech to university students, in which he declares that "storytellers are a threat. They threaten all champions of control" (141). Within days, just as Ikem, editor of the newspaper, has started to take his own role as a voice of the people seriously, he is murdered by government agents. Shortly afterwards, Sam himself is overthrown in a coup.

In a country where storytellers are routinely jailed, Achebe's warning about the risks of narrative has a sobering credibility. But he envisions a possible way out through the figure of a reluctant narrator who refuses to be other than what she is. Beatrice is a high-level civil servant, a modern career woman who shuns the false roles others assign her: her office rivals call her an ambitious Madame Pompadour; her father regards her as an unfeminine and rebellious soldier-girl; her lover sees her as a demure damsel hiding depths of passion; Ikem idealizes her as a down-to-earth woman in the kitchen who in a flash can become a village priestess with a gift for prophecy (96). But if Sam sealed his doom with too much role-playing, Beatrice survives by refusing to embrace conventional political, social, or sexual stereotypes of women. She doesn't even seek out the role of storyteller: "Who am I that I should inflict my story on the world?" she asks (80).

As a survivor who helps nurture new beginnings (in the form of Ikem's posthumous child), Beatrice finally emerges as the novel's primary narrator, reassembling the fragments of her friends' history. It is significant that an urban woman becomes Achebe's chief storyteller, taking up a role usually associated with a village man. Similarly, at the novel's end she also takes on the untraditional role of baby-namer, a position normally reserved for a man. In both instances, the power of naming, of interpreting the world through language, falls to her unbidden, because she is a woman in touch with the many sides of her humanity, her rural roots as well as her urban aspirations. The contradictions that others sense in her are simply the different sides of a fully realized individual. And just as many tales comprise this one novel, so Achebe suggests that many identities can peaceably coexist in one person—as long as they are acknowledged with humor and compassion, and not repressed by the quest for a smooth urban facade.

What conclusions can we draw from this brief look at urban role-playing? These authors explore the question of how people adapt to a new environment that makes unfamiliar demands upon them. Their characters all realize that the protean quality of city life requires people to shed their old personae and to invent new ones. No longer living out inherited roles among familiar faces, urban dwellers must learn to identify themselves in new ways among a multitude of strangers.

But the challenge, as all three writers attest, is to maintain a stable sense of self in the face of the disorienting pressures of urban life. Ekwensi seems to argue that there *is* an essential self to be found beneath the fabrications that his characters self-aggrandizingly weave, yet his implicit moral—"be true to your roots and rural values"—is repeatedly undercut by his own evident delight in how word-spinners can create their own realities, at least temporarily. Emecheta, on the other hand, implies that a woman like Nnu Ego, cut adrift from the village culture that shaped her for its own patriarchal uses, has no clear role to play in a city that is even less solicitous about female self-definition. A victim of social forces beyond her control or comprehension, she is, as her name suggests, a person of "No Ego," no sense of self. The most literarily sophisticated of the authors considered here, Achebe, posits a complex role for the morally conscientious urban dweller to play. He or she must indeed adopt the often artificial roles that urban society demands, but only up to a point. Honesty, compassion, personal loyalty, and a sense of justice all take precedence over the desire to make a good impression, or even to save one's life. For Achebe, these are not only the qualities needed to look "beyond survival," in its narrowest sense. They are also the qualities that the truthful storyteller needs in order to show his troubled audience how a more rewarding urban society can be achieved.

WORKS CITED

Achebe, Chinua. *Anthills of the Savannah*. New York: Doubleday-Anchor, 1988.

Ekwensi, Cyprian. *Lokotown and Other Stories*. London: Heinemann, 1966.

Emecheta, Buchi. *The Joys of Motherhood*. New York: Braziller, 1979.

Beyond Streetwalking:
The Woman of the City as Urban Pioneer

by Heather Henderson
Mount Holyoke College

In much of African fiction, the city has been portrayed as a threatening location. Cities represent a break with the past, not only because of their modern technology, but also because the bizarre combination of anonymity and intimacy found in cities cuts people loose from the protection of traditional family life. Thus, rural suspicions of the city embody broader cultural conflicts between old and new, traditional and modern, the community and the individual. Often these various threats are imaged in specifically sexual terms: the city is feared as a place of corruption, of loose morals and loose women.

What is the nature of the connection between cities and sexuality? For one thing, maintaining control over women's sexuality is a lot harder to do in a sprawling urban environment. And so the threat to traditional society is envisioned very specifically as a threat to and through female sexuality. Women will become prostitutes, even child-murderers, and their "fall" will be a keystone of a larger social breakdown. Thus, the man who strolls city streets is a *flaneur*, as the French say; the woman who does so is a streetwalker. The very expression, "to walk the streets," is synonymous with prostitution.

Frequently, such conflicts are dramatized through the stories of young women who go to the city in hopes of finding a job and some excitement, only to be betrayed or ruined. Reflecting on the dangers of urban temptation, the contemporary Malian singer, Oumou Sangare, sings "songs in which a conflicted young woman, with the approval of God, chooses to stay home and obey her parents instead of fleeing to the city with her boyfriend" (*NYTimes*).

In her novel, *L'appel des arènes* (1982), Aminata Sow Fall represents the threat to traditional village culture by describing the plight of Anta Lo, a young girl seduced and abandoned in the big city; the desperate girl murders her own illegitimate baby, and dies in prison. The episode takes on mythic dimensions, symbolizing the rapacious impact of modern cities on traditional rural life (126-29).

In "Minutes of Glory" (1975) Ngugi wa Thiong'o tells a similar story. Beatrice is a barmaid and part-time prostitute, and she is miserable with her life. Her partial education had made her discontented with life in the village, but when she left in search of an office job, her lack of skills made her unemployable. A man with a fancy car promised that "in a big city there would be no difficulty," but he seduced her and disappeared. "That's how she had started the life of a barmaid. And for one and a half years now she had not been once to see her parents" (80).

Beatrice "was tired of wandering" from job to job (74); "What she wanted was decent work and a man or several men who cared for her." She thinks nostalgically of her parents: "She wept late at nights and remembered home. At such moments, her mother's village ... seemed the sweetest place on God's earth. ... She longed to go back home to see them. But how could she go back with empty hands? ... Fallen from grace, fallen from grace. She was part of a generation which would never again be one with the soil, the crops, the wind and the moon" (75).

Like Anta Lo, Beatrice ends up in the custody of the police. Her break with her community and her roots has led to a downward spiral of disaster, of innocent hopes betrayed. But in "Two Sisters" (1970?), Ama Ata Aidoo tells a somewhat different story, this time of a young woman who already possesses the very things Beatrice longs for: good looks, an office job, a steady suitor. But Mercy is bored with her typing and believes her taxi-driver boyfriend is beneath her. An older married sister watches helplessly as Mercy's ambitions for glamor and status lead her to become the mistress of a well-known politician old enough to be her grandfather. When a coup overthrows the government, the older sister hopes Marcy will come to her senses and return home. Instead, she simply switches to a new lover whose star is rising, an officer in the coup. Like the politician, the officer is a married man with grandchildren.

Certainly there are distinctions to be made among these women. Unlike Anta Lo, a helpless victim of seduction, or Beatrice, a reluctant part-timer, Mercy actively chooses her new life, and she has the luxury of being the mistress of only one important man at a time. But there is a sense of moral despair that pervades all three stories, a kind of hopelessness about the future. In each case, the values of family and continuity are actively imperiled by the new order represented by the city and by its dangerous, amoral ways.

Another story by Ama Ata Aidoo, "In the Cutting of a Drink" (1970?), takes the process one step further, dealing as it does with hardcore remorseless prostitution. The story perfectly captures the gulf dividing urban and rural perceptions. Back in his village and surrounded by assembled relatives, the narrator recounts his trip to the city to search for his younger sister, Mansa, who disappeared a dozen years earlier. He is the classic country bumpkin, bewildered by the motion of traffic and the size of the crowds, astonished by city lights, puzzled by the sight of a water fountain. His carefully controlled narration avoids overt moral judgement, but each detail builds an ever-more-damning picture of city life: his cousin, now an urban sophisticate, sleeps away Saturday afternoon in cramped quarters, and introduces a girlfriend, whom "he wants to marry against the wishes of his people." Tradition is violated with a laugh: the girlfriend eats with the men, and when they go out dancing, she orders beer: "I sat with my mouth open and watched the daughter of a woman cut beer like a man." The narrator is reluctant to dance because the city folks "all dance like white men," but the urban cousin reassures him that "in the city, no one cares if you dance well or not....."

That message of urban alienation—"no one cares"—is at the heart of the story. Throughout his narration, the young man is anxiously aware of the effect of his words on his audience, which includes his mother and other relatives. He knows his story will shock them, and he fears their judgement: "My Uncle, do not say that instead of concerning myself with the business for which I had gone to the city, I went dancing." In the village, unlike the city, everyone cares deeply what you do.

The villager tells how he danced with a woman and only later realized that she and her friends "were all bad women of the city." This thought troubled him: "Have they no homes?" he brooded. "Do not their mothers like them?" He danced with another woman, and asked about her work. She screamed, "Let me tell you that any kind of work is work. You villager, you villager, who are you?" Suddenly he recognized her as his lost sister, Mansa. Bitterly, the narrator tells his relatives not to cry for her. "What is there to weep about? I was sent to find a lost child. I found her a woman. Cut me a drink ... Any kind of work is work ... That is what Mansa told me with a mouth that looked like clotted blood. Any kind of work is work ...."

In his book, *Women Writers in Black Africa* (1981), Lloyd Brown comments on this ending:

> The once naive storyteller seems to have understood something about her world of city prostitutes. His search for Mansa turns out to have been his own quest for worldly wisdom .... He and his rural audience have been exposed to

a new order that seems, incomprehensibly, to flourish beyond the well-defined
boundaries of village and oustom. (102-103)

But this "new order" is not merely beyond the village; it is specifically
located in the city. In story after story, women who go to the city almost
automatically become prostitutes.

But if the city is a dangerous place for women, in turn city women
"with their too-knowing ways" can mean a dangerous, uncontrolled
sexuality, particularly if such women return to the village, as Mansa
threatens to do at Christmas. Her return will force the community to
confront this "new order" more vividly even than her brother's story is
done.

Perhaps the best example of the sexual threat posed by the prodigal
prostitute can be found in Bessie Head's short story "Life" (1977). The
main character returns home after an absence of seventeen years. "Life had
had the sort of varied career that a city like Johannesburg offered a lot of
black women. She had been a singer, beauty queen, advertising model, and
prostitute. None of these careers were available in the village." The
neighbors are impressed by her glamor but dubious about her money and
her morals. "What caused a stir of amazement was that Life was the first
and the only woman in the village to make a business out of selling
herself." She attracts lots of customers, and "very soon the din and riot of a
Johannesburg township was duplicated."

Surprisingly, one of the most admired men in the village decides to
marry her. But he expects her to behave like a traditional wife, and she can
hardly bear the humdrum routine. "Custom demanded that people care
about each other .... It was the basic strength of village life." But Life cares
about no one except herself. Out of sheer boredom she goes back to her
freewheeling ways, and when her husband finds out, he kills her. She
brought novelty and interest to the village (hence, perhaps, her unusual
name), but her behavior disrupted the entire social fabric.

But perhaps there is more to the question of women in the city than
this vicious cycle of cities corrupting women, who themselves become
emblematic of the oity's corruption. Can we move beyond these stereotypes
to examine other possible interpretations, as well as new images and new
roles for women in the city? As Lloyd Brown has pointed out,

> The archetypally "liberated" woman of the city represents a broader cultural
> challenge to the older order from a brash, alien life-style .... The "bad" women
> of the city are symbols of a new uprootedness that is both exhilarating and
> destructive. Above all, the woman of the city bears a radically subversive
> image precisely because she can no longer be perceived or described within a
> conventional family context. (103-104).

As we think about the theme of this conference, "Beyond Survival," it may be helpful to consider Brown's thesis. The woman of the city is both exhilarating and destructive. She represents a new world that is both "alluring and forbidden" (104). Prostitution is, certainly, one of the worst forms of human degradation, a symbol of a person reduced to mere survival. Yet even in Mansa's raucous bitterness and Life's frenzied hedonism, we may perhaps find signs of something more hopeful. Anta Lo, Beatrice, Mercy—all are searching for the possiblities of a life lived beyond the margins of survival, even when their search ultimately ends in disaster.

In his book *The Sociology of Urban Women's Image in African Literature* (1980), Kenneth Little provides an extensive survey of representations of prostitutes in African fiction. He meticulously details a range of types, from the poor, half-educated village girl taken advantage of in the big city, to the worldly office girl in pursuit of flashy clothes, expensive cars, and glamorous nightclubs. He describes a range of motives, from economic desperation to Hollywood fantasies of glamor. He devotes considerable attention to Cyprian Ekwensi's Jagua Nana, perhaps the most famous prostitute in African literature (76ff). And in the end he asks, "Why are women other than prostitutes so underrepresented in African fiction?":

> We refer to the virtual absence from the literature of women involved in the professions, the public service and business, other than market trading. True, in real life there have only been a few female cabinet ministers; but today there are female diplomats, and women's part in the professions and in the civil service is certainly not negligible. How, then, is this omission to be explained? .... Why is it so difficult to find as a central character a female doctor, lawyer, high-ranking civil servant, director of a public service, and so on? In real life, such persons do exist. (154, 157)

Kenneth Little poses an interesting question (although his conclusion, that male chauvinism is primarily to blame, leaves something to be desired). One answer may be that the prostitute continues to be a very powerful symbol of the conflicts between old and new, rural and urban: the image of the prostitute works on a gut level to express a sooiety's fear that it is spiralling out of control, prey to outside anarchic forces.

Another answer may be that the resonance of the role lends itself to other, more complex uses. In his film, "Guelwaar" (1992), Ousmane Sembene portrays two prostitutes, Sophie and her girlfriend, whose lives represents not a flight from family but a positive contribution to family life: both are supporting their parents and one even manages to send her brother to medical school. Their histories repeat the by-now-familiar tale of inadequate education followed by a hopeless quest for a job in Dakar, and the inevitable descent into prostitution. But the moral Sembene draws from their situation is surprising. For while Sophie's family feels shame at her degradation and their economic dependence on her, they also believe that prostitution is infinitely preferable to begging. Sembene, then, uses the two prostitutes, not to oondemn urban values or lament the loss of tradition, but rather to underline his theme that it is foreign aid which is the true culprit in corrupting contemporary African society. He does not paint a rosy picture: one girl admits that she is "soared stiff" of getting AIDS. Nonetheless, Sembene has moved "beyond survival" to transform the familiar role of the prostitute in an unexpected way.

Finally, despite Kenneth Little's contention, there are indeed other women in African fiction; perhaps not cabinet ministers, but women who deal with urban life without succumbing to prostitution. One thinks of Buchi Emecheta (whom Little doesn't mention) as an example of a writer more concerned with portraying the nitty-gritty reality of life in the city than with using the city primarily as a symbol of loss and corruption. Her autobiographical novel *In the Ditch* (1972) presents London slum life from the perspective of a Nigerian woman with five small children to raise. Adah is a highly educated modern woman with a job in the Civil Service, but when her husband abandons her she is forced to quit work to look after her children. The family sinks further and further into poverty. Adah is not a prostitute, but her fertility sets her up as another potential female urban victim. However, this is a role she refuses to play: instead, she resists by helping to create a makeshift community of other women in similar plights. Rather than giving in to despair, these women gradually find ways to get out of the slums. Adah too finally moves her family to a nice flat in a good neighborhood. But the cost is high in terms of even greater social isolation and loneliness: "In flats like those, you couldn't holler to your neighbors in the mornings when you were hanging the babies' nappies out to dry. In fact, sometimes you got the feeling that you were a Robinson Crusoe, all by yourself" (122-23).

Adah escapes sexual fall, but she cannot escape urban alienation. One way or another, the city exacts its price. She leaves the slums, but only when she is also willing to leave behind the social network that had sustained her: "she moved out ... away from the ditch, to face the world alone .... It was time to become an individual" (121). Cut off from family and friends back home in Nigeria, Adah epitomizes the extreme isolation of the urban individual. Yet by the end, she is ready to embrace this fate, rather than lament endlessly for a nurturing communal culture that no longer exists.

More recently, Nadine Gordimer has offered another example of a woman who transforms her reluctant uprootedness into an exhilarating future. In the novel *My Son's Story* (1990), Aila must leave her job and her familiar neighborhood when her husband insists on moving to Johannesburg. His political involvement soon lands him in jail, and when he gets out he begins a prolonged and passionate affair with a white political activist. For years, Aila endures his neglect with patient devotion. She goes though the motions of domestic harmony, but her life comes to seem increasingly like a hollow sham.

But quietly, beneath the surface, a change is taking place. The outward signs are few: a new haircut, comfortable clothes instead of nylons and heels, a budding though mysterious social life of her own. We begin to suspect she has found a lover. But the truth is far less predictable: this long-suffering middle class housewife has become a revolutionary, hiding guns in her sewing basket. When she goes to jail, her husband assumes she must have been set up by others, so unwilling is he to credit her with independent initiative:

> How, without his having noticed it, had she come to kinds of knowledge that were not for her? And what was it she knew? Whom did she know whose names she couldn't reveal? What was Aila doing, all those months, without him? (222)

Though her husband can hardly grasp it, his wife has become a key player in the political struggle. When he and his son visit her in prison, they are forced to acknowledge her transformation:

> Through the familiar beauty there was a vivid strangeness. Boldly drawn. It was as if some chosen experience had seen in her, as a painter will in his subject, what she was, what was there to be discovered ... In secret, in prison—who knows where—she had sat for her hidden face. They had to recognize her. (230)

"My turn, now," she tells them, laughing. Aila has become "happy for battle" (233, 234). Without any help from her astonished husband, her comrades arrange her triumphant escape from the country.

Perhaps it would not be too optimistic to conclude with the hope that the city is finally beginning to be seen as a place that offers at least the possibility of economic and political enfranchisement for women rather than just sexual victimization. Buchi Emecheta's welfare mother in London battles poverty and emotional isolation, determined to create a new life for her family. Nadine Gordimer's neglected wife in Johannesburg finds her identity through political activism. Paradoxically, even Ousmane Sembene's prostitutes in Dakar keep their families from what he sees as the greater shame of dependence on foreign aid. All of these are women who could be said to be moving "beyond survival" in urban contexts.

WORKS CITED

Aidoo, Ama Ata. *No Sweetness Here.* New York: Doubleday, 1971 (originally published 1970).

Boto, Eza [Mongo Beti]. *Ville Cruelle.* Paris: Presence Afrioaine, 1971.

Brown, Lloyd. *Women Writers in Black Africa.* Westport, CT: Greenwood Press, 1981.

Bruner, Charlotte H., ed. *African Women's Writing.* London: Heinemann, 1993.

Ekwensi, Cyprian. *Jaqua Nana.* London: Heinemann, 1961.

Emecheta, Suohi. *In the Ditch.* London: Allison & Busby, 1972.

Fall, Aminata Sow. *L'appel des arènes.* Dakar: Nouvelles Editions Africaines, 1982.

Gordimer, Nadine. *My Son's Story.* New York: Penguin, 1990.

Head, Bessie. "Life." in *The Collector of Treasures and other Botswana Village Tales.* London: Heinemann, 1977.

Little, Kenneth. *The Sociology of Urban Women's Image in African Literature.* Totowa, NJ: Rowman & Littlefield, 1980.

Miles, Milo. "Sinewy Sweetness From Mali." *The New York Times.* February 20, 1994, 30.

Ngugi wa Thiong'o. "Minutes of Glory." *African Short Stories.* Eds. Achebe & Innes. London: Heinemann, 1985. (originally published in volume of short stories, *Secret Lives,* 1975).

Sembene, Ousmane. *Guelwaar* (film). 1992.

From Rue Cases-Nègres *to* A Dry White Season: The Evolution of Resistance *in Euzhan Palcy's Film*

by Gerise Herndon
Nebraska Wesleyan University

Julianne Burton suggests in her article "Marginal Cinemas and Mainstream Critical Theory" that national culture is defined not only by the origin of its elements, but by its content as well. Filmmakers from countries in Africa and the Caribbean engage in oppositional practice when they "attempt to infuse indigenous content into borrowed forms, adapting the cinema spectacle to their own national/ideological ends" (9). Euzhan Palcy, director of *Rue Cases-Nègres (or Sugar Cane Alley* as it is entitled in English) and *A Dry White Season*, seems to participate in such oppositional practice by valorization of identity as a Martinican and a person of African descent. Such a legitimization produces what Burton calls social pleasures:

> ...those pleasures which derive from and generate a sense of ethnic, community, class, national and gender-based rather than purely individual identity, as well as a sense of common goals and progress towards them. In such circumstances, cinema assumes a kind of auto-ethnographic impulse; it becomes a tool in the discovery and expression of previously unrepresented and under-represented aspects of the "self" as social and cultural being. (18)

Yet is this in fact what Palcy does in both her films? Is it in fact possible in narrative film to adequately represent a social construction of the subject? Does narrative film, especially within the confines of a European or U.S. studio system, automatically generate an ideology of bourgeois individualism? Are stories more often about this particular woman or this particular man rather than a social or cultural self? Using Palcy's two films as examples, I wish to consider these questions while examining the possibilities of representing political resistance both outside and within the Hollywood system.

Palcy's first film, *Rue Cases-Nègres,* tells of the intellectual awakening and coming of age of a poor Martinican boy, José, who, with the inspiration of an old man, Médouze, and the hard labor of his grandmother, moves from rural Martinique to school in Fort-de-France. Palcy was inspired by fellow Martinican Joseph Zobel's autobiographical novel *Rue Cases-Nègres* which she read at age fourteen; she says: "It was the first time that I read a novel by a black man, a black of my country, a black who was speaking about poor people" (cited in Linfield 43). When as a young adult Palcy moved to France to attend university, she consulted with Zobel about turning the novel into a film. She had some difficulty finding a producer and was finally successful in finacing the film because people of Martinique, Aimé Césaire among them, contributed. The film was produced for six million francs and included only two professionals: Darling Legitimus and Douta Seck of Senegal. The rest of the performers were discovered by Palcy as she searched the districts of Martinique to discover the faces she wanted.

The film shows the ideological state apparatus of the educational system as the only means of escaping poverty. In escaping poverty and the cane fields, José also risks losing traditional African-Caribbean cultural history as represented by the elderly cane-cutter and storyteller Médouze. The film shows a narrative and geographic movement *away* from Médouze (who educates José through riddles and stories outdoors by the glow of a firelight) *towards* a bright orderly building in Martinique's largest city where José learns classical Greek drama. It is no accident that one of his first vocabulary words is "territoire." Education proclaims the doctrine of civilization where, as Yvon Leborgne says, "L'Antillais a appris qu'il descend de gaulois et a meublé son imagination de neige, de chateaux, de cathédrales" (541). Perhaps this is why the film remains safest when representing José's childhood. Were the narrative to follow José to adulthood, it would find him leaving the Caribbean for the metropole, another lost to "genocide by substation" as Aimé Césaire described the immigration pattern of his people.

José is sort of a Martinican version of the Horatio Alger story: once his talent is recognized, he achieves a full scholarship. His friend Léopold, however, child of a white overseer at the cane factory and a black mistress, provides the viewer with an alternative response to his situation. Léopold steals the ledger of the white overseer (béké) who succeeds his late father. Léopold wishes to prove that the békés are cheating the blacks of their wages. Here Palcy shows the bleak consequences of political resistance. Léopold is beaten—punished publicly by being dragged through the streets tied to a horse. The community members attempt collective action, but guards prevent them. Is Léopold's suffering then brought about by open political resistance? José learns in school that "L'instruction est la clé qui ouvre la deuxième porte de notre liberté." Had Léopold the proper instruction, could he have succeeded in stealing the béké's ledger unnoticed? And what is *la premiere porte?* Does this absence function as a silence that structures Palcy's film? Is this the political struggle Palcy could not represent?

In Joseph Zobel's subsequent novel, *Quand la neige aura fondu*, José does in fact move to Paris to continue his studies. Given that Zobel followed José's migration but Palcy did not, Palcy's filmic text can be seen as an unfinished process. Rather than concluding this tale definitively, Palcy chose to concentrate on the struggle of South African blacks in her second film. *A Dry White Season,* the adaptation of Andre Brink's novel, also tells the story of intellectual awakening, but this time of an Afrikaner schoolteacher and his son. Unlike *Cry Freedom* and *A World Apart,* which examined apartheid through protagonists who were liberal whites of English background, Palcy's vehicles for consciousness-raising are an Afrikaner, Ben du Toit, his black gardener, Gordon, and their sons. The story is set in 1976, with a student uprising taking place. Gordon orders his son not to participate in any demonstrations. When his son is killed, Gordon determines to find his body. He appeals to Ben for help, to no avail. But when Gordon dies and the security police explain away his body with the fiction of a suicide, Ben begins to believe that he must take action—the conviction has spread from Gordon's son to Gordon to Ben and eventually to Ben's son. Thus, Ben and his son have their consciousness raised by the political action and deaths of first Gordon's son then Gordon himself. Palcy attempts to find a balance between, as she says, "the black world and the white world." (New York *Times* review 17).

Palcy, like the directors of *Cry Freedom* and *A World Apart,* has been accused of compromise because of her supposed focus on white South Africans in the film. However, her broad focus results not purely from ideology, but from material realities of financing a film: "Very clearly nobody wanted to put any money into a black filmmaker making a movie about blacks in South Africa" (Freeman 18). Palcy used South African actors (Winston Ntshona, Zakes Mokae, John Kani), yet she also employs Donald Sutherland, Marion Brando and Susan Sarandon so that white ticket buyers in middle America normally unsympathetic to political films might find someone on screen with whom they could identify. Critic Victoria Carchidi chastises Palcy for choosing actors "not even remotely imaginable as Southern Africans" (21). Carchidi claims that the glossy high-profile packaging is symptomatic of the film's ambivalence, given that, as she claims, the film exploits apartheid for money. True, the film has the unmistakable stamp of Hollywood, and while Hollywood studios will gladly exploit any fashionable political struggle for profit, Palcy most certainly intends to awaken viewers, not to merely capitalize on the struggle. Given the constraints of the financial realities of reaching an audience through film, however, what possibilities did Palcy have? In conventional Hollywood fashion, Palcy uses a traditional linear adventure narrative to reach a broad audience. However, she explains her purpose in framing the story the way she did:

> I originally had a story which portrayed a Black family in South Africa, but I couldn't find any financial backers. I had to find a way to tell the story the way I wanted to tell it, let the world see the reality of apartheid, and keep the studio happy. So in order to say what I wanted to say, I decided to tell the story of two families, one Black, one white. . . . For me, it wasn't really a compromise, because if you want to make a truthful movie about the apartheid regime, you cannot exclude the white people. (interview with Spare Rib).

Palcy also claims that black filmmakers don't need to go against Hollywood; they need to try to deal with Hollywood. She advises independent producers to help Black filmmakers make their first film a hit so that Hollywood will focus on them: "It's all to do with money," she says, "purely a question of business." (*Spare Rib*). Anticipating charges of assimilation, she cites Spike Lee as an example of an African-American filmmaker who worked hard to make the movies he wanted to make and fought with Hollywood studios until they would accept his movies without changes. But is her analogy valid, given that Spike Lee is an African-American? In interviews Palcy talks generally of "black filmmakers" as though the conditions were the same for filmmakers in the U.S., the Caribbean, and Africa. Is this a misplaced emphasis on a generalized black filmmaker's experienced? or perhaps a misplaced emphasis on big-budget Hollywood productions? Should filmmakers' visions be dictated by Hollywood's idea of a hit? And given that Palcy clearly attempted a commercial success, how successful was her own film? What's more, how can we define "success" when discussing a film with clear political intentions?

While *Rue Cases-Nègres* was very successful financially in Martinique (it sold 125,000 tickets, far outselling E.T.'s 35,000) and received favorable reviews in France and the U.S., Palcy's attempt to internationalize her perspective and broaden her audience with her second film met with lukewarm reception in the U.S. Reviewers criticized *A Dry White Season* as "clichéd; explicit" (Kauffman 245); "heavy-handed; didactic; and obvious," (Kael); "predictable"; while other reviewers had praised *Rue Cases-Nègres* for its humanism, universalism, and charm: *Rue Cases-Nègres* was not didactic (interview with *Cineaste*), "apolitique"; not "engagé" (Bassan); it was a coming of age story (Greenbaum 526); José is like Adam "gaining possession of the world with each new thing he names." (Klawans). Andrew Sarris says it was "remarkably free of bitterness and spite" (Voice 50); "universal" (Toubiana); "humanist" (Bassan 47); never falls into "the pitfalls of shrill propaganda!" (Variety). Stanley Kauffmann says "It told the ancient, always moving story of a poor boy fighting his way upward" (24).

Clearly film critics in France and the U.S. enjoy seeing themselves everywhere they look, rather than deal with the profound difference represented in this auto-ethnographic film *(Rue Cases-Nègres)*. Critics fit it into Western or Northern criteria for aesthetic value, an aesthetic that is as familiar as the American Adam and as old as the notion of self-reliance—pulling oneself up by one's bootstraps, so to speak. Perhaps this difference in reception in the two films betrays a modernist demand from critics that, as Jane Tompkins has written in *Sensational Designs*, includes criteria such as "psychological complexity, moral ambiguity, epistemological sophistication, stylistic density, formal economy, finely delineated characters" (xvii). However, Palcy sees her filmic text *A Dry White Season* as an agent of cultural formation rather than an object of interpretation and appraisal: "I didn't make this film for the critics, I made this film for the people." *(Spare Rib)*. She sees her film as an attempt to redefine the social order rather than to fit into European and American values (such as ambiguity, complexity) from the Formalists and New Critics. Political works of art attempt to redefine the social order; as Tompkins says, they articulate and propose solutions for the problems that shape a particular historical moment. In this case, Palcy has a design on her audience, in the sense of wanting them to think and act in a particular way. She claims that the film "cannot be subtle because the system is not subtle. I decided to do away with the idea of subtlety." Palcy sees film as a weapon, and asserts that her duty is "to restore black people's dignity on screen, for Black people, for all the world to see [here we see her dual audience]. And I believe that all Black filmmakers have this duty, because white filmmakers have sold an image of us which is not true" *(Spare Rib)*. Yet given the reviews, how successful was she in reaching either of her two audiences?

Perhaps part of the problem is that Palcy misjudged her U.S. audience. Even the use of famous faces and a suspenseful plot cannot sell a tragedy, which is basically what the film is. As Stanley Klawans, writing for the *Nation*, claims, *A Dry White Season* is something rare and unfashionable, a tragedy. Yes, it is predictable, because that is the nature of the genre. Klawans writes: 'The protagonist pursues his doom for the best of motives, challenging an authority that is deadly in both its force and its laws. The formula for this genre is 'Do the right thing [Spike Lee ref.], then die'—not a welcome lesson for most American audiences" (Klawans 507). While tragedy may not be welcome in U.S. multiplexes, parables certainly are. As pointed out by a *New York Times* article on films about South Africa, South Africa has become a parable in the minds of Americans, in which clearly "good" black characters battle clearly "evil" white characters. Apartheid satisfies a moral hunger among white Americans, a yearning for "clear choices on issues of race that America itself has not offered since the height of the civil rights movement" (13). The article contends that the closest thing to a complex Afrikaner figure in Hollywood's limited repertory is Ben du Toit. Yet, the film is criticized by South African blacks for implying that blacks need a white rescuer and by Afrikaners for failing to capture the cultural and historical ties of their community. One might respond that Palcy is simply showing that blacks and whites need to work together, not that one needs a rescuer. But here one might remark that Palcy is herself a visitor. Yes, she had to go undercover in South Africa to do research, but was that research sufficient to convey the reality of relationships between blacks and whites in South Africa? While the character Ben may be realistic, the friends and relatives around him are so clearly evil that his decision to "do the right thing" seemed easy.

"Doing the right thing" in *A Dry White Season*, unlike in *Rue Cases-Nègres*, involves using force to fight injustice. Palcy's move away from the educational solution of *Rue Cases-Nègres* to the violent one of *A Dry White Season* may be indicative of her inability to conclude definitively José's narrative of upward mobility. Because José's story parallels her own story and perhaps that of Martinique, she turns to a narrative that she can rewrite with a clearer purpose in mind. In *Rue Cases-Nègres* Palcy represents two children's paths to enlightenment: Léopold, the "mulatto" boy, chooses open resistance to white employers as a means to social change in Guadeloupe and is destroyed by that choice; however, the "black" child, José, chooses the more socially acceptable path of education, and the narrative rewards him accordingly. Palcy, however, does not conclude José's story definitively, and the reason may be interpreted from *A Dry White Season* , in which Palcy also demonstrates two boys' paths to enlightenment. The black child chooses overt political resistance to the South African government in the 1976 Soweto uprising and is murdered as a result. Unlike in *Rue Cases-Nègres,* however, in this film the other boy learns from the first boy's death: the black child's murder indirectly leads the Afrikaner boy on the path to political consciousness-raising: the white boy chooses covert political resistance and thus learns how to fight the government stealthily. While Palcy's first film remains within the "safe" realm of promoting education, the second film shows that real education is not always available within the walls of the ideological state apparatus of educational institutions (especially given Ben's role as a schoolteacher of Afrikaner history). Although a black character in *A Dry White Season* claims that "hope is a white word; it's not hope we need," this film nevertheless demonstrates that hope resides within politicized children who in turn politicize adults.

The adults also resist colonial oppression openly. This is where Palcy rewrites Brink's novel through her filmic text. Instead of escaping to Swaziland to join the armed resistance as he does in Brink's novel, Stanley shoots the security police captain responsible for the deaths of so many blacks. The shot with which she concludes this narrative indicates a change in her politics since the filming of *Rue Cases-Nègres:* "This is the first time in a major motion picture from Hollywood that a black man kills a white man and that is the end of the story" (Aufderheide 21). Brink, however, did not like this ending: 'You don't end a system by killing a cop. It's too glib and easy." And reviewers such as Klawant say she "introduces a false note at the end." This raises the question of whether the medium of narrative film can adequately represent political struggle. Given recent Hollywood productions such as *Philadelphia* and *In the Name of the Father*, Hollywood shows a tendency to dilute collective action by encapsulating it into sympathetic individuals that audiences in the heartland can safely identify with. These audiences are generally threatened by difference and are firmly ensconced in a bourgeois humanist individualism that insists on the sameness of individuals and the universality of experience. Given this, is it possible to reach such an audience through the medium of Hollywood film? Is it possible to portray a fictional narrative concerning the Irish Republican Army, AIDS Coalition to Unleash Power, or the African National Congress, without turning a radical message into something sanitized and innocuous?

Limitations of celluloid South Africa are more conspicuous now that the real South Africa is becoming politically more complex. Will films now deal with the negotiations, economic struggle, and class conflict that affect a post-apartheid government? Will these subtleties make for good cinema? "I don't expect Hollywood can give us a film on South Africa with any insight" said Thabiso Leshoai of the *Sowetan*, South Africa's largest black newspaper. "That requries a new sensitivity of some sort, and it will come from South African film makers, especially the new, young black flim makers" (*NewYorkTimes* article). What would be wonderful would be if they have an American budget to do it with.

A comparison of *A Dry White Season* and *Rue Cases-Nègres* raises important issues. Palcy clearly has a qualified vision of hope for Africans and people of African descent, as well as a message of warning in her second film that violence will be met with violence. It is significant that Palcy chose not to end her film with Ben du Toit's death but with Stanley killing Stolz. She says that for her "It's an empowering ending, and it's a kind of hope at the same time.

WORKS CITED

Bassan, Raphael. Revue de *Rue Cases Nègres*. *La Revue du Cinema* 125 *Hors serie* XXIX sommaire 1984. (and no. 387, Oct. 83.)

Burton, Julianne. "Marginal Cinemas and Mainstream Critical Theory." *Screen* May—Aug. 1985: 2-21.

Carchidi, Victoria. "Representing South Africa: Apartheid from Print to Film." *Film and History*. Feb. 1, 1991. V. 21, no. 1. 20-27.

Freedman, Samuel G. "Black Agony Pierces the Heart of an Afrikaner." *New York Times*. Sunday, Sept. 17, 1989. 17+

Greenbaum, Richard. "New Directors New Films" *Films in Review* 3519 nov. 1984: 525-9.

Kael, Pauline. Review of *A Dry White Season*. *New Yorker*, v. 65, n. 33, Oct. 2, 1989.

Kauffmann, Stanley. "Turbulent Lives: Review of *A Dry White Season*." *New Republic*. V. 201, n. 15. Nov. 18, 1989. 353-4.

Keller, Bill. "Is That Really South Africa?" *New York Times*. Oct, 16, 1993. 13+

Klawans, Stuart. "Films. Review of *A Dry White Season*." *The Nation*. Oct. 30, 1989. v. 249, n. 14. 505-8.

Linfield, Susan. "*Sugar Cane Alley*: An Interview with Euzhan Paley." *Cinéaste* 13/4 (1984): 42-45.

Paley, Euzhan. "Interview." *Spare Rib*. Feb. 1, 1990. 12+

Sarris, Andrew. "Oscar Hangover, Third World Crossover." Review of *Rue Cases-Nègres*. *Village Voice* 29: 49+ (Apr.24, 1989)

Toubiana, Serge. 'Les Monstrables' Revue de *Rue Cases-Nègres*. *Cahiers du Cinema* 352 8-13. Oct. 83

Healing Life in Death
Through Narrative:
The Power of Womanspeak
in Maryse Condé's
Moi, Tituba, Sorcière Noire...

by Maude Adjarian

> The world's earliest archives or libraries were the mouth to ear, body to body, hand to hand. In the process of storytelling, speaking and listening refer to realities that do not involve just the imagination. The speech is seen, heard, smelled, tasted and touched. It destroys, brings to life, nurtures. Every woman partakes in the chain of guardianship and transmission.
>
> —Trinh T. Minh-ha, Woman, Native, Other

To contain, heal, transmit; to make and unmake: these are the qualities Trinh T. Min-ha ascribes to women storytellers. *Moi, Tituba, Sorcière Noire...* by Maryse Condé is a fictionalized autobiography about a 17th-century Barbadian slave-woman which actively celebrates these qualities. Both Minh-ha and Condé are concerned with the relationship of the (third world) woman writer to written and oral discourse; and both explore the concept of difference. But where Minh-ha speaks from the generalized position of a theorist, Condé speaks in particularities. For it is her goal not only to affirm the power of black female colonial voices, but also to suggest how they, along with the various discourses to which they are heir, have helped to promote over 300 years of personal and cultural survival in the hostile environment of the New World.

Remembering and speaking in *Moi, Tituba* begins with the mother. The novel begins: "Abena, ma mère, un marin anglais la viola sur le pont du *Christ the King*..." [p.15]. The image Condé presents here suggests a double violation of both a woman and her homeland. Tituba, then, is not simply a slave-woman's child; she is the child of Europe's rape of Africa. To recall the mother is to recall not only cultural origins and the violence of personal beginnings, it is also to recall a larger history of which she (Abena) was part. Speaking the mother's name also affirms connections through lost acts which have not only preceded Tituba, but which have been beyond her control—the dispossession of her mother and her mother's people from Africa and her eventual death by hanging. If Abena is used as the starting point of Tituba's story, then, it is because she simultaneously represents both the part and the whole: she is the physical origin from which Tituba derived her own existence as well as the source of Tituba's first contact with the African culture she attempts to preserve during her lifetime.

Abena, then, is Tituba's first "home." Though "furnished" with cultural lore and personal and community history, it is one from which the half-white—and therefore tainted—Tituba is often turned away as a child. But Tituba is granted access into the "home" represented by Man Yaya, which itself contains a "library" of female learning passed on through generations of women and exists within a single living referent. Condé suggests that this "library" is constructed from intimate knowledge of the "discourse" of the great Earth-mother, origin, home and end of all human life, a knowledge gained from both oral communication and sensory experience. This kind of natural literacy is powerful in the same way that cultural literacy is powerful: both provide means to the end of personal and/or community empowerment. In a world where black colonials as well as the society in which they live are subject to white control, natural knowledge becomes essential. It provides them with the means to ease the physical and emotional manifestations of the daily brutalities visited on them and gives them what they need to survive what colonial culture cruelly enacts on their bodies, minds, and spirits.

By acting as a liaison between nature and the slave community, Tituba therefore assumes the role of a kind of "translator," one who "reads" Nature for the benefit of those who have little else on which to ameliorate, if only slightly, their condition. This renders Tituba fluent in two types of discourse: one, cultural (of human making), and the other, natural (what pre-dates human constructs). As a result, she stands between two discursive worlds, much as she was conceived between two cultural ones. Thus however beneficial she may be to her community, the duality of her status makes her suspect to slaves, who fear her power, and especially to whites. For Tituba is privy to knowledge not actively pursued, defined and *controlled* by the colonizers. She is thus a threat to both white masculine and colonial privilege, that is, to the New World order named into existence by white European males.

Ironically, while it is her Nature "literacy" that keeps her poised in precarious safety on the edge of colonial culture, it is also her nature as a desiring heterosexual woman which finally pulls her away from her liminal position and into a more culturally involved one. As she becomes "enslaved" to John Indien, her first lover-companion, she sacrifices her social status as a free woman and joins him in servitude. John attempts to make Tituba literate in Christian teachings; as he tells her, "Le devoir de l'esclave, c'est de survivre. Tu m'entends? C'est de survivre" [p. 43]. In John's actions as in his speech, a reversal of the mother-paradigm becomes clearly evident. An unconscious agent of colonialism, he tells Tituba about the male-figured European god, and his message—bitterly apt for slaves— of endurance through tribulation. This is in stark contrast to, for example the invocations to Nature that Tituba learns from Man Yaya and the playful animal stories that Abena learns from "la mère de ma mère" [p. 18]. Seen in another light, survival, for John Indien, signifies thinking through, naming, and speaking the words of a (false) father, be it the colonizer's god or by extension, the colonizer himself.

Indien thus initiates Tituba into an ideology which for slaves signifies adopting a double cultural position—one overt, as a yea-sayer to whites, the other covert, as individuals all aware of their status as racial others in colonial society. It is also an ideology to which Indien himself has unconsciously fallen victim, which becomes especially evident during the couple's stay in Salem. To save his life and his personal credibility, Indien, like so many of the white inhabitants of the city, fabricates accounts of demonic possession and accuses innocent people of collaboration with Satan. In other words, John Indien, having astutely "read" the bigoted society of which he finds himself part, repeats back to his masters what he has learned from observing their behavior. In so doing, he insures his own survival, even if what he says might eventually implicate Tituba, as she well knows: ".."n'aurait'il pas été capable de crier: 'Ah! ah! Tituba me tourmente! Ah oui! ma femme, ma femme est une sorcière!'?" [p.171].

Colonial ideology not only severs the ties among members of the same community by gradually supplanting their culture; it also weakens forces to hold apart individuals who might find reasons to ally themselves together. For example, in Elizabeth Parris, the wife of her American slaveholder, Tituba finds one who, though white, also suffers under patriarchal oppression. Both bleed at the hands of their mutual white master after Elizabeth's husband hits them both for "disobedience." Tituba attempts to help Elizabeth through herb-medicines she concocts—symbolic milk to nourish the woman for whom she cares—and through the telling of folk-stories that help alleviate the dreariness of her life. But Elizabeth, like John, stands between two worlds. Elizabeth is white but female and John is male but also a black slave: in other words, neither of the two is both white *and* male and both are therefore among the culturally disempowered. Like John, if Elizabeth is to survive white patriarchy, she must at times conform, even if such actions require her to break allegiances with others, as she eventually does with Tituba.

In Elizabeth Parris, Condé provides one example of the bind in which white heterosexual women find themselves with regard to white heterosexual men. In the figure of Hester Prynne, a character Condé borrows from Nathanial Hawthorne's *The Scarlet Letter*, the writer explores the problem that male-directed desire poses for all women. Hester is Tituba's cellmate during her stay in prison. The cell itself recalls the social isolation in which Tituba herself lives before her involvement with John Indien; it also brings to mind the fact that, prior to her "marriage," Tituba, though alone in the world, was also free. To allow expression of heterosexual female desire may end in a betrayal of the mother-origin-home, of other women and/or of the self. For Hester, however, the answer to this dilemma lies in the creation of a woman-centered, woman-governed society, where men would simply be the means to the end of (female) reproduction. Tituba identifies with Hester's outcast status, as signified by the blackness of her hair and eyes; however, she *cannot* identify with the ideas Hester sets forth. This conflict arises in part from the fact that to do so would mean denying the man-desiring part of herself and committing what she sees as an act of desecration against her nature, itself the product of the larger Nature whose guardian she has become. In other words, Tituba cannot reconcile her own totalizing thinking to the fragmenting one propounded by her cellmate.

It is interesting to note that at one point, Hester becomes frustrated enough with Tituba's insistence on her love of bodily *jouissance* that she exclaims "je ne ferai jamais de toi une féministe!" [p. 160]. This comment is significant because it recalls the distinction Alice Walker makes in *In Search of Our Mothers' Gardens* between "feminist" and "womanist." Through her definition of the latter term, Walker implies that "feminist" refers primarily to educated white (middle-class) women and their struggle for equal social and economic rights with white men. By contrast, "womanist" refers primarily to women of color, both heterosexual and lesbian, and their efforts to preserve "the survival and wholeness of an entire people, male and female." [p. xi]. Condé's depiction of Hester might itself suggest the writer's own attitude toward feminism and toward "feminist utopias" like the one Hester describes: they are attractive, but non-viable as options for heterosexual women of *any* race trying to live in the real world. Hester, it seems, is aware of this; a short time after Tituba leaves prison, she commits suicide. In evaluating Tituba's actions, then, it would seem as though she embodies Walker's notion of "womanism." For not only does she attempt to maintain connection with her foremothers while forging bonds with other women; she also uses her songs, stories and herbal lore for the benefit of the slave community as well as anyone else outside of it who may benefit from her store of knowledge, especially those who have in one way or the other been "wounded" by colonialism and its fraternal twin, patriarchy.

In examining Tituba, her life, and Conde's novel in light of the idea of "womanism," I would also like to suggest that Walker's idea could be revised and particularized with respect to language. Tituba is a womanist in the way in which she acts for the betterment of the colonized and the oppressed. How she speaks—what she says—be it to characters in the novel or to text readers, ultimately works toward the same end. Her utterances reveal the dilemmas of and commonalities and differences between black and white women while they often critique the status quo. They celebrate female heterosexual desire and possibilities of lesbian fulfillment. Seen in a larger historical context, Tituba's words also present another way of looking at history: through the mother and from a highly personal perspective. Building on Walker's idea, then, what Tituba says—how Condé presents it—could be termed *womanspeak*; for like the larger term from which I derive it, *womanspeak* works towards the same end of community-building and identity affirmation.

Tituba's life is a tapestry of suffering, betrayal, separation and loss. But as Man Yaya predicts when Tituba is still very young, "Tu survivras!"—words which are themselves echoed and re-echoed throughout the story Tituba tells. This is precisely what Condé seems most interested in depicting: how she survives. Among the powerful personal resources on which Tituba draws to achieve this end are her deep spirituality, her ability to communicate with the shades of Abena, Man Yaya, with her adoptive father Yao and later, with Hester Prynne. This along with a strong attachment to Barbados, which comes to represent the locus of her identity, a remembered past and a hoped-for future. Ultimately, what Condé seems to be suggesting here is that the survival of the spirit is a task which necessitates the positive engagement of the imagination. The children and adults in Salem are individuals who crush imagination and attempt to repress it, associating it with Satan. But in the end, imagination returns, distorted and perverted by the dominant ideology, to destroy the community.

By presenting Tituba's life as she does, Condé also seems to be addressing the question of what life itself might have meant to the enslaved, especially those who were not far removed from their original homeland and memories of it: a journey from the womb into the living death of slavery and then to the grave. And for slave women like Tituba, the journey was fraught with perhaps especially great peril due to their status as both black and female. Indeed, Tituba questions the imperative to survive at all costs throughout the narrative. During her stay in Salem, she aborts the child she would have had by John Indien, afraid that she would be doing it far greater harm than good by bringing it into such an intolerant world. Yet during the trials she undergoes while in America, she realizes the importance of continuing on, particularly after Hester's suicide. For only in that way can hope and the *possibility* for change exist. Seen in another way, she understands that, in order for the powerless to have any chance of altering the *status quo,* they must demonstrate their ability to endure *as well as* resist. And as Tituba discovers, creating life can impel an individual toward the kind of action which, in and of itself, may not effect change but which may serve as the impetus for other, perhaps more successful actions taken by other people during more auspicious times. Hence her satisfaction at learning, after her death, that her name and deeds are known to other Barbadians though songs sung about her life.

While the words uttered by others are of importance in Tituba's self-replication through time and space, the significance of the words she utters about herself must also be examined. As the fictive speaker from beyond the grave of her own life, she is a kind of oral autobiographer. She is able to look back at life events and make sense of them from the larger cosmic perspective she did not have during her lifetime. As she comments, "Qu'est-ce qu'une vie au regard de l'immensité du temps?" [p. 271]. She is also able to perform another, very important task of curing herself from the colonial malady of maladies: despair. Others may sing of her accomplishments on earth; but she offers her own words about the sufferings she experiences. In this most public way, her spirit effects both a personal purgation and a reconciliation with what was a troubled earthly existence.

If Tituba is able to "speak" to us, it is, of course, as a result of the writerly intervention of Maryse Condé, who states in the preface how she and the sorceress lived in a metaphoric "étroite intimité" during the year Condé wrote—or, better, "took down"—the narrative of Tituba's life. Such a relation would suggest that Condé is attempting to construct herself as a kind of spirit-conjurer who helps a historical "sister" manifest her presence in the present and enact personal healing through the written word. Condé thus becomes a Tituba-like figure who heals through the act of writing. Just as Tituba "reads" Nature and its vegetal products to create physical and spiritual curatives, so Condé reads culture and its *textual* products to derive what she needs to heal Afro-Caribbean—indeed, world—history and make it more whole. For Tituba signifies what has been marginalized and/or left out of this kind of discourse. By specifically choosing this figure from the 17th century as her other-worldly contact, Condé carries a "message" from past history to the present. Women of color should not be content to *just survive* and live their lives unmarked by any accomplishment with regard to their respective communities. For each woman represents the possibility of evolution, of movement *beyond* stasis and all the personal and social debilitation this motionlessness and tolerance of the *status quo* implies.

By forging links between herself and the historical Tituba, then, Maryse Condé establishes herself and her subject as part of an historical chain of storytellers and of mothers and daughters which, to quote Trinh T. Minh-ha, "has no beginning and no end." By re-imagining the sorceress' story and putting it into written form, Condé not only guarantees Tituba's survival in Afro-Caribbean and New World history, but also her own survival as a writer already marginalized by race and gender. Like Tituba, she will speak from the shadowy world of death through those (black women) writers who will come after her and inherit her literary mantle. Condé thereby establishes herself as one of Tituba's 20th century heiresses: a woman who "makes magic" and heals through printed words as Tituba once made magic and healed through spoken ones.

WORKS CITED

Condé, Maryse. *Moi, Tituba, sorcière Noire...* Paris: Mercure de France, 1986.

Minh-ha, Trinh T. *Woman, Native, Other.* Bloomington: Indiana University Press, 1989.

Walker, Alice. *In Search of Our Mothers' Gardens.* New York: Harcourt, Brace, Jovanovich, 1983.

The Poetry of Antonio Jacinto and Jose Craveirinha:
JOURNEYS BEYOND SURVIVAL

by Don Burness
Franklin Pierce College
Rindge, New Hampshire

Writing of his own time, the Russian poet Osip Mandel'shtam lamented "Moy prekracny, jhalky, vek," (my beautiful pitiable age, an age dominated by the blood builder). Mandel'shtam was to be exiled to a concentration camp in Siberia where he died in 1938. The communist beast roared for most of this parasitic century before dying from economic and psychological and moral osteoporosis. In the meantime millions were sacrificed to the blood eating deity including poets like Nikolai Gumilev and Mandel'shtam. Beyond the struggle and the horror, literature survives the living memory of a people. Reading Mandel'shtam today, one admires the man who could sing and would not be silent even though the bear's claws were at his throat. Reading Mandel'shtam, one admires, even loves his poetry, the beautiful ordering of words that speak to us still and warn us of demons that never seem to go away.

Much has been made of the differences between the socially committed African writer and the Western writer dancing in his garden of daffodils for daffodils' sake, but think that Mandel'shtam is not such a rare exception; that, in fact, many writers in the West have been prophets as well as sources of memory: Blake, Neruda, Paul Celan, Akhmatova, Milosz, Petofi, Martí, Yeats,—these are poets who live in the center of society's struggles and hopes.

We are well aware of the tradition of the griot, the praise singer in Africa, a tradition that has inspired modern poets of the pen to remain faithful to the call of the community. Surely in the march to independence, African poets were in the center of the arena. In the nights of disillusion that followed the cheerful morning of independence, the poets have continued to sing to the sound of the gong, and in many instances, like Mandel'shtam they have had to face exile and prison and even death. They have not chosen ease or security. They have marched forward into battle knowing the power of the word to awaken in man the best that is in him, a sense of brotherhood and justice and the vision of a better day. And when the poet dies his language survives to preserve the past and to remind us that the word is holy.

This is perhaps the chief function of poetry. But like the masquerade, poetry must be seen from different angles to appreciate the richness of the performance. If poetry is a social act it is also a personal one. Poetry offers the poet a flight beyond borders of banality. Poetry offers the poet community and companionship and, dare I say it, love. There is great joy in the creative process, there is magic in the muse's message, a magic without which life itself can be reduced to saharas of routine, Kalaharis of the quotidian. Writing poetry is simply an act of love and if there is pain there is also pleasure, offering the poet both joy and necessary solace. A Nigerian soldier and poet, Lt. Colonel Roland Nosukhare Omoregbe Emokpae, expresses this succinctly:

> All I know I sing
> Be it ballad distasteful or requiem sonorous
> Because it brings joy to me, a vent out of
> sorrows
> And fills a vacuum of part of my life.

Omokpae could be speaking for all poets, be they socially committed or not.

Let us look at two of Africa's most decorated poets, Antonio Jacinto of Angola and Jose Craveirinha of Mozambique. They have dedicated much of their lives to social and political struggle. Jacinto, first poet of Noma glory, was imprisoned for twelve years at Tarrafal in Cape Verde by the Portuguese for his activities in the national struggle for independence. As a leading member of the MPLA, Jacinto chronicled the oppression of colonialism from the cry of the contract worker to the suffering of Mother Lemba who weeps for her absent husband, gone to war. Jacinto's poetry was put to music and sung by soldiers in Cabinda and Luanda and along the waters of the Lukala. Along with Agostinho Neto, poet-president of Angola, Jacinto has come to be regarded not only as a spokesman for Angola but as a leading figure in the literary and social history of the continent.

Jacinto summarizes the personal and social dimensions of his art in his poem "Autobiography":

> Your smile
> dancing before my eyes, Mother;
> A bit of Poetry
> to transcend the here and now;
> And life smiling as well
> at the human future that awaits.

Poetry serves the human future, but poetry also is manna to transcend the here and now. While in prison the poet refuses to be enslaved in cages of sterility, despite the bars, the dull repetition of days and nights and days. He entitles one of his poems, "Oh if you Could see Here Poetry That Does Not Exist." Bored, depressed, he tries to recapture images of his mother, that dominant figure of his profoundly simple and clear "Autobiography." This is the woman who used to recite to him by heart, often singing, Portuguese poems of Joao de Deus, Soares dos Passos, Antonio Nobre, Feliciano de Castilho, Tomás Ribeiro, Junqueiro. Recalling his childhood, Jacinto remarked, "In truth, one can say that I sucked the milk of literature from my mother's breast."[1]

There is no apparent poetry in prison in Tarrafal. The poet writes, "Mother, there is no poetry, none." Yet for the poet, the imagination, the flight of metaphor, cannot be destroyed. Suddenly the poet looks up from his cell into the evening sky, and noticing the clouds, magical clouds, poetry is born again:

> Riding a horse of white clouds
> The moon on fire removes shrouds
> Bringing to my pale and listless face
> Kisses, Mother, from you. Kisses.

Through poetry, Jacinto overcame the physical and psychological assaults on his freedom, on his imagination. I am reminded of Wole Soyinka's observation in *The Man Died* that for a person of imagination, what is horrible about prison is not just physical incarceration but also the stifling of the intellect. Without books Soyinka was starving, dying of kwashiokor of the mind.

Jacinto, ingenuous, clear, quintessentially alive, writes poetry as naturally as a bird flies—he calls it "personal discovery under the maternal wing of the world." "Writing," says the poet, "when the soul is not small, is for us, for friends, and for the people...."[2] In Angola the dawn of independence did not bring the sun, but years and years of darkness, of civil war, of death, slaughter, suffering. Jacinto died in 1991 but even though the desired human future that awaits did not materialize in his lifetime, he found life a smiling friend and through poetry, the great gift of his Mother, his life went beyond survival. Reading Jacinto's poetry one feels here was a man who loved life, loved people, loved nature and surely loved words.

One does not feel the same sense of wonder in the poetry of Jose Craveirinha, the only lusophone African writer to be awarded the Camoes prize. In his early years the drum of anger echoed in his lines of protest. Anger at racism, anger at the plight of the "magaica," the Mozambicans

---

[1] Antonio Jacinto, "We are Other People" in *Echoes of The Sunbird: An Anthology of Contemporary African Poetry*, ed. Don Burness, (Athens Ohio, Monographs In International Studies, no. 62) p.103.

[2] Ibid.

who work in the mines of South Africa only to know unremittant poverty and absence from home and family. The titles of some of his early poems suggest his point of view, "Manifesto," "Black Protest," "I Want to be a Drum." Reading these poems of vitriol and challenge, I am reminded of the proud voice of protest of David Diop whose "Coups de Pilon" reflected the need to challenge European devils who demeaned and destroyed the body and soul of African people and African lands.

The later poetry of Craveirinha is an ongoing song of sadness, rooted primarily in responses to the death of his wife Maria. Refusing to let her go and reclaiming her through poetry, Craveirinha, the tender, finds in poetry a vehicle for personal salvation. "Absence," "My Mourning," "In Memorium," "Unjust Saturday," "Ze Craveirinha by Himself"—these titles tell their own story. Maria is everywhere, sorrow finds no refuge. He opens a bureau drawer and sees her kerchiefs and pulls out a poem:

> Your favorite kerchiefs
> without a single crease.
> Kerchiefs dear to me.
> Pure silk
> Kerchiefs that speak to me of tenderness
> making me a widower in the bureau drawer.

Yet for Craveirinha, as for Jacinto, the act of making poetry is pleasurable—it goes beyond psychological survival. It is a form of play. Craveirinha has stated, "For me poetry is an act of passion. It is an act of love. I do not believe that it is possible to write poems without enjoying the taste of words. I enjoy words much as one enjoys a woman's body."[3] Beyond combating personal pain and sadness, writing poetry for Craveirinha is serious sport.

A poet-friend of mine, Niyi Osundare, once told me that his farmer father told him when he was a boy that education should give a man wings. Surely, writing poetry is a form of flight. For the poet cannot live removed from the core of life's essential pain and pleasure; the poet lives with steady intensity. Life is not just survival. There is gaiety in the creative process. For social poets like Jacinto and Craveirinha, literature offers a path to a new and better life, a path from colonization to independence, a path from human folly to human fulfillment. Beyond survival there is hope. They confirm Chinua Achebe's view that "We should be able to ask of poetry that it treat us not as life does or worse, but better."[4] The poet may be exiled or even murdered for his words as Mandel'shtam's life shows, but the poet

---

[3] José Craveirinha, "Poetry is Playing With Words," in *Echoes of The Sunbird*, p. 58.

[4] Chinua Achebe, "When Something Stands, Look Well: Something Else is Standing Right Beside It," in *Echoes of The Sunbird*, p.4.

cannot be silent. Beyond survival, there is commitment to others. Beyond survival there is the imagination, soaring singing beyond the seasons and the gates, always the young bird at the passage.

THE VOYAGER
And The Quest For Atonement

by Obi Maduakor
University of Mainz

When Kofi Awoonor visited the University of Texas in 1971 he was asked whether America had had an effect on his work, and he answered: "It is going to affect my work in terms of my absorbing what I believe will be the totality of my American experience."[1] *Comes the Voyager at Last* (1992) is one of the works that came out of that experience. The action is inscribed within the heady years of the fifties and the sixties in African American history.

Awoonor arrived in the United States towards the close of the turbulent sixties, in November 1968 to be exact. Robert Kennedy had been murdered and Richard Nixon was priming himself for a victorious entry into the White House, having won the Presidential elections of that year. The Vietnam War was in its most escalatory phase. The Civil Rights Movement was still gathering momentum. The Reverend Martin Luther King, Jr. had just been assassinated. His death evoked memories of his achievements as a Civil Rights leader which include the successful Montgomery Bus Boycott of December 1955 and the great March on Washington in 1963 during which he made the famous "I Have a Dream" speech. The radical Black Panther party had been formed in 1966. The Great Black Power Conference in which over seven hundred delegates adopted unanimously the resolution calling for a separate and independent homeland for Black Americans had taken place in the summer of 1967. The trauma of the Africa-American "connection" was bound to affect the imagination of a sensitive African writer-intellectual living in the States in

---

[1] "Interview with Kofi Awoonor" in Bernth Lindfors et. al., eds., *Palaver: Interviews with Five African Writers in Texas* (Texas: African and Afro-American Research Institute, 1972), p.47.

those turbulent years. This was a period, writes Awoonor, "when I sought to understand the mightiest power on earth, grasp my own place as an African, nay, a 'black man,' in the global scheme of things, and expand perhaps the frontiers of human understanding and our common destiny."[2]

The novel focuses on the life of African Americans during the early years of the Civil Rights Movement. The two activists of black nationalism (as the movement is represented in Awoonor's book), Elijah Muhammad and Malcolm X, were leaders of the Nation of Islam, known to many as the Black Muslims cult, a militant religious and quasi-political organisation claiming to have been entrusted with a divine mission to "lead Negroes out of slavery in the wilderness of America."[3] Its teachings were thought to instill racial hatred and to endorse revolutionary violence, while denouncing the Bible vehemently and holding up Islam as the true religion of the black people, celebrating Africa as the spiritual home of black folk all over the Diaspora. The Nation appealed to the down-trodden, the hungry, the poor, the unemployed and the outcasts such as ex-convicts, to whom it gave a sense of belonging and hope.

This characterization of the Black Muslims takes form in the novel. Sheik Lumumba Mandela, the book's young hero, is the prototype of the angry young men of the urban ghetto of the sixties. Harassed and molested by Babylon, he finds redemption in the Black Muslims. Like most of the members of the organization including their leaders, he is an ex-convict, jailed for an offence he did not commit, and like some of the members, he too returns to Africa on a spiritual pilgrimage. Malcolm X made such a pilgrimage in 1964, visiting Mecca as well as Nigeria, Ghana and other African countries.

Lumumba's return to Africa is the culmination of the wayfarer motif that has featured prominently in Awoonor's works. The speaker in most of the poems in *Night of My Blood* is a poet-persona like the narrators in the novel. He has witnessed many journeys and is concerned with the need for an individual or a community to make a ritual crossing in order to bridge the gap between the physical self and the spiritual self. In the poem "Exiles" he dismisses as "lost souls" those who lack the will to dare transition. In "Night of My Blood" he celebrates the "burning feet" of a whole community emerging from a ritual journey bearing tokens of their symbolic death, a "million crucifixes" which they bore "across the vastness of time." In "I Heard a Bird Cry" he deplores the cudgel wounds of a

[2] "Kofi Nyidevu Awoonor," in *Contemporary Authors Autobiography*, vol. 13 (Detroit: Gale Research Inc., 1991), p.47.

[3] Simeon Booker, *Black Man's America* (Englewood Cliffs: Prentice-Hall, Inc., 1964), p.121.

caravan of sorrow returning to the fetish hut after years of spiritual separation:

> My people, where have you been
> And there are tears in your eyes?
> Your eyes are red like chewed kola
> And you limp towards the fetish hut.
> My people, what has happened
> And you bear many cudgel wounds
> and rope marks cover your naked bodies?[4]

The poet speaks of his own Middle Passage in reverse in the poem "The Wayfarer Comes Home" when he returns to Africa by sea after a sojourn of seven years in the United States:

> I too have come home to be born in the wake of the seed.
> In the single way journey upon the sea.
> My companions the flying fish
> heading towards the coast to Senegal. We rode, we rode
> taking the waves as we traced the Middle Passage backwards
> in the smell of vomit
> our light bent for home
> grey in the August moon.[5]

All these references to journeying are brought to a climax in the three epic journeys in the novel: Lumumba's ancestors' journey from the Savannas to the sea, and from the sea via the Middle Passage to the new world; and Lumumba's own passage to Africa.

The narrative method recalls the technique of *This Earth, My Brother*. Passages of intense poetic beauty are juxtaposed with prose narratives but this perhaps does not do full justice to the book's poetic tonality. The entire narrative is poetic in its totality. Each of the three narrators is a poet, although the third narrator, whose circumstances are close to Awoonor's, is somewhat too conscious of his poetic abilities. The book is made up of three narrative plots each told by a separate narrator and unified by the presence in two of Lumumba himself and by the presence of his ancestral forebears in the first, that is, the plot of the slave caravan. The story of the slave caravan and the story of Lumumba's experience in Babylon told by himself run side-by-side up till the middle of the book, where they merge into one, fused together by a dream symbol. The second half, constituting the third plot, follows Lumumba to Africa. An earlier version of this part of the book was written much earlier and had appeared in the Nsukka journal *Okike* in 1975.

---

[4] Kofi Awoonor, *Night of My Blood* (New York: Doubleday, 1971), p.44.

[5] Kofi Awoonor, *The House By The Sea* (Greenfield Centre, New York: Greenfield Review Press, 1978), p.65.

The story is told all through in segments of unnumbered chapters, which in their undemarcated totality would appear, in this author's estimation, to have achieved a greater effect of wholeness and unity than would have been the case if they had been separated by a numbering device. Awoonor did deplore the numbering of the chapters in *This Earth* as a publisher's error. That device, he said, imposed too rigid a form on the structure of the novel.[6] Here in *The Voyager* a sense of interconnectedness is achieved for all the sections in the fluid structuring which eschews chapter numbering. The story of the slave caravan is indicated by italics and Lumumba's story in Babylon and Africa is put in regular type.

Lumumba's story is a catalogue of the woes to which black people are heir in Babylon. He has lived through four centuries of oppression in that wicked land. His ancestors were forcefully transported into the new world as slaves to work the land and do domestic chores. Since then it has been with them four centuries of sacrifice and of giving to a god who knows how to take but gives nothing in return except pain and death. Two of Lumumba's ancestors fought in the Civil War. One was killed in action a few days before the war ended. The other was among the one thousand Negro soldiers who perished at the Battle of the Crater when "they marched in valiantly against superior fire after three white divisions had refused to advance."[7] Lumumba is worried by the fact that the names of these heroes are not commemorated on even a wooden plaque.

Lumumba's father drudged his life away as a railway nightguard. His mother worked as a cleaning lady. In Lumumba's own generation the suffering and the sacrifice have not abated. If anything, they have been intensified. Lumumba works a nine-hour shift in a plastics factory, for "we would never become executives in suits in these establishments" (p.40). And there is the ever-threatening imminence of lynching and of violent death: "You carried the smell of your own violent blood and death in your wide nostrils." (p.8)

Lumumba's passage leads him through three initiations: his initiation into the discovery of personal freedom at his father's death; his initiation into a personal experience of the realities of Babylon; and his initiation into a personal discovery of the meaning of Africa.

He had been brought up under a strict parental tutelage with a father who was a bully and a pious mother who imposed a religious discipline upon the children. His father's death liberated him from a futile

---

[6] Lindfors *et al* , p. 61.

[7] Kofi Awoonor, *Comes the Voyager at Last* (Trenton: Africa World Press, Inc. 1992), p.10.

domestic routine and initiated him into a discovery of personal freedom: "I was in a new world, in the throes of new sensations. I was discovering myself and my potentialities. My father had died so that I might be saved" (p.22). But this freedom is attended with an intellectual comprehension of his destiny as a black man; it sharpens his sensitivity to "the Negro question": "I seemed to be more aware of the world then. My senses of smell, touch and taste became keener .... My heart began to stir from a deeper slumber of four centuries .... I was aware of the historical wilderness in which I and my people had lived" (p. 21).

New York, the scene of his next initiation, is the "city of god" (p.34), the "un-real city of redemption" (p.31). Lumumba had gone there to savour his new-found freedom. But within six months of his arrival there Lumumba was jailed. Six months later the case against him was dropped and he was released. In prison Lumumba meets thousands of other black youths who have been made victims of the arbitrary and high-handed system of justice in Babylon: "There were and still are kids in that jail whose lives are blighted because they are black and poor and no one will ever care about them" (p. 48). To the agents of the law black people are part of the statistics of urban crime.

Lumumba is critical of his countrymen's apathy towards their destiny in Babylon. He blames it on what he calls the "Good Lord syndrome" which has sapped their will and emasculated their energy. Simeon Booker has noted that for some time the Negroes believed that they had only got to pray to be delivered from the white man's cruel world:

> Church, to him, was a place to pray to the white man's God that he some day could go to heaven and put on a pair of silvery wings.8

And Stokely Carmichael and Charles V Hamilton add that until the Civil Rights Era the history of the country shows that black people could come together to do only three things: sing, pray, dance.[9]

Lumumba mocks the "Good Lord" syndrome with gentle irony. His people, he says, are men

> whose only claim to humanity seemed to have been their signal endurance record under the whip, men who sought refuge in the good book, and actually

---

8
Booker, p. 108.

9
Stokely Carmichael and Charles V Hamilton, *Black Power: The Politics of Liberation* (New York: Vintage Books, 1967), p.100.

believed that they too, as God's children, will be given brightly coloured robes to cover their nakedness on that glorious judgement day (p.8).

He dissociates himself from the crippling apathy and embraces the Black Muslims soon after his release from prison. The Black Muslims encourage the kind of questions that have begun to stir Lumumba's mind, questions bordering on his destiny and his origin. Lumumba says of Malcolm X that "he gave us a vision of ourselves, of our true homeland Africa before he died" (pp. 83-84).

The homeland question is one that touches a sensitive chord in the life of every Black American, opines Robert S Browne.[10] Its absence, he says, exacts a severe price from his psyche. He is unique in the sense that among the many cultural groups of the world he is the only one that has no homeland. America cannot be his homeland because he senses from a very early age that he is different and that he is victimized. He is in a desperate need of a place where he can experience the security which comes from being a part of the majority culture. In this regard, Africa is welcomed as the homeland which he so desperately needs.

Thus, Lumumba goes to Africa in search of a homeland. It is here that his third initiation takes place, and it is at the point of his departure that his story merges with the story of the slave caravan.

That story is an even more harrowing tale of woe than Lumumba's account of his misery in Babylon. The narrator describes the caravan as "a silent processional unto death and degradation" (p.25). About one hundred African captives chained together and tied to a common leash are dragging their way southwards from the northern savannas towards the sea that will take them to the New World. They are tortured and beaten by their cruel captors. One old man with the "magical word" collapses under the impact of the beatings. A phantom woman, half human and half spirit who protests against the enslavement of her children (she is mother Africa enraged by the humiliation of her children) is butchered in one fell swoop.

In all these stories Awoonor endows blood with sacrificial potency. The spilt blood of the old man with the "magical word" and the blood of the phantom woman is invested with sacrificial potency: it is the blood of sacrifice. The old man is described as the caravan's "lamb of sacrifice" (p.3). We are told that "he kept his bleating on through the village lane behind the priest on his way to the shrine where his throat will be cut" (p. 3). The blood of the phantom woman liberates the captives from their chain

10 Robert S Browne, "The Case for Black Separatism: 1967,11 in Bradford Chambers, ed., *Chronicles of Black Protest* (New York: Mentor Books, 1968), pp. 234-235.

and binds them together with a common knowledge of their destiny: "it released our long manacled spirits and sets them soaring in the knowledge that this is perhaps the ultimate end of our journey" (p.29). It is this brutal knowledge that the poet speaks of as "the allegory becoming the truth" (p.29), that is, the symbol (their chain, the journey) has coincided with its referent (death). Over there in Babylon many blacks have been lynched and hounded to death but the sacrificial blood is provided by the symbolic death of Malcolm X, murdered as a martyr.

The immediate event that leads to Lumumba's flight into deeper recesses of the African heart of darkness is not so important in itself as in the leverage it has given the author to get even with fellow novelist Ayi Kwei Armah. Nothing could have been lost if the poet had gone straight to the celebration of Lumumba's homecoming. But the extended structural scaffolding upon which the African episode is built enables Awoonor to catch up with Armah who had portrayed him as "Asante-Smith" in *Fragments*. In the original version of the episode published in 1975 Armah is referred to as a "Harvard African novelist ... set ablaze by the call of revolutionary blood."[11] Here in the novel he is called "the journalist fellow from Brown" (p.85). The revision is not thorough, for Harvard surfaces occasionally as a slip of the pen (p. 90).

After the riotous episode at the Osu Bar in which Lumumba attacks a group of Europeans, killing their African bodyguard (the Europeans reminded him of Babylon), he flees with the poet-narrator to his hometown in Eweland. The flight is a homecoming for Lumumba. The narrator's uncle, who is both a priest and a diviner, divines outright that Lumumba is a lost son who has come home: "he is one of those people who left us long ago" (p. 111). Lumumba attends a ceremony of healing taking place in the dark amidst the wailing of ceremonial drums. The noble savage ingredients of an African nightfare are here invoked to the full and invested with dignity: The frightening darkness, the hooting owl, the magic drums transmitting their mystical rhythms, the tangible darkness and the mercurial echo of the drums, sounding very close and yet far away. These are instruments for initiating Lumumba into the reality of Africa. In "Voyager and the Earth," Awoonor holds brief for African traditional customs, stating that they "possess a nobility of body and gesture, if not of mind," and that they must be "protected from imminent extinction."[12] About the entire experience Lumumba says:

---

[11] Kofi Awoonor, "From *Comes the Voyager at Last*-Fiction" *Okike* 7 (April, 1975), p.43.

[12] Kofi Awoonor, "Voyager and the Earth," *New Letters*, 40,1 (1973), p.85.

There was something eerie, weird about it, especially the shrill
female voices of the chorus that seemed to be suspended on the air
waves long after the drums had ceased to be a voluble echo of the
deep and fearful night .... I was not afraid for my life, I was
apprehensive of the powers of this dark night, powers that the
voices and the drums seemed to be releasing into the world
(p.133).

The little girl undergoing the healing ritual is a reincarnated replica
of Dede of *This Earth, My Brother.* Lumumba and the girl are attracted to
each other by mutual empathy. Lumumba was fascinated by the girl's
beauty when he saw her for the first time and thought that he had seen her
before (in the world of myth, of course). On her part the girl welcomes
Lumumba as her husband who has come home from the journey to the
forest and a desert land where he had gone to hunt (p.121).

The climax of the homecoming occurs at the moment when
Lumumba, captivated by the bewitching rhythm of the mystical drums,
hurls himself into the centre of the magic circle to embrace the girl dancing
within the circle. This is for him a magical moment of self-discovery,
rebirth and homecoming. The contentment he feels at this moment recalls in
its healing and restorative wholeness Amamu's final encounter with the
woman of the sea. And it looks as if Awoonor intends the reader to make
this connection. Contentment and fascination register visibly on the face of
the returning lovers in each case: "There was a look of fascination, and an
indescribable contentment upon his face" (p.121). The girl is again another
image of the maternal essence bedecked with the same healing concoctions
for the returning lover as is the case with the woman of the sea: "she
brought into the room the beautiful smell of camwood and some other
spices" (p.114).

Lumumba is physically and emotionally healed with the beautiful
girl serving him food and rubbing the herbal ointment all over his body with
her delicate fingers. But the spiritual aspect of the healing is much more
important. It is the spiritual bond that catapulted Lumumba into the magic
circle to embrace the dancing girl. The implications of this moment are
expanded fully in the final chapter, which celebrates universal harmony in
surrealistic terms.

Lumumba is given to much dreaming. The two things that matter
to him most impinge themselves on his subconscious as dreams: his slave
past and his expectation (since his contact with the Black Muslims) of the
black millenium. Three of the dreams link him with his slave past (the
dreams on pages 40-42, 51-52, and 130-132). The other two dreams (the

final dream and the one that occurred at Lenox Avenue) telescope the millenium. Outside the premises of the mosque at Lenox Corner Lumumba sees a procession of redeemed Moslem faithfuls converging from all corners of Babylon towards Lenox Corner. From there they move in a slow procession (singing and dancing) towards the festival of blackness singing nuptial songs. They are expecting the King who will come to redeem them.

This dream is extended into the final apocalyptic evocation of universal harmony. In that final dream the expected King has come. The millenium is here. In content and detail this millenium is nothing short of the New Jerusalem of the Christian apocalypse[13] except that it is not the Lamb that leads the celebrants this time but the poet who releases with his mouth "the hidden essence of all things, restoring the unity of ALL by the power of the WORD" (p. 137). The dream indeed echoes the vision of universal harmony in the "I Have a Dream" speech made by the Reverend Dr. Martin Luther King, Jr.:

> I have a dream ... that one day ... little black boys and black girls will be able to join hands with little white boys and white girls as sisters. I have a dream that one day every valley shall be exalted, every hill and mountain shall be made low. The rough places will be made plain, and the crooked places will be made straight. And the glory of the Lord shall be revealed, and all flesh shall see it together.[14]

Oppression and racial hatred/difference have no place either in Dr. Martin Luther King's vision or in this festival of universal reconciliation:

> Then, as if in response to the music's call, the whole valley burst into life. There poured into it from nowhere a host of men, women, children, and flocks of birds that darkened the face of the moon ... The people were of all colours of the earth, pale, pink, red, brown, black, Europeans, Jews, Asians, Africans, each group in its colourful clothes (p. 137).

Lumumba himself is born anew having been cleansed of four centuries of racial hatred: "The suspended and preoccupied moon, destitute passion of my rebirth, was the cleansing force washing away the hate and calamity I once bore" (p.137).

But the occasion is also a celebration of Lumumba's marriage with the beautiful girl. That is why this celebration is an extension of that

---

[13] See the book of *Isaiah* 11: 6-8.

[14] Martin Luther King, Jr., "I Have a Dream," in Bradford Chambers, ed., *Chronicles of Black Protest*, p.186.

magical moment of union at the magic circle. Lumumba is given a place of honour at the festival. The wedding is blessed by the whole of creation. Gods, humans, and animals pay him homage, bringing their wedding presents.

This is the moment of atonement which in the special Awoonor context of the word means "at-oneness," the individual's attainment of "oneness" both with himself and with his community: "My poetry has sought not only to achieve this reintegration, an 'atonement' (at-oneness) with my culture, but also to make that the elemental basis of my literary statement."[15] "Art," Awoonor writes in a different context, "assays a reassemblement, the establishment of a harmonic order."[16] Awoonor designs the end of his novels to correspond with his vision of the ultimate harmony which art ought to generate.

But is the millenium something to be sublimated through fantasy? At the beginning of the novel the vision has lost its magic and Lumumba is returning to Babylon. This confirms Robert S Browne's observation that the value of Africa as a homeland for Black Americans is merely symbolic:

> They had been away from Africa for too long and the differences in language, food and custom barred them from experiencing the 'at home' sensation which they were eagerly seeking. Symbolically, independent Africa could serve them as a homeland, practically it could not.[17]

The language of the novel is dense, myth-embryonic and potent. What matches the symbolic reverberations of language particularly in the caravan story, is the evocation of Amamu's pre-birth and the womb of origin in *This Earth*. Awoonor has properly designated this story "a poetic tale."[18] His creative imagination is essentially poetic so that when he attempts the novel genre his sensibilities as a poet intrude upon the effort as all his stories bear out. Awoonor is aware of his peculiar addiction to the poetic which tends to interfere with his effort at the prose-fictional: "I was aware that I was not essentially a prose-fiction writer."[19]

Myth and oriental magic combine to enrich the language, providing it with much of its charm. This is perhaps to be expected from the allusion to Keatsian oriental emperors at the beginning of the novel. In one

---

[15] "Kofi Nyidevu Awoonor," *Contemporary Authors Autobiography*, vol. 13, p.46.

[16] "Voyager and the Earth," p.90.

[17] Browne, p. 234-235.

[18] Publisher's blurb.

[19] Lindfors *et al*, p.61.

of his dreams Lumumba catches a vision of "young riders on gaily caparisoned horses" wielding "leather flutes of Arabian nights" and galloping towards "the black nirvana" (p.14). There was also a "procession of young nubile maidens naked from the waist down, but veiled from the destructive power of the noon-day sun and the desert wind. On their feet were sandals shod in pure gold" (p.64).

In one of the caravan episodes earth is apostrophised as "the divinity that oversees our days, maternal essence of invisibility, the only certainty we know. Her divine sister was the echo among the trees, generated by footsteps on cracking twigs" (p.46). Perhaps all this is overdone, but the celebration of mysteries and the beauty of iridescent moonbeams make this story a magic tale.

Post-Apartheid Drama

by Donald Morales
Mercy College

In Esiaba Irobi's play, *Gold, Frankincense and Myrrh* [1989], the Nigerian playwright turns the long-standing debate on Wole Soyinka's linguistic complexity into high comedy. The setting is an African Writer's convention at the Ibadan University Staff Club where Soyinka is on trial for "crimes" of "private obscurantism," and "gratuitous conundrums" (25). To underscore these charges, Irobi gives Soyinka, "Ogun" in the play, an interpreter to paraphrase his remarks for an attending audience of writers and scholars.[1] However, in the midst of this comic debate, a South African woman proffers a sobering thought, "Do you think all this howling about elitist and traditional literature would arise if you were in South Africa? If you were suffering the abject negation of man...?" (44).

Such a literary debate and satiric play would seem improbable in South Africa—at least in the South Africa of Apartheid. Apartheid has etched such an indelible mark over South African life that it serves as a palimpsest over which writers try to fashion new ideas. Athol Fugard's drama, *A Road to Mecca*, for example, contrasts two Afrikaner women who stand on opposite poles of social conformity and rebellion, yet apartheid's presence is never absent. One brief meeting of a dispossessed black woman[2] and child in the Karoo desert reinforces the ideas of desolation and moral censorship placed on the Afrikaner women.

Writing in South Africa has not been able to escape the assumption of politics. Fugard observes:

> if you're a black person in South Africa, and an opportunity comes up to tell a story on stage, any real separation of arts and politics is impossible. The black person's sense of silence, of not having had a voice, is colossal. (Engstrom 22)

Thus without a means of redress through the political process, the South African artist becomes, willingly or unwillingly, the artist/politician.

---

[1] Among the participants are Chinua Achebe [Achibiri], Ayi Kwei Armah [Baako], J.P. Clark [Clerk], Femi Osofisan [Osofolo], Ngugi Wa Thiong'o [Kariuka], Chinweizu [Chekwas].

[2] The play's original title—*My English Name Is Patience*—is a reference to this black woman who has been widowed and forced to move on (O'Quinn 43).

"Culture is," playwright Matsemela Manaka comments, "one of the last weapons we have to mobilize society for change" (Horn vii). But as South Africa heads in the direction of an excruciatingly slow democratization, what happens to the nature of a theater that relies so heavily on political metaphor? As the remnants of apartheid are buried deeper into the palimpsest, in what direction does South African theater move for black and white playwrights?

Very little writing has come out of South Africa since the February 11, 1990, release of Nelson Mandela. There seems to be an unconscious literary moratorium while awaiting the outcome of South Africa's political quagmire and acclimatization to a new order. It would be pure speculation to predict the nature of future writing. Breyten Breytenback, in a new travelogue, *Return to Paradise* [1993], warns:

> To my mind only a fool would pretend to understand comprehensively what South Africa is really about, or be objective and farsighted enough to glimpse its future course (xviii).

But based on what little has emerged in and outside of South Africa, plays like Fugard's *Playland* [1992] and *My Life* [1994], Duma Ndlovu's *Black Codes from the Underground* [1993], Tug Yourgrau's *Song of Jacob Zulu* [1993], Mbongeni Ngema's *Sheila's Day* [1993], Hilary Blecher's *Daughter of Nebo* [1993], one can at least venture into possibilities. Surely there will be a sense of negotiation in the plays, an awareness by artists of the datedness of past themes. Afrikaner writing is understandably paranoiac, guilt-ridden and conciliatory—when the Afrikaner woman in *A Road to Mecca* offers the nomadic black a ride, it is offered culpably and not with a sense of wanting to effect change. Dennis Brutus recently commented that reconciliation is "part of the national psyche and part of the process of creating a new South Africa" (Personal Interview). If this national psyche is explored honestly, it can lead to great drama rather than drama that has become predictable and static.

Writing by black South Africans may move into a more self-revelatory mode, casting off overt political writing since apartheid may no longer be an obvious target. Irobi's play is an in-house investigation of Nigerian writing. While politics is and has always been a vital ingredient in Nigerian life, it is in the background of this play, a play where cultural choices move to the forefront. Percy Mtwa's *Bopha* produced in 1986 and turned into a 1993 film, and Ngema's new drama *Magic at Four AM* move slowly away from straight political theater and more into self disclosure.

Coleen Angove in a constructive essay, "Alternative Theatre: Reflecting a Multi Racial South African Society?," observed South African drama from the Grahamstown Festival and considered whether the society on stage reflected a South Africa moving towards unification or polarization. She witnessed current theater falling into three classes: an Afrikaner drama preoccupied with white fears over a black controlled government; a black theater that primarily aired black grievances aimed at black audiences; and an alternative theater that rejected polarization while attempting to graft a distinct South Africa, a theater of reconciliation.

The first class of plays comes out of a conservative Afrikaner mindset. Norman Coombs' *Snake in the Grass* [Feb. 1988] depicts elderly whites living in a colonial style hotel. The heavily symbolic play uses a melancholic and nostalgic setting that signals the end of white control in Africa. Ian Bruce's *My Father's House* [1989] is set in post-revolutionary South Africa now populated with white ghettos under the repressive forces of blacks. *Scorched Earth* [April 1988] by Pieter Dirk Ulys tackles the homeland question. An Afrikaner family's ownership of an estate given them for their service to the English is threatened by the new post-apartheid black government (41). These plays illustrate the paranoiac fears of the Afrikaner for a black-centered government and the diminished role whites play. They are agitprop types geared obviously to a very specific white conservative clientele with an iron resolve to give up nothing.

A more problematic class is the theater of reconciliation, liberal Afrikaner writing that runs across racial barriers with varying levels of communication. Each character is allowed "a voice, an opinion, an indulgence" (43). One example Angrove cites is the March 1989 Market Theater production of Pieter-Dirk Ulys' *Just Like Home*. It is a play of exiles: Cathy September, a black domestic who travels to London with her South Africa employers; Hector Price, a white political exile and Trevor Juries, a nephew of the domestic in London fighting for the revolution. Cathy, after twelve years in London, decides to return to South Africa for non-political reasons and finds herself justifying her return to both Hector and Trevor (43). The final irony is that South Africa unites each character because in the end it is home to all.

What is troubling is the facile treatment of an endemic South African problem. Because apartheid separated society so conclusively, there was and still is very little opportunity for cultural exchange, more so for whites, and this can become a problem when Afrikaner dramatists voice what they presume are black aspirations. The Afrikaner playwright often writes from the perspective of an outsider, leading, in some cases, to political stereotypes that lack human dimensions, or plays that contain misleading desires of its black characters.

A play that comes to mind is *The Song of Jacob Zulu* which opened at Chicago's Steppenwolf Theater in late 1992. Tug Yourgrau, a white South African documentary filmmaker and television producer who came to the US when he was ten, conceived the musical. It was originally a courtroom teleplay based on the 1985 bombing of a shopping center near

Durban that killed five people and injured fifty. The accused, Andrew Zondo, a nineteen-year-old son of a black minister, was convicted and hanged (Waites 25). Yourgrau examines this transformation from a bright and quiet religious man to an ANC member turned terrorist.

The play ruminated for some five years before it was reconceived for the Steppenwolf Theater in 1990. Yourgrau collaborated with Ladysmith Black Mambazo, the nine male-member a cappella group known for Isicathamiya, a folk form that combines traditional Zulu, varied gospel, R&B, doo-wop with stomping dance movements (Pareles 1). The playwright uses Ladysmith as a Greek chorus to comment on the action of the play, but the group, led by Joseph Shabalala, becomes instead the heart and soul of the drama which in turn exposes Yourgrau's bare and polemical script. Frank Rich of the *New York Times* wrote that the anti-apartheid drama "lack [ed] the poetic texture, eloquence, surprises and deep feeling— in short, the voice—of its music" (Rich "Sad Song" 17). There is a level of arrogation of Ladysmith because Yourgrau, of necessity, writes from the vantage point of an interloper. Rich lauds the mining camp origins of the music but is not as generous with Yourgrau's writing which he describes as "utilitarian" and "pedagogical" (17). Yourgrau's comment about Ladysmith's inclusion is telling: "I think it [Ladysmith] made a difference, I think Ladysmith was our trump card" (Waites 25). The character of Jacob Zulu is never illuminated but regresses into a blurry metaphor for South African injustice. Mr. Yourgrau's distance from his subjects produces a static work that does not move beyond cliché.

The most prominent of the Afrikaner playwrights is Athol Fugard. He is at once committed to change yet ambivalent about this commitment. After a career of anti-apartheid plays that subtly attacked the way he envisioned apartheid affected blacks—*Bloodknot* (1961), *Boesman and Lena* (1969), *Statements* (1972), *Sizwe Banzi Is Dead* and *The Island* (1973)—Fugard changed perspective. *A Lesson from Aloes* (1980) portrayed the effects of the growing South African violence upon an Afrikaner family. *Master Harold and the Boys* (1982), largely autobiographical, recounted the growing chasm that inevitably occurs between master and servant. *The Road to Mecca* (1984) focused almost exclusively on the isolation of two Afrikaner women. Most surprisingly, *A Place with the Pigs* (1987), described as a personal parable of a Russian deserter in self-imposed exile for forty-one years, was set outside of South Africa. When questioned about this change he responded:

> obviously politics is one of the elements in my playwriting...[but] sometimes create [s] a wrong anticipation on the part of critics and audiences who wait for a certain sort of thing when I'm doing something else" (Engstrom 22).

Politics often forces an individual to take positions that compromise ideals. In Fugard's case he was castigating his own sense of identity. Living in South Africa under apartheid created for him a "monumental guilt trip...by being white, by being an Afrikaner...circumstances have made me harshly judge South Africa, and I am judging something I love. I am judging my own people" (Freedman 1). In writing *Boesman and Lena*, Fugard reflected, "Can I align myself with a future, a possibility, which I believe in (hope for) but of which I have no image" (*Notebooks* 179). In his *Notebooks* he questioned his commitment to a changing South Africa: "Could it [change] be sooner if I chose to sacrifice. But I can't" (161).

Fugard's *My Children, My Africa* [1989] seemingly returns to the political front—the 1984 school boycotts. A black school teacher and student trade political differences, but stationed between the two is a young Afrikaner student whose debating team is brought in from a private boarding school as an experiment meant to lift the shadow of ignorance between the races. Young Isabel has virtually no contact with blacks accept for an "auntie" and a boy who delivers medicine for her chemist father. She initially views her relationship with Thami, the black student, as a great liberal experiment, but during the course of the drama, her character grows as she realizes "there is a whole world without [her] imprint." The play is essentially an argument where Fugard's persona, the black school teacher, debates education over politics. Fugard, like Yourgrau, is writing as an observer and imposing his vision of reality over something very distant from him. This distance sometimes questions the credibility of his plays, especially among black observers. Producer/playwright Duma Ndlovu points out that Fugard writes what he thinks is a political priority for blacks. Ndlovu looks at the themes of *Bloodknot*, *Boesman and Lena* and *Master Harold* as priorities low on the political agenda for blacks (Personal Interview).

One of the dramas to emerge from Fugard since Mandela's release is *Playland*, originally produced at the Market Theater in July, 1992. *Playland* is set in a traveling amusement park bordering a Karoo town in South Africa. The time is New Year's Eve 1989, several weeks before the February 11, 1990, release of Nelson Mandela. Its two characters, a black night watchman and a white Defense Force soldier, pass the evening attempting to hide the sins of their pasts: Martinus Zoeloe, the watchman, killed an Afrikaner for raping the woman he loved, while Gideon Le Roux gunned down dozens of black rebels in his border confrontation with SWAPO while in the South African Defense Force. Fugard spreads the guilt equally so that their confrontation can end in optimism, an optimism Fugard would like to extend to a new South Africa.

One New York critic, complained that Fugard has been writing the same play since *Bloodknot* in 1961 (Simon 71). The criticism suggests that since South Africa has changed, should not there be changing themes in Fugard's writing? So many of his plays investigate an existential landscape using Port Elizabeth as backdrop; there is not the writing of an engaged artist fully aware of the full-bodiness of its black characters. He has always been more concerned with man's isolation in an alien universe than with the volatile political predicament in South Africa. South African poet/activist Dennis Brutus has always sensed a degree of dishonesty in Fugard's "committed" theater:

> I always felt that there was an element of exploitation in his [Fugard's] work, that he really was, in a sense, writing about the predicament of blacks without completely supporting them so we've had various disagreements about various plays of his. (Personal Interview)

Similar attacks are leveled at his most recent drama, *My People*, a metaplay using the voices of young women. One critic complained that Fugard does not have a voice for the new South Africa (Gevisser 5).

The ambiguity an Afrikaner faces when working under the burden of apartheid is overwhelming. *Playland* wishes the problem away through good will on both sides. Rich commented that the play is "reductivist to a fault...almost fanatically tidy. It's as if Mr. Fugard felt he could contain his society's messy, careening history and even more miraculously, push it to a hopeful denouement by maintaining rigid control over everything that happens on a patch of stage" ("Boiled" C15). Martinus and Gideon are metaphors of defined positions, not fully drawn characters with unequaled histories. The one-act work reveals a South African playwright searching for an image of himself in an alien environment.

Fugard is more credible when he details an Afrikaner sensibility. His film, *The Guest*, confirms this. Fugard plays Eugene Marais [1871-1936], a South African poet and naturalist who exposes political corruption working as a newspaper editor. Marais' stay on a farm run by an Afrikaner family poignantly unveils the nuances of their stark Calvinistic existence. This film illustrates that Fugard is better served in defining the Afrikaner sensibility than projecting a black world view unless, of course, it is done in a collaboration as was the case with *Sizwe Banzi Is Dead* and *The Island*.[3]

Society can never dictate to an artist what he or she should write. But as a new order comes into being, new terrain needs to be examined dramatically by the Afrikaner: the Dutch Reform Church's support of apartheid on biblical grounds, the existence of an Afrikaner Broederbond set up in 1918 to "prevent the disappearance of the Afrikaner volk as a separate political, language, social and cultural entity"; the Afrikaner of

---

[3] Actors John Kani and Winston Ntshona improvised their own limitations under apartheid before the scenes were finally put down on paper.

1948 caught between the rich, educated Englishman and the black South African; the psychological impact on Afrikaners over changing symbols— flags, anthems, holidays—as a new South Africa develops. A growing world audience needs to understand the thinking of the Afrikaner that pushed him into such an untenable racial predicament. The Afrikaner theater of post-apartheid South Africa will have to exorcise demons and not lobby for political justice for its black future citizens out of a sense of guilt.

Angove's description of black plays developed at the Grahamstown festival—*Kuyase Africa* [People's Cultural organization], *Kuma* [Fuda Centre, Soweto Oct. 1988], *Ababhemi* [Darlington and Mnembe Black Sun Oct. 1988], *Dankie Auntie* [Mda], *Kode Kubeneni* [M. Memela Makhanya], *Kagoos* [Jan. 1989] (42)—fall under the umbrella of urban ills created by apartheid. They are not unlike the 1986 Woza Afrika theater festival that introduced a New York audience to township plays— Maishe Maponya's *Gangsters*, Matsemela Manaka's *Children of Asazi*, Mbongeni Ngema's *Asinamali!*, Percy Mtwa's *Bopha*. Township theater is revelatory and message oriented; it is as Maponya says a "theater of the fist," a theater born of political repression. It would be senseless to argue aesthetics when a theater's aim is to effect political change. But as the landscape changes, it is up to the artist to find new ground to accommodate a new social order.

Some voices in South Africa who see a new South African theatre emerging argue that art not be so tied to politics. Albie Sachs, a member of the legal department of the ANC before his death in 1995, said back in 1966 [*The Jail Diary of Albie Sachs*] and most recently at the New Nation Conference, that the arts should not become a prisoner of the struggle and ignore themes of the human condition (Chapman 2). Nadime Gordimer has warned "Agitprop binds the artist with the means by which it aims to free minds of the people. It licenses a phony sub-art" (137). Njabulo Ndebele at the 1986 Second Stockholm Conference for African Writers "Refining Relevance" said, "post-protest literature... should probe beyond the observable facts, to reveal new worlds where it was previously thought they did not exist" (Gray 25). Zwelakhe Sisulu [New Nation Writers Conference, Wits University-Dec. 1991] spoke of reconstructing South Africa anew through literature. This kind of thinking, however, is on a theoretical level, for it has not surfaced in the drama written by black South Africans since Mandela's release.

Thuli Dumakude's *Buya Africa* has run intermittently at various locations in New York over the past two years. Ms. Dumakude, the lead vocalist in *Cry Freedom*, served as the vocal coach to the young actors in *Sarafina*. *Buya Africa* is a series of dramatic monologues accompanied by songs that recount her growing up and coming of age in South Africa. Her eclectic style draws from traditional, South African, gospel and contemporary music. The content of *Buya Africa* is overtly political. Julius Novick of *Newsday* commented, "Dumakude's heart is in the right place, but her political analyses does not get much beyond 'Apartheid no! Freedom yes!'" The playwright's call for a communal song at the play's end cries of 1960's participatory theater.

Duma Ndlovu and Layding Kaliba collaborated on *Black Codes from the Underground* that ran at Barbara Ann Teer's Harlem-based National Black Theater during the summer of 1993. This is Ndlovu's second play where he synthesizes South African and American experiences in an attempt to find parallels in oppression. In *Codes* there are several men awaiting execution for terrorist acts in the US during the sixties. Each recounts, in monologue, his reason for being there. The South African prisoner, in the midst of his story, finds parallels in the sixties' Civil Rights battles with that of Steve Biko's black consciousness movement, and this is Ndlovu's input since he was intimately a part of that movement before coming to the US in 1977. The American monologues are predictable and Biko's invocation forced.

A more developed work is *Sheila's Day*. The musical was workshopped for an eight-week period in 1989 by Ngema, Ndlovu, and Dumakude who choreographed the work; later, Americans Ruby Lee and Ebony Jo-Ann created the American element. The play is a celebration of domestic workers both in South Africa and in the United States, who are, as Ndlovu states, the "spiritual center of the African continuum...the keepers of tradition and the intercessors with the ancestral spirits" (BAM Program Note). The title is a reference to the name white employers give workers whose names they refuse to learn; the name is also a reference to Thursday, the traditional day-off for South African domestic workers. Ndlovu says the day is additionally a gathering day for women who come together in prayer, song and testimony to heal and renew themselves. Metaphorically they are the liberating force within Africa and throughout the African Diaspora.

The twelve-women musical is also based on the deaths of two men: Jimmy Lee Jackson who, in 1965 Alabama, died at the hands of the police while protecting his mother from police attack, and Mthuli KaShezi who was beaten and pushed in front of a moving train while defending domestic workers harassed by white men in Johannesburg, South Africa. The four authors point out that both men were refused treatment at local hospitals and later their tombstones desecrated. The authors contend the deaths changed "the collective consciousness of their nations" (Note).

Song and dance are the play's force as the women make use of traditional Zulu chants, tribal anthems, gospel/Pentecostal screams and the blues. The American and South African women's stories are told chronologically and sequentially. The Civil Rights and anti-apartheid movements are juxtaposed through dramatic monologue and music. The women are not heroic but merely in the way of historic boycotts and protest; they are rather humble people who simply want to work and eat but are caught up in the sweeping history of the moment. Once caught up, however, they quickly fall in step with their American and South African a cappella choruses and become part of the struggle.

Sheila's Day has undergone subtle changes since its workshop period and was last performed at the Grahamstown Theater Festival in Grahamstown, South Africa by the Crossroads Theater Company in the summer of 1993 [July 6-11]—the first Actor's Equity organization to perform in South Africa in thirty years. The audience reaction varied according to age. Older white South Africans resented an American company coming to South Africa to interpret the situation in their own country. The critical reception was mixed. Terry Herbst of the *Eastern Province Herald* commented: "I can't remember when I last saw a theatrical event so richly deserving of this ultimate accolade." Barry Ronge of *Cue* voiced doubts about the plot's credibility: "this plot device is...contrived...barely believable, even allowing for the suspension of disbelief, that two women could, between them, stumble into every major civil rights event that occurred on two different continents." Dumakude anticipated this reaction because she understands how sensitive South Africans are about being analyzed from abroad. But she adds that South African writing is no longer subject to the censorship of previous years which forced actors to memorize parts so scripts could not be judged by censors, although that's how *Sheila's Day* started out, i.e. as guerrilla theater. Now situations have changed. "South Africans aren't speaking between the lines anymore... [there are] no more double meanings to get a point across," she says (Collins).

Although the music is riveting, the *Sheila's Day* collaboration is along the lines of *Codes*. It does not break new ground dramatically and really is a reshuffling of old themes—a modern-day Civil Rights pageant.

Patreshettarlina Adams, the Crossroads' stage manager, was able to sample several other works while in Grahamstown, including a South African cast performing Ntozake Shange's *Colored Girls*. Much of the program of black South African plays revolved around life in the townships, hostels or mines, similar to what Angove observed at the festival several years before. Ms. Adams recalled one play, however, that moved in another direction. *Daughter of Nebo* is a Hilary Blecher, Victor N'toni and Rashid Lanie music theater collaboration based on a documentary made by Sara Blecher and James Mthoba. The story is a traditional tale of village people who place communal responsibility high on their list of priorities. In the drama, a young girl is murdered and it is incumbent upon the village to find out what happened and act upon it. They discover the murderer is her father who claims that he was possessed by demons. He is given over to the white government who do not sentence him to death. Ms. Adams indicated the play's theme is that black South Africans have created their own communal laws and must believe and fight for them. Accordingly, the father is sentenced to death by the village. What surprised Ms. Adams was the apolitical nature of the play, the absence of anger or shock that is so common with agitprop theater.

Other members of the Crossroads cast who saw more political black plays complained of the graphic language and violence. Ms. Adams thinks straight political theater is limiting and sees so many other possibilities available to playwrights. "You know intellectually as well as emotionally there are so many stories that should be told; they've only begun to realize that they have the power to tell them" (Personal Interview). In this context she mentioned Ngema's new work, *Magic at Four A.M.*, a play about men gathering in the ungodly hour of four a.m. to watch a Muhammad Ali title match. The men see Ali's heroic qualities in themselves and become the magic at four a.m. The two plays, *Magic* and *Daughter*, are plays Ms. Adams sees as moving towards the internal concerns of black South Africans without reference to the white antagonist that has dominated their lives.

In discussing the Market Theater productions and 1994 Grahamstown festival, Mark Gevisser noticed another trend developing: the revival. Jerry Mofokeng directed Fugard's 1959 *Nongogo* at the Civic Theater in Johannesburg; the Market Theater revived Malcolm Purdy's *Sophiatown*. Mofokeng also revived Can Thembe's *The Suit* at Grahamstown. Revivals bring up a certain irony that is inescapable. Gerisser, referring to Sophiatown, ruefully comments: "at the moment of liberation we [are] moved by a white woman living with black people in the bad days of early apartheid...we...find comfort, not in possibilities of tomorrow but in the struggle of yesterday" (5).

Bill Keller, the present *New York Times* correspondent in South Africa, writes of the paucity of real images about the South Africa he covers and knows. And although he is talking primarily about films like *Bopha*, *The Power of One* [1992], *A Dry White Season* [1989], *Cry Freedom* and *Sarafina*, what he says applies to the theater as well. Keller quotes Barry Ronge, the cultural voice of South Africa, who accuses American directors of coming to South Africa with "imaginations paralyzed by apartheid" (13). Plots must revolve around attacks on apartheid and are "immobilized by a reverence for the struggle" (13).

Another journalist, Michael Clough, in a review of David Ottaway's *Chained Together: Mandela, de Klerk and the Struggle to Remake South Africa*, writes, "The grand struggle is over. Stark contrasts between good and evil have blurred. The ennobling challenge of ending apartheid has been replaced by a host of more mundane tasks. Many of the heroes have been tarnished. Most of the old villains seem less evil and less menacing" (3). Ottaway, who was the *Washington Post's* correspondent in South Africa from 1990-1992, finds Mandela a rather mundane politician whose view of the world belongs to another generation. This gray hue of the present is what confronts the writer of post-Apartheid South Africa. The fixed targets of the past are no longer there. What each group may do is go back to cultural and psychological roots and develop strong and vital stories of what makes them who they are.

Breyten Breytenbach is an example of what becomes of a writer so consumed by politics. He has not lived in South Africa since 1959 and spent seven years in a South African prison from 1975-1982, two in solitary confinement. During that period he felt abandoned by the ANC who saw him as a romantic militant. This bitterness with South Africa penetrates almost every page of *Return to Paradise*. Towards the conclusion, his South African host accuses him of being a "poseur, a misery sponge, a bird of doom come here for the satisfaction of high and holy moral indignation to spew disgust over the assembly, flying off to lick imagined wounds in 'exile'" (215).

Now that South Africa approaches a new period, Bryetenbach cautions like some punch-drunk boxer, "the war is invisible" (Finnegan 3). He searches for new illusions to insure his survival, a "psychological necessity." He sees politics and writing as coming out of the same source: "they both use the same means of deception, the same words, the same concepts, dreams" (Finnegan 3). A writer's function, for Breytenback, is to "contest" ideas, to make uncomfortable the comfortable. This frame of reference places him outside any idea of reconciliation: "I [forfeit] the repose of belonging to 'my country' with 'my own people,' I [deform] my past and [destroy] my future." It is because politics is "voracious, deadening all else" (*Paradise* 218).

Dennis Brutus' comments at an October '93 poetry reading might begin to round out this discussion. He alluded to the 1991 New Nations Conference at Wits University where a suggestion, maybe even a prescription for future South African writing was made. First, there should be no writing about suffering of the past, that new writing should only focus on the creation of a new society. Brutus' response was that he found it "troubling that some people [are] trying to prescribe to the writers what their themes should be in the future" (Personal Interview). He hastily rejects this literary censorship to "buy" a peaceful South Africa. "You cannot," Brutus warns, "come to grips with the present if you pretend that the past doesn't exist" (Interview).

Somewhere there has to be compromise or politics will consume all of South Africa along with its artists. Their record of literature will be of period works that mark a decade but do not reveal a generation or a culture.

Nigerain playwright Femi Osofisan has warned of the writer's limitation, "It is not the writer who will correct [in his case] Nigeria's...situation. The writer can help diagnose and increase awareness; he can protest, and move others to protest; he cannot cure or heal" (Dutton 68). There are so many powerful dramas in South Africa. Perhaps an Irobi satire is one of them.

WORKS CITED

Angove, Coleen. "Alternative Theatre: Reflecting a Multi Racial SA Society? *Theatre Research International* 17 (Spring 1992): 39-45.

Breytenbach, Breyten. *Return to Paradise.* New York: Harcourt Brace, 1993.

Brutus, Dennis. Personal Interview. 8 October 1993. [Poetry Reading: Artists Ilse Schreiber & Dennis Brutus MJS Books & Graphics 9 E. 82nd St.]

Chapman, Michael. "The Critic in a State of Emergency: Towards a Theory of Reconstruction (after February 2)." *On Shifting Sands: New Art and Literature from South Africa.* Ed. Kirsten Holst Petersen and Anna Rutherford. Portsmouth: Heinemann, 1991. 1-13.

Clough, Michael. "Now What? A Reporter Ponders Life after Apartheid in South Africa." *New York Times Book Review* December 1993: 3+.

Collins, Karyn D. "'Sheila's Day' Heads Back to Spiritual Home." *Ashbury Park Press* 10 June 1993: NP [New Jersey Clipping Service]

Dunton, Chris. *Make Man Talk True: Nigerian Drama in English Since 1970.* London: Hans Zell, 1992.

Engstrom, John. "A 'Lesson' from Athol Fugard." *New York Times* 16 November 1980, Arts & Leisure: 3+.

Finnegan, William. "The Post-Apartheid Power Scramble: Return to Paradise" *New York Times Book Review.* 28 November 1993: 3+.

Freedman, Samuel G. "Fugard Traces a Dark Parallel on Film." *New York Times* 10 June 1984, Arts and Leisure: 1+.

Fugard, Athol. *Notebooks 1960/1977 Athol Fugard.* Ed. Mary Benson. London: Faber and Faber, 1983.

Gevisser, Mark. "South African Theater Faces a New World." *New York Times* 14 August 1994, Arts and Leisure: 5.

Gordimer, Nadime. *Essential Gesture.* New York: Alfred A. Knopf, 1988

Gray, Stephen. "An Author's Agenda: Re-visioning Past and Present for a Future South Africa." *On Shifting Sands: New Art and Literature from South Africa.* Ed. Kirsten Holst Petersen and Anna Rutherford. Portsmouth: Heinemann, 1991. 23-31.

Herbst, Terry. "Stirring Stuff by US Equity Group" *Eastern Province Herald* 8 July 1993: No page. [New Jersey Clipping Service]

Hinckley, David. "Voices of Freedom." *Daily News* 23 March 1993: 37.

Horn, Andrew. Introduction. *The Plays of Zakes Mda.* by Mda, Zakes. Johannesburg: Raven Press, 1990: Vii-Liv.

Irobi, Esiaba. *Gold, Frankincense and Myrrh* Enugu: ABIC Books, 1989.

James, Caryn. "Around Town with Breyten Breytenbach: Writing in English, Crying in Afrikaans." *New York Times* 25 November 1993: C1+.

Keller, Bill. "Is That Really South Africa?" *New York Times* 10 October 1993, Arts & Leisure: 13+.

Lee, Felicia. "Expanding Perceptions of Family in Film" *New York Times* 27 September 1993: C11.

Ndlovu, Duma. Personal Interview. 9 December 1986.

Novick, Julius. "South African Songs Sung True." *Newsday*

O'Quinn, Jim. "Theater: Human Highway" *Seven Days* 20 April 1988: 43.

Oberhelman, Harley D., Ed. *Gabriel Garcia Marquez: a Study of the Short Fiction.* Boston: Twayne, 1991.

Ottaway, Marina. *South Africa: the Struggle for a New Order.* Washington, D.C.: The Brookings Institution, 1993.

Pareles, Jon. "Ladysmith Raises Its Voice on Broadway" *New York Times* 21 March 1993, Arts & Leisure: 1.

Patreshettarlina Adams. Personal Interview. 17 September, 1993.

Program Notes. *Sheila's Day.* BAM 2-6 June, 1993.

Rich, Frank. "A Sad Song of Grief, Violence and Apartheid." *New York Times* 25 March 1993: C17+.

Rich, Frank. "South Africa's Conflict, Boiled Down to 2 Men." *New York Times* 9 June 1993: C15.

Ronge, Barry. "Sheila's Heyday." *Cue* 7 July, 1993: N. pag. [New Jersey Clipping Service]

Simon, John. "Invasion of the One-Actors" *New York* 21 June 1993: 71.

Sisulu, Zwelakhe, ed. *New Nation Writers Conference December 1-6, 1991.* DJ Du Plessis Centre, Wits University, 1991.

Waites, James. "A Whole Generation Sacrificed to History. " *ABC Radio 24 Hours* n.d.: 24-5.

CONTRIBUTORS

M. M. Adjarian is an independent scholar. Currently, she is working on a book dealing with women's writing from the anglo-, franco- & hispanophone regions of the Caribbean that will examine allegories of self, community and desire in relation to issues of gender, (im)migration and the concepts of history, nation and race.

Akosua Anyidoho, Senior Lecturer in the Department of Linguistics at the University of Ghana, Legon, has published significantly on Akan texts.

Fahamisha Brown is associate professor of English at Austin Peay State University. Her paper in this volume is part of a larger study on Black poetry.

Don Burness is Coordinator of English Studies at Franklin Pierce College. Author/editor of eight books on African literature, his work includes Lusophone literature.

Ezenwa-Ohaeto is Professor of Literature at Anambra State College in Nigeria and is author of *Contemporary Niegerian Poetry and the Poetics of Orality* (1998).

Heather Henderson is Associate Professor of English at Mount Holyoke College. She is the author of *The Victorian Self* and co-editor of the Victorian section of the new two-volume *Longman Anthology of British Literature* (1998).

Gerise Herndon teaches English, Film and Women's Studies at Nebraska Wesleyan University, including courses on Culture, Ethnicity and Film. She has published on Euzhan Palcy, Maryse Conde, Jamaica Kincaid, Simone Schwarz-Bart, as well as feminist pedagogy in the midwest.

Peter Hitchcock is a Professor of Literary and Cultural Studies at Baruch College and the Graduate Center, City University of New York. His books include *Dialogics of the Oppressed* and *Oscillate Wildly*, with a third, *Imaginary States* forthcoming.

Oliver Lovesey's recent articles have appeared in *Research in African Liteatures*, *Ariel*, and *Journal of Commonwealth Literature*. He is completing a book on Ngugi wa Thiong'o for Twayne. He teaches at Okanagan University College in Kelowna, British Columbia.

Obi Maduakor is Professor of English at the University of Nigeria, Nsukka.

Edris Makward is Professor of French and Afircan Literatures at the University of Wisconsin-Madison. He is author of *Contemporary African Literature* and co-editor of The *Growth of African Literature: 25 years after dakar and Fourah Bay*, and of numerous articles and chapters in books on African literatures and cultures.

Fredric Michelman is a professor of French and African literature at Gettysburg Coillege. He is the author of numerous articles and essays on Francophone African literature.

Judith G. Miller is Chair of the Department of French and Italian of the University of Wisconsin. She has edited and translated, with Christiane Makward, *French and Francophone Women's Theatre*, and has authored numerous articles on French and Francophone theatre. She is now working on a book on African and Caribean Francophone productions.

Donald M. Morales is Professor of Literature at Mercy College in Westchester, New York, with a specialization in African and African American drama. His essays have appeared in *The Literary Griot*, *African American Review and Journal of Afro-Latin American Studies and Literatures*.

Bob Newton was Fulbright researcher in Mali from 1992-94, working on the epic tradition of the empire of Bamana Segu in its present forms. He is currently an arts and media project coordinator for the African Studies Program at the University of Wisconsin-Madison.

Kwadwo Opoku-Agyemang is Senior Lecturer at the department of English at the University of Cape Coast, Ghana.

Niyi Osundare, professor of English at University of Ibadan and visiting professor at University of New Orleans, is Nigeria's most internationally recognized poet. His ten volumes include *Waiting Laughters* (Noma Award) and *The Eye of the Earth* (Commonwealth Prize).

Renee Schatteman is pursuing a PhD in postcolonial literature at the University of Massachusetts in Amherst and is currently writing a dissertation entitled "Caryl Phillips, J.M. Coetzee, and Michael Ondaatje: Writing at the Intersection of Postcolonialism and Postmodernism." Her publications include an article in *Scope: A Journal of African American Thought* entitled "Ethical Dilemmas and the Use of Deception in African American Slave Narratives."

William Sharpe teaches urban culture and American Studies at Barnard College, Columbia University. He is the author of *Unreal Cities* (1990) and a co-editor of the new *Longman Anthology of British Literature* (1998).

Ousmane Souley, lecturer in the English Department at the University of Ghana, Legon, has completed a manuscript, "The Cosmic World of Soyinka's Drama."

Marie Linton Umeh specializes in Literature of the African World at John Jay College of Criminal Justice of the City University of New York. She is the editor of *Emerging Perspectives on Buchi Emecheta* (1995) and *Emerging Perspectives on Flora Nwapa* (1996).

EDITORS

Kofi Anyidoho is professor and head of the department of English and Director of the African Humanities Institute Program at the University of Ghana, Legon. Best known as a poet, he has also contributed to many scholarly journals and books on African Literature and Culture, as well as edited a number of anthologies. His areas of specialization include oral poetics and interrelations between literature and other disciplines. His most recent publications include "Akpokplo" [a play in Ewe] and "The Word Behind Bars & The Paradox of Exile". He is 1998-99 President of the African Literature Association.

Anne V. Adams is associate professor of Africana Studies at Cornell University, where she teaches in the area of Comparative Black Literatures. Her current research interests are the contributions of women to African intellectual thought, and definitions of African Diaspora, from which a manuscript "The Sankofa Factor: Recollecting Africa" is in progress. Her publications include *Ngambika: Studies of Women in African Literature*, co-edited with Carole Boyce Davies, the English translation *Showing Our Colors: Afro-German Women Speak Out*, as well as *Mapping Intersections: African Literature and Africa's Development*, co-edited with Janis A. Mayes. She was president of the African Literature Association 1989-90.

Abena P.A. Busia is an associate professor of English, Comparative Literature and Women's Studies at Rutgers, the State University of New Jersey, New Brunswick. In addition to being a teacher, she is a poet and short story writer. She has published numerous articles on black women's literature and colonial discourse, and her poetry has been anthologized in journals and anthologies in Africa, Europe, and North America. Her first volume of poems, *Testimonies of Exile*, was published by Africa World Press in 1990. She is the editor, with Stanlie James, of *Theorizing Black Feminisms: The Visionary Pragmatism of Black Women* (Routledge, New York: 1993), and co-director, with Tuzyline Jita Allan and Florence Howe of the "Women Writing Africa" project.

INDEX